M000033229

Ulrich von Hutten's
Arminius

Richard Ernest Walker

Ulrich von Hutten's
Arminius

An English Translation with
Analysis and Commentary

PETER LANG

Oxford · Bern · Berlin · Bruxelles · Frankfurt am Main · New York · Wien

Bibliographic information published by Die Deutsche Bibliothek
Die Deutsche Bibliothek lists this publication in the Deutsche
Nationalbibliografie; detailed bibliographic data is available on
the Internet at ‹http://dnb.ddb.de›.

British Library and Library of Congress Cataloguing-in-Publication Data:
A catalogue record for this book is available from The British Library,
Great Britain, and from The Library of Congress, USA

ISBN 978-3-03911-338-5
Cover Design: Tracey Brockwell. Peter Lang Ltd.

Contents

Acknowledgements   7

Chapter One   Introduction   9

Chapter Two   Hutten's *Arminius* and Eobanus Hessus's Preface   21

Chapter Three *Arminius* Analysis and Commentary   41

Chapter Four   Hutten in Literary Contexts   83

Chapter Five   Hutten in Cultural and Political Contexts   131

Chapter Six   Conclusion   165

Appendix I   In Hutteni Arminium Eobanus Hessus   173

Appendix II   Arminius Dialogus   175

Bibliography   187

Acknowledgements

This translation and analysis of Ulrich von Hutten's *Arminius* dialogue and the preface by Eobanus Hessus, both published post-humously (1529), could not have been completed without the support of a number of individuals and institutions. My special thanks and appreciation to the Director of the Herzog August Bibliothek, Wolfen-büttel, Dr. Helwig Schmidt-Glinzer, and the Research Director, Dr. Gillian Bepler, whose invitation enabled me to spend a month in residence there, during which the initial translation of this material was completed. As on previous occasions, the HAB staff was extremely helpful, generous, and supportive in providing a most wonderful environment for work and reflection. Other libraries provided resources and facilities without which this study could not have been accomplished. My special thanks to The Folger Library, Washington, D. C. and the McKeldin Library of my home institution, the University of Maryland College Park. A significant portion of the writing on this study was completed at the East Columbia Branch of the Howard County Public Library System, Columbia, Maryland, which offered enormously valuable workspace and resources for the work I was doing; my special thanks to the Branch Director, Nina Krzysko, and her staff. To my wife, Lucile, who facilitated my use of Inter-Library loan services for various resources through the Baltimore County Public Library System, her employer, and who has shown admirable patience and understanding of my endeavors for a number of years, my sincerest appreciation and gratitude.

Chapter One
Introduction

Towards the end of March, 1945, the struggling Wehrmacht under-
went the thirty-fifth and final regrouping of forces, which included the
formation of a new division under the name of 'Ulrich von Hutten.'[1]
The newly constituted Hutten Division saw its first action against
American troops on April 12, 1945, in the vicinity of Bitterfeld, first
supporting the Eleventh Army and later as support units for the
Twelfth Army moving up to defend Berlin. By the end of April, the
Ulrich von Hutten division had been captured by the Americans near
Tangermünde in the state of Saxony Anhalt.[2] Given that the war by
this time was for all practical purposes a lost cause for Germany, the
question arises why a unit engaged in such a futile effort would
have been designated by the name of the man who had come to sym-
bolize German patriotism. While virtually meaningless as a strategic
or tactical maneuver, the naming of such a division can only be seen
realistically as a symbolic gesture in the face of certain defeat. If the
point of symbolism, or symbolic gestures, is to awaken associations
or connotations that go beyond the literal, explicit sense, then the
creation of the Ulrich von Hutten division, however ineffective it may
have been, made a statement which on some level addressed meanings
going beyond men and materiel. We will never know the impact such
a gesture did or did not have on the individual soldiers, but it is not
unreasonable to suggest that the use of Hutten's name in this way
aimed to draw forth the same propagandistic associations which Hitler

---

1   For brief confirmation of the creation of this division, see W. Victor Madej,
     German Army Order of Battle, 2 Vols., Allentown, PA: Game Marketing
     Company, 1981, Vol. I, 90. See also www.axishistory.com. The 18th Infantry
     Division was disbanded in March of 1945 in the region of East Prussia. The
     Division staff was reformed as Stab/Division 'Ulrich von Hutten' on April 4,
     1945.
2   Ibid.

and his supporters had used on earlier occasions.[3] That such a tactic would be used at this late date in the faltering war effort speaks to the desperation of the leadership and the hope of governments, then and now, that resorting to patriotism would blind citizens, however briefly, to the political blunders that had brought a nation into chaos and despair.[4]

In a similar context, but one with rather more complex motivations and implications, the name of Ulrich von Hutten came into play again in the 1960s. The *Gesellschaft für freie Publizistik* (GfP), founded in 1960 by former SS members and former officials of the NSDAP and with ties in more recent times to the NPD,[5] annually awards the 'Ulrich von Hutten Medaille' to persons such as the last adjutant to Propaganda Minister Joseph Goebbels and the Rightwing-extremist publisher Wigbert Grabert; Udo Walendy, a Holocaust-denier, has also been a Hutten Medaille recipient.[6] The 2005 recipient of the Hutten medal, Austrian writer Konrad Windisch, expressed his fascination with the man whose name the medal bears and anyone who, like Hutten, has the courage to take a stand outside his class or against his class for the sake of his own convictions. According to Windisch, Hutten turned away from his class to act in support of the peasants, a characterization which is acceptable only in a limited sense and poses a challenge not only to what we know of Hutten's political

---

3   See Wilhelm Kreutz. *Die Deutschen und Ulrich von Hutten. Rezeption von Autor und Werk seit dem 16. Jhdt.*, München: Wilhelm Fink Verlag, 1984, 230. Hereafter cited as Kreutz.

4   It is not inappropriate to mention in this respect the characterization of American anti-war proponents in the Vietnam era and after the invasion of Iraq as unpatriotic and those who see Iraq as a failed war policy as being un-American.

5   The Nationaldemokratische Partei Deutschlands (NPD), is a legitimate political party, which espouses ideas and attitudes supportive of and identifiable with Neo-Nazism.

6   The Annual Report (2000) of the Federal Office for Protection of the Constitution, Bundesamt für Verfassungsschutz, described the *GfP* as the most significant rightwing extremist cultural organization in Germany. Similar reports in Nordrhein-Westfalen (2001) characterized the *GfP* as having a defensive position as regards the National Socialist regime.

activities but also to the alleged interest in historical truth of the organization which awards the Hutten medal.[7]

The creation of the Ulrich von Hutten division, as a historical phenomenon, fits into the context of the propagandistic initiatives of the Nazis, but the Ulrich von Hutten medal, having been awarded annually now for more than forty years, has historical implications that go beyond the symbolic gesture of 1945. How does the life of Ulrich von Hutten and his literary reputation relate to the uses made of his name in contexts such as last-ditch patriotism, the alleged search for historical truth, and class protests that are, at best, a distortion of the reality of Hutten's political interests? How can the person and persona of Hutten be stretched to such an extent to serve purposes with which he may or may not have agreed? Just as Hutten and others used the Arminius figure to represent views and behavioral modes that were anachronistic at the least for the Germanic-Roman warrior, so have subsequent generations, as we have seen above, made of Hutten a man for all seasons as regards German patriotism. A subsequent question, of course, is how the patriotism expressed by the creation of the Hutten division relates to the patriotism of the awarders and recipients of the Hutten medal? The effort to understand how and why such interpretations and re-interpretations occurred is an important aspect of this translation and study of Hutten's *Arminius*.

Among the many prominent personalities in the history of sixteenth century Germany, perhaps no one had a more tragic life or, arguably, was more misunderstood than Ulrich von Hutten. A very controversial figure in a number of ways, Hutten nevertheless shared common features and close relationships with many of his contemporaries but at the end of his life was alienated and exiled from most of them as well. A strong voice for German nationalism, or ethnic chauvinism, long before there was a German nation,[8] Hutten's success and effectiveness may well have been hampered significantly not only

---

7   Interview archived in the on-line press of the NPD, *Deutsche Stimme*, May, 2005, *Konrad Windisch im Gespräch über Vergangenheit und Zukunft der Deutschen.* http://www.deutsche-stimme.de/

8   The appropriateness of this term for Hutten's attitudes and beliefs will given closer attention in the analysis of the *Arminius* dialogue.

by his commitment to the Latin language, of which he was an acknowledged master stylist, but also by his late recognition of the value of writing and communicating in the vernacular, German. His fluent Latin skills, his interest in the history and literature of Classical antiquity, and his concern for the moral, cultural and political values of Germany brought him into close contact with many personalities whose names, ideas, and attitudes served to define sixteenth century Germany. It is noteworthy, however, that among his many prominent contacts, Emperor Maximilian I, Archbishop/Prince-Elector Albrecht of Mainz, Johannes Reuchlin, Emperor Charles V, Erasmus, Willibald Pirckheimer, Martin Bucer, and many others, he never met the one with whom he is said to have felt a close affinity, Martin Luther.[9] The fact that their understanding of one another developed and was sustained by means of the written word, underlines two important aspects of the contemporary society: the cultivated solidarity of communities of like-minded personalities, scholarly and /or religious, and the role of letters or other forms of *written* correspondence in the proliferation of intellectual discourse; Hutten's support and participation in each of these areas was significant. The tragedy of the loneliness and isolation of his last days stands in contrast to the gregarious, convivial associations of his student days, the joyous outpourings of respect and admiration he received when traveling in Italy and France, and the devoted friendships he cultivated among humanists in Germany and other parts of Europe throughout most of his life. The posthumous publication of the *Arminius* dialogue also stands in contrast to the considerable corpus of his other writings, though it may embody more than any other work the attitudes for which Hutten is remembered, if he is remembered at all.

The decision to prepare an English translation of this relatively unknown work,[10] and Eoban Hessus's introduction to it, arose from a

9   For an illuminating view of this relationship, see Eckhard Bernstein, *Ulrich von Hutten mit Selbstzeugnissen und Bilddokumenten*, Reinbek bei Hamburg: Rowohlt Taschenbuch Verlag, 1988. Hereafter cited as Bernstein.
10   Gerald Strauss translated into English and published excerpts from Hutten's *Arminius* in his study *Manifestations of Discontent in Germany on the Eve of the Reformation*, Bloomington: Indiana University Press, 1971, 75–82.

12

desire to address three broader issues that seem to be relevant to Hutten's life and work: first, to examine the conventional view that a German national identity found its first and fullest expression in nineteenth century German nationalism, and to challenge at the same time the use of the term 'nationalism' to characterize Hutten's sentiments; secondly, to highlight the implications of the neglect of Neo-Latin writings in modern assessments of German literature and culture of the sixteenth century;[11] and thirdly, to offer a more objective focus on what are, in my view, misjudgments and unduly biased characterizations of Ulrich von Hutten by writers who, while identifying with his expressions of pride in being German, tend to gloss over the broader implications of his pronouncements on ethnic identity and cultural superiority. On another level, the treatment of his literary and political life, that is to say, looking at the broad outline of his activities as suggested by the Hutten biography of David Friedrich Strauss,[12] is an effort to provide some perspective on the significant events of Hutten's life while placing that brief life in a broader German and European historical context. The latter objective made it necessary, given the unfamiliarity of some of the authors in Hutten's circle of friends and the limited access to some of the texts in German, not to mention their non-availability in English, to provide some excerpts either in the original Latin or in German translation. In all cases, English paraphrases of these excerpts will appear in the body of the text with reference to the relevant original sources. The *Arminius* translation will speak for itself; however, as mentioned above, an extensive commentary on and analysis of the text was deemed necessary to establish a context within which the ideas and attitudes flowing from Hutten's text can be assessed with respect to his own time and for their application to later periods as well.

11   For a notable exception, see Jozef Ijsewijn, *Humanistische neulateinische Literatur*, In: Horst Albert Glaser, Hrsg. *Deutsche Literatur: Eine Sozialgeschichte* (2) Von der Handschrift zum Buchdruck: Spätmittelalter Reformation Humanismus, 1320–1572, Reinbek bei Hamburg: Rowohlt Taschenbuch Verlag, 1991, 287–301.

12   David Friedrich Strauss. *Ulrich von Hutten*. Leipzig: F.A. Brockhaus, 1857/58, rev. ed. Otto Clemen, Leipzig: Insel Verlag, 1914. Hereafter referred to as Strauss.

The starting points for any study of Ulrich von Hutten are the collected works, edited by Edward Böcking,[13] and the detailed, though biased, biography by David Friedrich Strauss, who apparently had full access to Böcking's materials.[14] An equally valuable overview and supplement, though it too relied heavily on Böcking and Strauss, is the Hutten article in the *Allgemeine Deutsche Biographie*.[15] Hajo Holborn's shorter biography[16] is useful but perhaps not as objective as one would wish. While he acknowledged reliance on Strauss for the details of Hutten's life, as this study also does, his view of such details did not always lead to the conclusions one draws from the same materials today; in such instances, objectivity was the more important criterion. The more recent biographical study by Eckhard Bernstein, though smaller in format and more limited in scope, is nevertheless an important source for a more balanced view of Hutten.[17]

Hutten's life and works are inextricably bound up with the regions of Germany known as Rhenish Franconia and East Franconia, which includes the modern states of the Rheinland-Pfalz, Baden-Württemberg, Hesse, and Bavaria. Given the historical role of the medieval Catholic Church in these regions as represented by the bishoprics of Mainz, Bamberg, and Würzburg, it is not surprising that these cities and their Church officials also played a role in the religious and political activities that concerned Hutten in the early sixteenth century. Hutten's family origins also linked him intimately to the fortunes and misfortunes of the class of independent free knights, *Reichsritterschaft*, whose social and political survival were central concerns

---

13   Edward Böcking, *Opera Ulrichi Hutteni equiti Germani*, Five vols, Leipzig: B. G. Teubner, 1859–62, and two supplementary vols, Leipzig, 1864. Hereafter referred to as Böcking *Opera*.

14   Strauss, vii.

15   *Allgemeine Deutsche Biographie*, XIII, 464–475.

16   Hajo Holborn, *Ulrich von Hutten and the German Reformation*, [German, 1929], English translation by Roland H. Bainton (1937), New York: Harper & Row, 1965. Hereafter cited as Holborn.

17   In contrast to other studies, for example, Bernstein makes it clear that there was no personal relationship between Hutten and Luther; he also provides comments by Hutten that help to clarify the nature of the relationship, such as it was. This aspect will be discussed in more detail later. Bernstein, 93ff.

during the last years of his life. Most accounts of Hutten's life follow the outline of the Strauss biography, already mentioned here as a source. It will suffice briefly to mention some important dates and information relevant to the context:

1488, born at Schloss Steckelberg in Franconia into a family that claimed an ancestral provenance reaching back to the tenth century; by the sixteenth century, Huttens were found to have held some administrative, advisory and military offices as well as ecclesiastical appointments in Würzburg, Bamberg, and Eichstätt.

1499, delivered to the Benedictine monastery in Fulda to begin educational preparation to be a monk, a career choice made for him by his father.

1505–1507 departure without permission from Fulda, allegedly aided by his friend, Crotus Rubeanus. Both Hutten and Rubeanus appeared in the matriculation register of the University of Cologne for that year.[18] Attendance at the University of Erfurt and later the University of Frankfurt/Oder.

1508–1512, traveled in northern Germany; complained in 1510 of having suffered from fever, boils, fatigue, and weight loss for about two years; this suggests that by this time he had already contracted the syphilis that would plague him for the rest of his life.[19]

1512–13, after a brief stay in Vienna, Hutten began study of law at the University of Pavia; in connection with the Italian wars of this period, Hutten was taken prisoner, first by the French, then by Swiss troops; he returned to Germany to take employment at the court of Archbishop Albrecht of Mainz.

1515–1517, various cures for his syphilis attempted with only temporary relief; literary indictment of Duke Ulrich of Württemberg for the murder of Hutten's cousin, Johann von Hutten; second trip to Italy; participation in the Reuchlin controversy; contributed to the satirical work *Epistolae obscurorum virorum* of which the first part was written by his friend Crotus Rubeanus; crowned *poeta laureatus* (1517) upon his return to Germany; probable time period (1517–19) of the writing of the *Arminius* dialogue.

18 Strauss, 13. It has been suggested that Hutten had actually left Fulda two years earlier (1503), having been sent to participate in the *Normstudium, biennium studii,* at the University of Erfurt; see H. Grimm, Ulrich von Hutten, Göttingen, 1971, 32f., but as Bernstein points out 'Beweise für diesen Erfurter Aufenthalt gibt es allerdings nicht!' Bernstein, 17.
19 Strauss, 39. For a study of Hutten's literary use of his affliction, see Lewis Jillings, *The Aggression of the Cured Syphilitic: Ulrich von Hutten's Projection of his Disease as Metaphor, The German Quarterly,* Vol. 68, No. 1. (Winter, 1995), 1–18.

1518, some relief from the pain and suffering of the syphilis from a medicine extracted from Guaiac wood.

1520–21, Hutten began to translate his Latin works into German and to write original works in that language; extended residence with Franz von Sickingen at Schloss Ebernburg.

1522–23 after Sickingen's campaign failed, Hutten and others left Schloss Ebernburg and Hutten left Germany for Switzerland; after failed attempts to contact Erasmus in Basel, Hutten moved on to Zürich where he found a refuge arranged by Zwingli. Huttens last days were spent on the island of Ufenau in Lake Zürich.

Ulrich von Hutten was a complicated person whose relationships, it seems, were never simple and straightforward. From the troubled relationship with his father, the curious love-hate relationship with Erasmus, the frustration of admiration for but estrangement from Martin Luther, to the futile efforts to establish productive relationships with various members of the imperial family, Hutten's independent voice set him apart from others and made his ultimate exile seem almost inevitable. But the factor underlying most of his personal life, his academic life, such as it was, and his unrealized political ambitions, was a strong sense of himself as a German. This identity, molded by anti-Roman feelings engendered by the role of the Catholic Church in Germany and, to a certain extent, by his treatment at the hands of Swiss and French soldiers during his peripheral Venetian war experiences in Italy, rather than being a positive, assertive expression of his inner feelings was more a reactive, defensive posture that evolved over time. Hutten's vicissitudes were not trivial, e.g., his role in a stifling, authoritarian family, the personal and legal abuses his family endured at the hands of Duke Ulrich of Württemberg, the mistreatment of him by the Lötz family. Add to this his imprisonment by Swiss Germans on suspicion of being a supporter of the French and imprisonment by the French on suspicion of being a supporter of the Swiss, his rejection by many of his class peers because of his friendship with and support of the failed political ambitions of Franz von Sickingen, and it would be understandable had he developed quite negative feelings about Germany and Germans. The curious fact is that none of this seems to have made a difference, and it makes his personal isolation and exile at the end of his life seem all the more poignant.[20]

This English translation of Hutten's *Arminius* does not in itself provide answers to the many questions raised by a consideration of his life. In fact, it is doubtful whether extensive analysis of any one work or group of works could do so. Making the *Arminius* text accessible, however, can do two things: first, it will provide an opportunity to assess Hutten's humanist interest in and knowledge of Classical texts and literary traditions and their relation to his own times; secondly, it may provoke deeper thought about the scope and meaning of ideas embodied in the *Arminius* text which have resonated with particular groups of like-minded thinkers over several centuries beyond the time of Hutten. Each of these aspects can be better appreciated, if not completely understood, by consideration of Hutten within the broader contexts of his roles as a literary figure and a political thinker. Consequently, this study will attempt, among various possible approaches, to provide a close literary analysis of the *Arminius* text, to examine and to assess some of Hutten's ideas in other selected works, to review and evaluate what has been said about Hutten as part of the German literary tradition, and to examine in some depth several of the many works spawned by Hutten's life and his ideas. In an effort to consider Hutten's humanist credentials and his view of history and culture, the intellectual environment of the period from the mid-fifteenth to the mid-sixteenth centuries had to be considered. Consideration was also given to the role of the humanist Aenea Silvio and others in the creation of an image of Germany that, building on Tacitus, persisted into later periods. Equally important for this study, however, were the issues raised by Hans Kloft in citing the positive and negative implications of the nationalist feelings engendered by the humanist images.[21] Kloft's outline of the interest in a historical and moral continuity in German culture ranging over the views of Tacitus,

---

20 Hans J. Rehfisch, ed., *In Tyrannos, Four Centuries of Struggle against Tyranny in Germany*. A Symposium. [The Club 1943], 'Ulrich von Hutten and the Humanists,' 26.

21 Hans Kloft, *Die Germania des Tacitus und das deutsche Nationalbewußtsein*. 108–109. Hereafter cited as Kloft.

Aenea Silvio, Celtis, Wimpfeling, Hutten, Pirckheimer and others is still valuable as regards the question of nationalism and German culture. The extent to which these fifteenth and early sixteenth century impulses fed into anti-Roman and anti-Italian attitudes, possibly given added impetus by the growing interest in religious reform, cannot be viewed simply as a matter of cause and effect. But, as Kloft pointed out, the role of such views in the later development of a national consciousness underlying the creation of a national state cannot be ignored.[22]

The difficulty of assessing Hutten's role as a patriotic icon is perhaps most evident in the contrasting views of Hajo Holborn, whose biography was mentioned earlier, and others of the modern enthusiasts enamored of Hutten. The polarity of the views is illustrative. Holborn saw Hutten as a synthesizer, the first to attempt to bring together humanism, nationalism, and Protestantism. He also endorsed the view of Wilhelm Dilthey, who saw Hutten as the first modern German, and that of Kuno Francke, for whom Hutten was the exemplary representative of German individualism in the Early Modern period.[23] The last paragraph of Holborn's Hutten biography in English translation illustrates the key role he saw for Hutten in the history and culture of Germany both in the sixteenth century and in modern times as well:

> His achievements and his frustration bear the marks of human greatness. Still a kindling force in modern German history is he who first wrestled with her deepest problem: that of a genuine synthesis of spiritual freedom with the external needs of the nation. Throughout the centuries with all their variations the appeal to [sic] Ulrich von Hutten belongs only to those for whom the nation is a way of ascent to 'Humanitas.' (Holborn, 202)

The German text reads:

> Huttens Erfolge und Niederlagen tragen das Zeichen menschlicher Größe. Auch in der modernen deutschen Geschichte strahlt seine Persönlichkeit noch eine zündende Kraft aus. Denn Hutten hatte mit Deutschlands tiefstem Problem gerungen, dem Problem, eine echte Verbindung zwischen geistiger Freiheit und den äußerlichen Bedürfnissen der Nation zu finden. In allen folgenden Jahr-

22   Kloft, 113–114.
23   Holborn, 1; 2.

hunderten übte er eine Anziehungskraft gerade auf diejenigen aus, für die die Nation einen möglichen Aufstieg zur 'Humanitas' bedeutete. (as cited in Kreutz, 226)

The English text, translated by Roland H. Bainton, lacks the force of the German and, especially in the last sentence, is somewhat misleading. To say that 'Throughout the centuries with all their variations the appeal to Ulrich von Hutten belongs only to those for whom the nation is a way of ascent to Humanitas' is not the same as saying that Hutten's appeal has been to those for whom the nation, i.e., patriotism, provided a possible path for the rise to 'Humanitas' as a level of human understanding. This interpretation of Hajo Holborn's final assessment is important in view of the role Hutten, the man, and his ideas had for the National Socialists and have for the more recent adherents of such views.[24]

The concept of patriotism, or, as seems more appropriate here, ethnic chauvinism linked to landscape, customs, and traditions, is a sub-text of the *Arminius* dialogue. It is a subject that is absent from all of the comments and observations made in the dialogue by Alexander, Hannibal, or Scipio, but it is the primary feature of Minos's praise for Arminius, the most German of the Germans. As it evolved into and through nineteenth and twentieth century nationalism, patriotism, or ethnic chauvinism, became what such modes of thought seem inevitably to become–prejudiced expressions of the arrogance of self, group, and national identity. It is inaccurate to suggest, as Holborn does, that Hutten sought to synthesize humanism, nationalism, and Protestantism. Hutten sublimated a humanist's cosmopolitanism, the hallmark of Erasmus, for example, while remaining committed to a world-view based on ethnic imperialism with token acknowledgement of the rise of Protestantism but lacking the fervor of religious con-

---

22   Wilhelm Kreutz, in his study of Hutten reception cited earlier, remarked that Holborn's comment about Hutten's appeal to those who saw the nation as a path to the ascent towards 'Humanitas' was intended to be a liberal endorsement of the tradition of freedom in German history in opposition to the totalitarian nationalism of the Third Reich. The irony is that those same Nazis and their ideological descendants came to admire in Hutten the same principles Holborn had seen as a counter to them.

19

viction that was a hallmark of Luther. In this respect Hutten became a victim of his own idealism, isolated and estranged from the intellectual and literary culture that had once held him in high esteem.

This study does not pretend to offer an exhaustive review and critique of the extensive body of scholarly literature dealing with Ulrich von Hutten in general and the *Arminius* dialogue specifically. The German-language studies, for example, are numerous and cover various perspectives; the on-line World Catalog lists more than one-hundred-fifty secondary works in various languages on Hutten and his works. An effort has been made, however, to incorporate wherever appropriate ideas that seemed relevant to the analysis of the *Arminius* and related works. Any works not mentioned directly in the text or in footnotes may be found in the bibliography.

Chapter Two
Hutten's *Arminius* and Eobanus Hessus's Preface

Arminius *Preface. Eobanus Hessus*

The fame and glory of many a nation has been preserved by the memory of the deeds and events of its people; hitherto each age has had its famous names. Even Rome, though dying, recalled memories of its earlier triumphs and saw therein traces of its former life. And Troy, unable to show evidence of its glory by its ruins, found its name renowned in Meonio's[1] songs. Jealousy was not sufficient to bury all of Thebes;[2] and the undying honor of Sparta[3] lives on. The sacred image of Pallas Athena[4] will never be totally destroyed, so long as Greece still enjoys special praise. The renown of the race of Pelle[5] still flourishes, and the fame of Perseus's[6] name endures.

Innumerable other peoples have similarly preserved their names, but to refer to them now would be both superfluous and futile. One group of people, however, the Germans, always deserving of honor, has not been spoken about much and has been deprived of its due praise. Why? Who begrudges the Germans this honor? Why such ill-will for the Germans and such honor for others? To whom is it not

---

1   Reference to the Greek poet Homer, whose birthplace some considered to be Maeonia, a part of Lydia in Asia Minor;
2   See Aeschylus. *Seven Against Thebes*.
3   Sparta was prominent among the states that never experienced tyranny, a fact noted even in antiquity.
4   The Trojan Palladium, the sacred image of the goddess Pallas Athena, believed to be the protectress Troy.
5   Refers to the ancient city of Pella (Pelle) in Macedonia, the birthplace of Alexander the Great.
6   Perses / Perseus (212/13–166B.C.), elder son of Philip V and last king of Macedonia (179–168B.C.).

clear that Germans are the sons of Mars?[7] Should Germans be ashamed of being victorious often? No! The matter could not be clearer, namely, that in the whole world or throughout time there has never been a greater people or one that suffered fewer defeats than the Germans. Why, then? For, it would seem that it was not the absence of deeds but rather the apparent lack of those who would write about such deeds. If only we could return to that time when German virtue flourished, the time before we had the luxury of wealth. Then, our ancestors managed to perform notable deeds; then, virtue alone was a just cause for action; then, when writers failed to record their feats, the glory of the German people sank into the waters of Lethe.[8] But not entirely; since the jealousy of others cannot suppress the fame of our deeds, the Romans have recalled those deeds here and there in their writings, in only a few instances at first, but then, as you will see, in more appropriate measure.

And if you ask who and which deeds, let me draw your attention to the name of Hutten, defender of our fatherland. He published a little book as a special monument to the fatherland and caused the Germans to be seen in a new light. For the unknown deeds mentioned here and there in Roman writings had escaped the notice of many; those who have read about them are few, as well as those who have the texts to read. Hutten made it possible for everyone to read the praise of the fatherland scattered in the various texts and there to read the names of worthy Germans unjustly eliminated or ignored. He wrote this little book himself but he did not publish it. Having been taken away by a premature death, the book remained to become a part of his funeral rites. If you do not find here what you are seeking, you will still find other parts that have merit. As I said, Hutten wrote the book but he did

7 While the Germanic peoples, according to Tacitus, traced their origins to the god Tuisto, an Earth god, they also worshipped a war god, Tiu, seen as an equivalent to Mars, or Ares, and whose name is carried forward in the English and German words for Tuesday, or Dienstag.

8 In the works of the Latin poets, *Lethe* is one of the five rivers of the Underworld. In Orphism, a Greek mystical religious movement, it was believed that the newly dead who drank from the River Lethe would lose all memory of their past existence. In Book X of Plato's *Republic* the souls of the dead must drink from the 'river of Unmindfulness' before rebirth.

not publish it; you may infer from this that in later years it was regarded as being better than Hutten thought it was. Moritz[9], a relative of Hutten, rescued the book for you from the eternal night.

The book is about fierce Arminius, conqueror in defense of the fatherland, who struck down your men of Mars, O' Rome. Arminius, he who, had he not perished while still young by the deceit of his own people, would have made the Rhine lord over the Tiber. Learned reader, if you own this little book devoted to the fatherland, you owe thanks first to Hutten, second to Moritz, third to Joachim,[10] and fourth, if there is still place left, to me.

Eobanus Hessus

9 Moritz von Hutten, cousin of Ulrich, cleric, Provost in Würzburg, Bishop of Eichstätt, died 1552.
10 Joachim Camerarius, (1500–1574) was a classical scholar and Lutheran theologian.

Ulrich von Hutten's Arminius

Speakers: Arminius, Minos, Mecury, Alexander, Scipio, Hannibal, Cornelius Tacitus

Translator's note: In a special region of the Elysian Fields, a gathering of illustrious generals had come before Minos to receive his judgment as to which of them most deserved the distinction of being the greatest. Alexander, Scipio, and Hannibal had been singled out by Minos for the top three ranks of distinction, without challenge, until the arrival of Arminius, who requests permission to make a case for himself.[11]

Arminius
This, O' Minos,[12] is an unfair judgment, if you were the one responsible for it.
Minos.
I welcome honest words, Arminius;[13] but tell me, what new complaint is this? Of what unfair judgment do you accuse me? What was the substance of this judgment? So, speak.
Arminius.
I will, but first, you must pardon me if my frank manner of speaking was offensive to you. It is a peculiarity of Germans to avoid flattery when speaking freely and seriously. My complaint is quite frankly this, that when you – with honor and as was your prerogative – set out to settle the dispute of who among the generals was most deserving of the highest honor, you overlooked me as though I never existed. For a long time now, here among the happy generals in this region of the

---

11   The literary context of Hutten's dialogue is the twelfth dialogue of Lucian's *Dialogues of the Dead* (A.D.2); this connection will be discussed in greater detail in the analysis section of this study.

12   A king of Crete and son of Zeus and Europa; Minos was killed in Sicily by the daughters of King Cocalus, who poured boiling water over him as he was taking a bath. After his death he became a judge in Hades. Cf. Homer. *Odyssey*, Book 11.

13   Arminius, (18BC–AD19) Leader of the germanic tribe, the Cherusci, whose defeat of Roman legions in AD9, near the modern city of Detmold, ended Roman domination in Germany.

Elysian Fields, the kingdom of the Blessed, and in accordance with your pronouncement, the first rank has been given to Alexander of Macedonia,[14] second honor to the Roman, Scipio,[15] and third to the Carthaginian, Hannibal;[16] I alone have no assigned place. Nevertheless, if one had to bet on them or on me, and if you were the judge, I have no doubt that I would be given first place.

Minos.

You certainly have reason to complain, German. But why didn't you seek to advise me when they first brought this competition before me for judgment?

Arminius.

First of all, I never thought that something like this could be the subject of a competition, nor did I doubt that at any time you would exercise any other than the highest equity in distributing appropriately what was deserved in life, good or bad.

Minos.

Indeed, and this is done intentionally; but for the most part we judge according to that which we are told, and we make decisions based on however much anyone has to say on their own behalf. Others, especially those seeking favors, we easily pass over, or neglect, as a consequence of the demands of our business. For you can see the difficulty we face, the burden of the numerous and varied judgments we make, and the limited amount of time left for leisure. However, if that which you are reminding me of now had been brought to my attention then, I would surely have called and heard you along with the others.

Arminius.

And now that you are giving me a hearing, don't you also want to recall those whose case you recently heard?

---

14   Alexander III of Macedonia (356BC–323), king, (336–323 BC).

15   Scipio Africanus Major, his full name Publius Cornelius Scipio Africanus, (236BC–184/183), general noted for his victory in the Battle of Zama (202 BC), ending the Second Punic War. He won the surname Africanus as a result.

16   Carthaginian general who commanded the Carthaginian forces against Rome in the Second Punic War (218–201 BC).

25

Minos.

Why not? Mercury, summon before me those generals who a few days ago were here contending against one another in matters military and of war.

Mercury.

As I recall, there were three of them. Here they are now.

Minos.

Noble ones, this man is Arminius, former leader of the Germans, who in the past fought for freedom against the Romans and was victorious. When he heard that you had been arguing about the excellence of generals, and that you had brought the matter before me for judgment, he claims that he was undeservedly left out. For if one considers his evidence in this matter, he says, no one will be seen to have more right than he to possess the palm.

Alexander.

If that is indeed the case, then, by all means, he should be allowed to speak.

Scipio and Hannibal agree that Arminius should have the right to speak, and Minos gives the order permitting him to present his case.[17]

Arminius.

If there are no objections, I would like to have that man Tacitus, formerly of Italy, come here because he knows what was attributed to me in his history.[18]

Minos.

By all means; call him, Mercury.

Mercury proceeds to call Tacitus before the group.

---

17 Such summaries of actions, given here in italics, are not part of the original text but have been added her for clarity.

18 Gaius Cornelius Tacitus. *Historiae.* ed. K. Wellesley, Stuttgart, 1989. The cited material is from *Annales.* See Michael Grant, Trans., *Tacitus. The Annals of Imperial Rome*, New York: Penguin, 1956, [1996], 69–91.

Mercury.

You, you there! Tacitus, come here to me so that you may speak. Here he is!

Arminius.

Your works are esteemed, O' Italian. Please recite here the praise of me that you made in your history.

Tacitus.

Do you mean the place where I also recount your downfall?

Arminius replied that that was the place he had in mind.

Tacitus.

After the withdrawal of the Romans and the defeat and banishment of Maroboduo, Arminius sought to be king over his people. But the people, loving freedom as they did, rose up against him. Arminius met their challenge and while contending with the changes of fortune, winning some battles, losing some, he finally fell victim to the treachery of close relatives. He was without doubt the liberator of Germany. He did not attack the Roman Empire in its infancy, like other kings and princes, but rather when it was at a high point in its prosperity; he had successes and failures in a number of treacherous battles but in war he was always victorious. At the age of thirty-seven, having been in power for twelve years and being much celebrated in the songs of the barbarians, Arminius was unknown in the annals of the Greeks, which only admired its own, and likewise was not at all celebrated by the Romans, who, while praising ancient events, pay no attention to things that are more recent.

Arminius.

Minos, was anyone more honest in his way of life than this man? Was he a good man?

Minos.

That he certainly was; but you, Mercury, are more familiar with the manner of his life, for he worshipped you especially.

Mercury.

Yes, that is true. He was more candid than any other, and no one was more honest or impartial in writing history than he, and doing so without emotion. Moreover, he had observed the Germans with an extremely keen eye and described the behavior and deeds of that people in great detail.

Arminius.

Therefore, if things were as he says and, being aware of my deeds, he described me in such an excellent manner that I have nothing to add, there should be no doubt that great importance should be given to this testimony from an enemy regarding me. First, he called me the 'liberator of Germany,' which I believe is something, to have taken away that Roman province by force of arms and to have led to freedom, against the will of the Romans and despite their greatest efforts, those who were decreed to be slaves. Moreover, it is most proper and fitting that he – Tacitus – says that I took that empire not when it was growing and developing, 'like other kings and generals,' such as Pyrrhus, or Antiochus, or Hannibal here, but rather when it was already well established and stood at the height of its prosperity. He points out further that I waged war against the Romans by provoking them, a war, unique among all others, in which I was never vanquished. And it is for these reasons that he believed that I was worthy to be celebrated in the annals of both the Greeks and the Romans.

So, if all agree that there was never any power greater than that of the Romans, nor in any age an empire so vast, and yet I vanquished it when it flourished and was most vigorous, then I must justly be considered the best general and in matters of war be judged to be the most outstanding, having overcome in battle the boundless power and greatest force of the mightiest empire. Nevertheless, I would not want to rob others of their fame or to do anything that would diminish the glory of their deeds. On the other hand, I have always felt that each ought to be judged by others according to his merits; and though I speak of myself in this regard, it is not from ill-will towards others. I have always honored the pursuit of virtue in itself. I have not cared much for fame, thinking that it would be sufficient to act according to ones conscience. But at the same time, I am not so arrogant as to belittle the deeds of other generals to benefit myself. I also do not suggest that no one of them is superior to me. To the contrary, if one of them is, then he too should have the opportunity to plead his case before you. But you'll forgive me, if in good conscience I refuse to cede a place to those who have competed here for merit. And I will

28

demonstrate that I am not speaking rashly, if they who promised to listen, will listen to me now and judge rationally.

Minos.

I can assure you that they will listen; I am responding for them.

Arminius.

First, let me address you, Hannibal, you whom many speak of as someone who rose from humble beginnings to achieve a rank of great distinction. I will show that if this be the measure of fame and renown, then I have more right to claim greatness than you or any of the others. For example, of those here today who lay claim to having performed illustrious deeds, no one had to struggle with greater difficulties or overcome more serious impediments on all sides than I. Indeed, what man would have been able to seize power in such a deplorable, lost cause? Even my age set a limit on my authority. Why, then, is Alexander seen to be the only one who managed to bear heavy burdens at a young age?

I was no more than twenty-four years old when I was forced to assume the active role of a soldier. I began as general of an army before there was an army, before we had come together as a unified force, and I was forced so quickly to conscript forces which were so dispersed that one could have justifiably doubted that it would ever become an army. I am not bothered by the suspicions of some who say money played an important role in my success at raising an army; this may be so, for at that time the Germans had no money! But I lacked men and resources, miserably impoverished, deserted by everyone, beset by obstacles on all sides, yet I had to find a way to restore our freedom. Without regard to the fact that I lacked resources, aid, or support, I had to rely on the one thing I had, my courage, and to reach within myself for the first step, something I had never done before: to undertake a dangerous war.

Many considered my situation hopeless and were far from my way of thinking; nevertheless, I provoked a war, leaving nothing to chance, but boldly challenging fate rather than fearfully awaiting my destiny, I was able to move more quickly than was expected. For, as you heard earlier, I declared war on Rome voluntarily, faced in my own house with the treachery of Segestis and Inguiomerus, and my own brother Flavius, whose armed force stood on the side of my great

29

enemy. I had soldiers who knew nothing about discipline or about military techniques, with arms that were practically useless, and other equipment of war so inadequate that there was not enough iron to make spears. But all of these insufficiencies were compensated for by courage, intelligence, and enthusiasm.

I converted my great contempt for my enemy into their military defeat. I rushed against them with such speed, while they were still wondering whether I would wage war, and launched the first murderous attack, before they even knew that I had put together an army! Truly, I was not concerned even for a moment that this dangerous undertaking would have any other than an auspicious end. First, I attacked and destroyed three legions, among them the Mars legion which, with its support forces, was considered one of the Roman army's best from the standpoint of military experience, strength, and courage. I then killed the generals and the legion commanders down to the last man. At that point, the safety of the country lay in my hands.

How can Scipio take greater credit for having restored a helpless and weakened Rome than I, who in the shortest time, restored a Germany that had been completely trampled and torn apart. Though I do not consider it necessary to try to equal the magnitude of this deed with my words, the old Romans themselves spoke about it daily, namely, that I brought misfortune upon them, that I brought misery to the most powerful city in the world, that I confounded a prosperous empire, and that no other had brought greater fear and alarm to these lords and masters, these people of the toga, than I had.

One thing is certain, Hannibal, that you, having ridden up to the very gates of the city, were unable to accomplish what I did, though I had been stationed at one of the farthest outposts in Germany, at such a great distance away, amidst rivers, marshes, and mountains interspersed with places not yet explored by man, and, as you know, separated from Rome by the highest mountains of the Alps. Nevertheless, I was able to force that city into such a desperate situation that even Emperor Augustus, he whom many considered to be the most fortunate of men and whose power and control all would agree was beyond question, resolutely decided that he would rather die than to see Rome seized and occupied by me, which of course I never intended to do. It is said that he beat his head against the gates, then

30

ordered guards stationed at all entrances to the city, posted extra guards, extended the authority of imperial governors, and dedicated great games to be held in honor of All-Powerful Jupiter in the hope that this might reverse the fortunes of the Republic. Thus, in short, he did what he was accustomed to do in such situations, in times of dire necessity, but not at other times, he anxiously took defensive actions for Rome. Never before were the people so seized by fear and panic that the city could be in danger; never before had the people's confusion led to such anxiety.

In effect, this was a most serious and destructive defeat for the Romans. I undertook and accomplished all of this when the situation in Germany was desperate, cut off and thoroughly disrupted internally, while the Republic was flourishing, its fortunes favorable, its growth and development great. Having taken the power, I did not receive a kingdom, as did Alexander from his father, nor, like others, did I receive an army from the senate. Then at home I had to suppress agitation within one group and then another. I demanded from people on all sides the names of those who were responsible for the revolts. Some I punished to comply with the wishes of the people, some I pardoned when entreated to do so. Those who deserted, I captured; those who surrendered, were accepted; those who had been disgraced, I forgave. Those who were paying tribute to foreigners I did not consider to be Germans, nor those who allowed other scandalous conditions to be imposed on them. And I proclaimed that the worst possible thing would be to see scepter or battle ax or even one Roman toga between the Elbe and the Rhine.

Then, when the spirit of the people became excited by the prospect of seizing their freedom, I promised that relatively soon not even a trace of the Romans would be left in Germany, even the memory of them would be obliterated. And much of this was quickly accomplished, being slowed down only by the bitterly persistent efforts of the enemy. Thus, to avenge the defeat of Varus, the conduct of the war against the Germans was handed over to those who were strongest and, because of their youth, Rome's primary hope. Tiberius Nero, a warrior not to be disparaged, Drusus, his brother, one of those exceptionally intelligent and prudent men, and others, who were to vie with me and reverse Rome's fortunes and return triumphantly. But in reality I grew in power and in days increased our freedom from taxes and regained the rights of the Germans. Then General Germanicus, a man of vigorous courageous spirit, and his lieutenant Caecinna, known to have had extensive experience in the use of military power, came up against me with a thousand ships, a force such as was used in the battle against Troy, but I held them back and inflicted a defeat that brought great misery to the Roman people. I also slew Cariovalde, leader of the Batavians and many other nobles among the Roman auxiliaries, and in a campaign of revenge I utterly subdued the Chatti and the Frisians. Meanwhile, as within our ranks my brother Flavius was devising a plot in connivance with Inguiomerus, a shameful thing took place: Segestis defected to the enemy. This traitorous criminal showed no consideration even for his daughter, my wife, who was pregnant, but carried her and other noble women off into shameful captivity, an act which the Romans saw as a triumph. Then Segimerus and his son took refuge with the enemy. Many members of my household were enticed by money and helped develop a plot to ambush me and take my life. Among the people a number of hostile plots were devised against me, primarily, however, by the Chattian leader Adgandestrius, who undertook to agitate the situation among the Germans thoroughly by committing a crime unheard of, namely, to obtain from the Romans the poison he would use to finish me off.

However, not being provoked by any of this, I stood firm in pursuit of that which I had begun from the start, to ensure the rightful, ancestral glory and honor of the Germans. I then drew upon the most effective way to move the Germans into courageous action: I relied on those who had wives being held in captivity; for nothing causes greater fear and anxiety among the Germans than the thought of being taken captive by ones enemy. I loved my wife deeply and she had mutual feelings of love and fidelity towards me, and I was concerned that her being pregnant and in captivity might lead to her death. Nevertheless, I remained true to my objective and would not allow my personal sorrows to lessen my love for my land and my people. Consequently, my sorrow turned into anger and I resolved to continue what I had begun. And Hell may be witness to the multitude of Romans who were daily vehemently destroyed and the various traitors who were constantly sought out and killed in the deadly, atrocious war to which I subjected them.

Thus I made it clear to the Romans that I was not intimidated by great acts of treason nor by the actions against pregnant women, but rather was challenged to oppose them openly armed and see them stung by a proper sense of and desire for revenge. In short, I was committed to driving the Romans out of German territories, and henceforth, even unto this day, no one of that empire has set foot there. Maroboduus, the Suebi – the Marcomani – formerly in league with me, was also bound by treaty to the Romans and, thus, my adversary; consequently he waged a dangerous war against me. This was a most serious and intractable war against a most powerful king, skilled and knowledgeable in matters of war and having as allies the enormous support of the bellicose Saxons. In addition to the wealth of the Romans, he also had the support of Inguiomerus, who had sought refuge with him, thus depriving me of a great number of fighting men. But then, after various attacks, with success first on one side and then on the other, fortune showed the will of the gods to support the more just cause, enabling us to defeat the enemy in a secluded spot in the Hercynian forest. Shortly afterwards, seeking to avoid a greater danger, Maroboduus – having been cleverly deceived by the Romans who had made him great and generous promises – his hopes frustrated and facing an inglorious old age, fled back into Italy. I, however, having brought the Germans together into a certain degree of unity and singleness of purpose, delivering to them that sense of freedom which they had so long desired, began to enjoy the benefits of our successful efforts. Anyone who would suggest that I should cede my rightful place or who would challenge my right to receive the palm branch, would have to be someone who had performed the greatest of deeds.

But if the matter in dispute here is that of skill in military matters, or knowledge of command, or the leadership of a diligent army, then is there one here who would be preferable to me or one who would deny that I possess these qualities? I, who did so much against a powerful enemy and who fought and remained victorious to the very end? I am not envious of the fame of others, but these others – let it be said without malice – were often only attacked by mediocre

33

powers with widely dispersed forces. For my part, I attacked the premier empire of the world at a time when, as I said earlier, it was at the peak of its power and had a more concentrated force than any other nation. For a long time I sustained a war against them and was reborn after each defeat, emboldened by my own courage, enduring the continuous vicissitudes of good and bad fortune; that I brought matters to a good end, even my enemies will not deny. I was triumphant, and I freed my country from the yoke of a foreign power. At a time when other nations were agreeing to become vassals of that power, the Romans, I fought for independence and reawakened an awareness of the idea of freedom.

Minos, honorable judge, Alexander has taken up your time trying to persuade you that he could have defeated the Romans in his time as easily as the weak, effeminate Asians, later defeated by a Roman and celebrated with those memorable words, *Veni, Vidi, vici,* or even the defenseless nations of India, which he only needed to approach, surrounded by an army of inebriated, wine-drinking, haughty warriors, in order to compel his enemies to flee and/or surrender. And as for the Scythians, of whom so much has been said, he merely appeared before them and that was enough. And no one can deny that at least his uncle, enlightened king of the Epirotes, when waging war in Italy but not against the Romans, at least it can be said that he was engaged with men; the nephew, however, seems only to have had women for adversaries. Moreover, the pursuit of virtue was always the highest calling for me, not the desire for fame, or greed. For me it was never about erecting monuments to myself after having defeated the Romans, nor did I fight for wealth or the acquisition of power and authority. But rather my goal, towards which all my efforts were directed, was to restore freedom to my countrymen, even if it required violence.

I devoted my entire life to the pursuit of the highest virtues, while being hard pressed by jealousy within my own family, a deceitful, outrageous ambush carried out by my own relatives. I stand here before you as a free spirit, victorious in all that I have pursued, knowing full well that I deserve the highest merit of my country, as one who lived a good life in all respects. So, it is now up to you, Minos, to decide whom you prefer over me; I, who by virtue of courage and bravery came through serious difficulties to achieve greatness; I, who waged a great battle against the Romans, exhibited skill in military matters, and ruled with equanimity. I, who took up arms in a just cause, went up against a great army, but in my life never gave in to the baser passions and stood firmly on the side of good. In summary, among those who have shown the qualities mentioned here, who in your judgment deserves to be declared the best?

Minos.

That was a noble speech, and not just that of the greatest of generals but rather one also worthy of a good man. And I know that all that was said was true, unembellished by Arminius. Indeed, I recall even now how I admired his military skill, the way he handled the barbarians. Consequently, since he was always committed to serving a higher cause, since his merit derived only from his spirit, his virtue, and his military courage, and since whenever he confronted danger it was in the interest of his country, with minimal concessions to vices, I cannot see, by Jupiter, who other than he ought by right to be called the best general. There can be no doubt, O' Alexander, that had he been competing with you here at first, then I would have awarded him the palm. However, since that which has already been adjudicated here by divine law cannot be rescinded, nor can the order determined by that judgment be changed, it must suffice for you, Arminius, to know how I think and to hear what I would have said, had you been competing with the others here.

Now, since you were indeed the liberator of the Germans, and since all will agree that you were unconquered in the wars of liberation you undertook, and since none here faced the dangers you did nor achieved greater advantages for the sake of your people, it seems appropriate to place you alongside Brutus and award you the primary place as a defender of liberty. Consequently, I hereby order, Mercury, to announce in the forums, the streets, the circuses, at the crossroads, in any places frequented by the gods and men, that Arminius the Cheruscan is the most free, the most victorious, the most German of the Germans, and I decree that he be known as such here and there and by all. By this decree this ranking is thus established and no one shall have any right to dispute it afterwards.

Alexander.

But, for some time he served as a vassal; I have always been a king, always been free!

Arminius.

But in my mind there was never a time when I felt subservient to anyone. The thought of being free was always with me, and my mind was devoted to this one ambition, to be prepared, should the occasion present itself, to free my fellow Germans who were bound by the yoke of servitude. Until the day when I was able to act, I kept my intentions and my desire for freedom hidden within.

Alexander.

Then it might seem to some that it was not permissible for you to desert those by whom you had been placed in servitude.

Arminius.

To the contrary; to those people I would respond that I never accepted the yoke of servitude nor consented to it in my mind. If there were times when I necessarily had to accept unjust situations, nothing prohibited me, on other occasions, from doing whatever I could to act in a contrary manner. What right does anyone have to take away from others one of the benefits of nature: freedom? Is it an injustice to use violence to retrieve that which has been taken away by violent means?

Alexander.

But you had given your faith, you had pledged your loyalty to your leaders!

Arminius.

But not to support unjust actions; I was prepared to serve honestly and freely those who would rule with civility and discipline. The fact is that the loyalty I showed was forced from me by violence and by injustice and, as life will generally affirm, when plunderers act against those who of necessity are easily forced to surrender, it is not they, the vanquished, who should show restraint but rather the vanquishers themselves. Furthermore, doesn't he who has held others in servitude for so long by violent means bear some guilt for having done so? Or, doesn't he who has been unjustly deprived of his freedom by the use of arms, have the right to use arms himself when the opportunity for redress presents itself?

If it is a crime against nature to enslave a free man, as I believe, then to have respect for that gift of nature – freedom – cannot also be a crime. In the end, loyalty is that which we give when we ought to. So, tell me, who should be expected to endure injustices such as the Romans inflicted upon Germany under the leadership of Varus, in my view, the most avaricious and unjust man the world has produced. He, who, after having plundered and despoiled all of Syria, decided to do the same to Germany. And it was he, a man of overweening pride and violent spirit, who came to conceive of the Germans not as men but as beasts, irrational brutes, for whom there could be no indignity so great so as to cause horror and disgust among us or force us to resist. Accordingly, his madness was unrestrained, all of the most disgraceful and criminal acts were tolerated. For this reason, it may be said that I committed a crime of conscience, but it was not that I failed to render loyalty to legitimate rulers, but rather that I sought to defend the common laws and rights of the country against a vicious tyrant. It is a natural and noble thing to defend ones cause, and I suggest that no one, bound to peace by an oath, when moved to act on behalf of such a cause, would not feel they had a right to try to bring about change.
Scipio.
Nevertheless, we can still reproach him for the excessively cruel and treacherous way in which he brought Varus to his defeat.
Arminius.
But Scipio, treachery is always involved in situations where one is attempting to replace tyranny with liberty and freedom. Especially in the case of your people, for example, they who rejected and expelledTarquin[19] and assassinated Caesar, but who by doing so have earned the highest praise and eternal fame. And finally, the most treacherous are those who, having observed changes of fortune, make corresponding, accommodating changes in their loyalties. In my case, it was the justice of my cause that compelled me to turn against my adversaries. But now I turn again to Minos; since the gods have pro-

---

19 Lucius Tarquinius Superbus, traditionally the seventh and last king of Rome, accepted by some scholars as a historical figure. His reign is dated from 534 to 509. Tarquinius Superbus was, in legend, the son or grandson of Tarquinius Priscus and son-in-law of Servius Tullius.

vided me an opportunity, is it not permissible for me to attempt to justify the atrocities carried out against Quintilius as reprisals for his earlier atrocities?[20]

Minos.

Indeed, Arminius, in my judgment such a defense of your situation is permissible.

Hannibal.

Can it be, Arminius, that you, who boasted that nothing was more important to you than to be recognized for your devotion to your country, were only pretending to want power? And you, who prided yourself on having removed the yoke of servitude from the people, only threatened to impose a yoke of your own? These are wrongs which could never have come into my mind, and for that alone I should be given the primary place.

Arminius.

Minos, if you wish to remain true to yourself, you will give no credence to what he says. For the desire for power was never part of my thoughts, but rather it was envy on the part of my enemies that led to the suspicions about me. We all know from human experience that the person possessing the greatest virtues will also be the one to engender the most envy and jealousy. The only one who does not experience jealousy is one whose virtue is not evident. The higher one has been exalted, the greater the jealousy he attracts. He who attends to the highest matters of state must necessarily have more influence and power over the people he rules.

How easily the people's freedom could have been destroyed, if I, their defender, being true to the perverse opinion everyone has of me, had simply abandoned them. In this instance, at the time when I held the power and was acceptable to those who would do good, I fell victim to the evil, false accusations of those who tried to portray me as a tyrant. Those who accused me of seizing power should ask themselves who would have been a more appropriate choice than I, the one who rescued the people from foreign servitude and brought them together under the rule of the fatherland? An equivalent act of gratitude on the part of the people, in return for my having restored

20   Publius Quintilius Varus, (*AD9) the primary adversary of Arminius.

their freedom and rescued them from an imminent demise, would have been voluntarily to bestow upon me the power of a ruler. After an interval of time the benefits of the memory of my deeds began to weaken and were replaced, first, by false accusations and then by the evil deed of being overthrown. Of such a course of events, I am not the first victim and will surely not be the last. Did you receive well-deserved thanks from the Carthaginians for your service, Hannibal? Or, to the contrary, was the hostile criticism of personal enemies in your own household the thing that finally overwhelmed you?

Hannibal.

I must admit it; the situation as you describe it was indeed the case.

Arminius.

And you, Scipio, I believe, were repaid by the people of Rome, those by whom you were widely honored but by whose illustrious deeds you were denied the right to die in Rome. Even you, Alexander, must acknowledge that jealousy within your own household brought about your death.

Minos.

Enough; this ends the matter. No one among you was immune to treachery and deceit despite your excellent virtues. But it is truly necessary now for those who have become acquainted with Arminius, his nobility and inborn qualities, to acknowledge him and admire him. Henceforth, German, it is fitting that your honor increase and it is our obligation and my command that we never forget your virtues. Now, go, Mercury, and with those who accompany you immediately announce my judgment. Return, all of you, to the places from which you have come.

Mercury.

Follow me.

Chapter Three
Arminius Analysis and Commentary

Discussing a posthumously published book can be difficult on one level because often there is no concrete evidence to explain why the book did not find its place among other works published during the author's lifetime. In the case of Ulrich von Hutten's *Arminius* dialogue, the delayed publication is especially perplexing. Eobanus Hessus, a lifelong friend of Hutten and first editor of his collected works, gives us one perspective on the problem in his introduction to the *Arminius* dialogue. At one point he said that Hutten 'published a little book as a special monument to the fatherland and caused the Germans to be seen in a new light'.[1] A few lines further on he corrected himself: 'He wrote this little book himself but he did not publish it.' The correction is then followed by an explanation, which also does not help much: 'As I said, Hutten wrote the book but he did not publish it; you may infer from this that in later years it was regarded as being better than Hutten thought it was.'

Such an inference is certainly possible and it may or may not be accurate, but unfortunately there is no concrete evidence of Hutten's attitude towards his book that may have justified withholding it from publication.[2] It is not clear, for example, whether Hessus saw Hutten's failure to publish the book as a judgment that was based either on its content, or on the effectiveness of his presentation of the argument, or any of a variety of other considerations that might have influenced him. The fate of the book, however, rescued from probable obscurity by a relative, was, as Hessus suggested, due to the efforts of others who may or may not have been aware of the writer's intentions. This

---

1   German translations of Hutten's dialogue render the term patria as 'fatherland'; I prefer 'native land' or 'native country'; however, since most German scholars discussing the work use the term 'fatherland' in its modern sense, this study also does so to facilitate taking issue with this nationalistic usage later.
2   See Strauss, 462–465.

is an example of a recurring motif as regards Hutten and his works: critics often allude to an inherent value in his works which earlier critics/readers have either ignored, downplayed, or praised, for reasons not always having to do with matters of content or intellectual insight. The fact of the dialogue's uncertain history does not bring Hutten's authorship into question, though the dating of Hessus's introduction (1528) seems to precede the time of the acquisition of the items from Hutten's library.[3]

The underlying assumption for presenting the two works together in this translation is that Hessus, as a friend of Hutten, was called upon to prepare a preface that would reaffirm Hutten's literary talent and justify publishing the work at a time when Hutten's death in exile was still a source of mixed feelings. On the one hand there were those who felt that his departure from Germany was an appropriate response to his troubling support of the unsuccessful Franz von Sickingen. There were others, however, such as Hessus, who despite their differences with his political views, still admired Hutten for his role as humanist poet and who may have felt that a literary monument may have been the only means to perpetuate his memory for later generations. Hutten's *Arminius* dialogue and Hessus's prefatory essay share a common theme, namely, that societies owe a debt to historians and other writers who preserve records of events and activities to which people in later years can pay homage.[4] The remembrance of things past, they suggested, is key to the current and future welfare of the nation or state. History, as a record of the fortunes and misfortunes of social groups, in their view, plays an important role in the development, maintenance, and perpetuation of cultural attitudes and national identities. The same themes, history and memory, are prominent in Conrad Celtis's inaugural lecture in 1492 when he was appointed professor of poetics at the University of Ingolstadt.[5] The

3   Camerarius, a middleman in the acquisition transactions, allegedly contacted Mauritz Hutten in 1529; the Hessus *Arminius* document is dated 1528.

4   All references to Hessus's *Armimius* preface and the dialogue itself are taken from the translation as given in Chapter Two of this study. The original Latin texts are in Appendix I and II.

5   Conrad Celtis (Celtes) (1459–1508), first German poet laureate, crowned by Holy Roman Emperor Friedrich III in 1487; for the *Oratio* see: Hedwig Heger,

three men were contemporaries, and though neither Hutten nor Hessus mentions the influence of Celtis, it is useful to consider how the three humanists were linked by thematic similarities in their writings. While Celtis's approach in the lecture was basically pedagogical, for example, using it to offer a fairly severe critique of German educational standards and negative attitudes towards learning, a secondary but important goal was to emphasize the valuable role of history and memory in the formation and perpetuation of cultural identity.[6] It is not enough merely to be familiar with and to digest the beautiful, noble thoughts of the ancients, Celtis suggested, one must also be able to imitate those thoughts in word and deed, to give expression to such thoughts and ideas in ones own tongue in the interests of edification and immortality; above all, one must do so eloquently. Celtis, like Hutten, confronted the problem of humanist commitment and ethnic pride. On the one hand there was a commitment to writing and speaking Latin as the common bond between European humanists; on the other, there was a consciousness of the need to use the vernacular language to express ones ethnic pride and to maintain ones sense of a cultural identity.

Celtis felt that history, as a cultural record of deeds and achievements, was dependent upon the eloquence of writers and the durability of the written word.[7] By chastising the young men in his audience both for a lack of interest in German history and a lack of the skills necessary to preserve German deeds in written records, Celtis made points that are subsequently underlined by Hutten in *Arminius* and other works and by Eobanus Hessus in the *Arminius* preface.

For Hessus, as for Celtis, the requisite points of reference were the history and literature of Greece and Rome. He suggested that the knowledge and understanding of those great empires and civilizations was not due primarily to their archaeological remains but rather to the

---

Hrsg. *Die Deutsche Literatur, Spätmittelalter / Humanismus / Reformation, Texte und Zeugnisse*, Zweiter Teilband, Blütezeit des Humanismus und Reformation, München: C. H. Beck'sche Verlags–Buchhandlung, 1978, Konrad Celtis, aus *Oratio in gymnasio in Ingelstadio publice recitata*, 5, 47–50. Hereafter referred to as Celtis *Oratio*.

6   Celtis *Oratio*, 6, 66–70.
7   Celtis *Oratio*, 5, 44–48.

written monuments memorializing their deeds, thoughts, and ideas. He suggested further that Rome's decline did not diminish the glory of its ancient past, nor did the lack of physical evidence of Troy's existence lessen in any way its history as recorded by the imagination of Homer. The Greeks, their gods, heroes, and generals, are known to posterity from records of the written word. Against this backdrop of memory and recognition through the ages, the lamentable state of the Germans and their attitude towards history came into view. There is an element of unfairness underlying the undeserved obscurity of German deeds and personalities, according to Hessus. It goes without saying, though he says it, that the Germans deserve better. Through a series of rhetorical questions, nameless enemies are blamed for the suppression of the renown and recognition due the Germans. Hessus's word choice is illustrative: those who have worked to keep Germany down are guilty of less than honorable behavior, *fraudata*, and they harbored ill-will, *invidit*, towards her; the general tone of victimization is noteworthy, a sense of having been deprived of something which others have been given freely. Having indicted those who had deprived Germans of their honor and fame, however, Hessus, like Celtis, then indicted his own people for not having produced writers who could play the role that posterity required. For the problem was not the lack of meritorious deeds, he pointed out, but rather a lack of worthy recorders of such deeds. Again, using a series of rhetorical questions, he set forth the parameters of his argument, and the implicit answers were buttressed by an assertion of ethnic pride that would also echo through later historical periods:[8]

> One group of people, however, the Germans, always deserving of honor, is not spoken about much and has been deprived of its due praise. Why? Who begrudges the Germans this honor? Why such ill-will for the Germans and such honor for others? To whom is it not clear that Germans are the sons of Mars? Should Germans be ashamed of being victorious often? No! The matter could not be clearer, namely, *that in the whole world or throughout time there has never been a greater people or one that suffered fewer defeats than the*

8   This study suggests that the term *nationalism* as used by scholars writing about Hutten and his works would be more accurate were it construed as ethnic chauvinism.

Germans. [emphasis added] Why, then? For, it would seem that it was not the absence of deeds but rather the apparent lack of those who would write about such deeds, [i.e., historians].

Hessus, like the Romantics more than 250 years later, yearned for a lost German, i.e., Germanic past, filled with heroic deeds and strong virtues which, lacking German writers to record them, 'sank into the waters of Lethe.' And here we see the other side of the alleged vindictiveness and jealousy responsible for suppressing Germany's claims to fame: the historical record, so neglected by Germans themselves,[9] was supplied, nevertheless, by the Romans:

> [...] the Romans have recalled those deeds here and there in their writings, in only a few instances at first, but then, as you will see, in more appropriate measure.

Noting the scarcity of historical texts and the small number of competent, interested readers, Hessus gave Hutten credit for using Roman sources to provide the German public a record of the worthy German deeds and the names of those undeservedly relegated to the realm of unrecorded history. Hessus set the work on its way with a cryptic reader's advisory: 'If you do not find here what you seek, you will still find other parts that have merit.' In other words, even though the work may not meet your expectations, there may still be serendipitous benefits to reward the time and effort spent reading the work.

Hessus's synopsis of the dialogue highlights a problematic aspect of Arminius's heroism: the defender of the fatherland who, according to Hessus and Hutten, might have made the Rhine triumphant over the Tiber, was murdered by members of his own family! This explicit contradiction embodies a problem that arises in other narratives which

---

9   Hessus's criticisms neglect to mention the contributions of Jakob Wimpfeling, *Germania,* 1501, and *Epitoma rerum Germanicarum usque ad nostra tempora,* 1505, or Thomas Murner's *Germania nova,* 1519. For a brief survey of historical texts in this period, especially as regards Tacitus, see also Dieter Mertens, *Die Instrumentalisierung der 'Germania' des Tacitus durch die deutschen Humanisten,* In: Heinrich Beck, Hrsg., *Zur Geschichte der Gleichung 'germanisch–deutsch':Sprache und Namen, Geschichte und Institutionen,* Berlin: De Gruyter, 2004, 80–96. Hereafter cited as Mertens.

use literary texts as vehicles for the expression of national feelings and virtues: coming to terms with the difference between fiction, historical reality, and the perception of reality. Whether one considers literary narratives such as *Das Nibelungenlied*, the *Chanson de Roland*, *Beowulf*, the *Poema del Cid*, or many other epic narratives, the stirrings of national pride that led to their reception and commemorization as national epics derived from a perception of heroism that either ignores central features of the works, or ignores basic flaws in the behavior of heroic groups or individuals, to concentrate on a more nebulous but self-serving code of values underlying their heroic actions. In the case of *Arminius*, though not specifically epic in genre but with an epic narrative implicit in its theme, the issue is not only the double treachery, i.e., Arminius's behavior towards Varus and the Romans as well as the actions of Arminius's kinfolk towards him, but also the conflation of purpose and intent that permitted the oppressive acts of the Roman Empire in the early Germanic period to be used as a metaphor for the relationship of the Catholic Church towards Germany in the sixteenth century.

Arminius, or Hermann, as his name was later Germanized, had adapted successfully to the Roman social and military structure, achieving both citizenship and the rank of equestrian. While there can be no question of the significance of the defeat of the Roman legions in the Teutoburg Forest, the circumstances before, during, and after the battle are frequently either overstated or confused. The treachery of family members leading to Arminius's death occurred seven or eight years after the Teutoburg battle and during a time when Arminius had attempted to replace the tyranny of the Romans with his own brand of autocratic rule. Similarly, the effort to create a confederation of Germanic tribes which would make the defeat of the Romans possible was not initiated by Arminius but rather earlier by Maroboduus, subsequently Arminius's vanquished opponent.[10]

---

10   Maroboduus, king of the Marcomanni, led his people into the region of present-day Bohemia where he initiated a confederation of Germanic tribes to thwart Roman domination. See: *Loeb Classical Library*, Velleius Paterculus, *Historiae Romanae*, trans. Frederick W. Shipley, London: William Heinemann, New

The choice of Arminius, leader of the Cherusci, and the well-known victory over the Roman legions in the Battle of the Teutoburg Forest (A.D. 9) seems thematically most relevant to an appeal to German patriotic feelings and a call for freedom from oppression. Interestingly, it was a choice that could only be exploited for Hutten's patriotic purpose by turning to sources created by the spokesmen of the Roman oppressors whose works would have been available to Hutten as a student, Caesar's *De Bello Gallico*, perhaps Velleius Paterculus,[11] and Tacitus's *Germania*, published in Germany in 1500 by Conrad Celtis. As mentioned earlier, given the fact that they were contemporaries and fellow humanists, it is certainly possible that Hutten was acquainted with Celtis's *Oratio* and its patriotic sentiments; at any rate, the two were linked by their interest in ancient Germanic values, German patriotism, and a humanist reverence for the culture and literature of ancient Greece and Rome. Unlike Celtis, however, who made some severe criticisms of Germans, especially the German princes, Hutten stressed the injustices Germans had experienced in the past and, by implication, continued to endure in the contemporary present. Himself a member of the knight class, Hutten directed some of his most biting criticisms at his peers while maintaining steadfastly the need for a strong monarch to uphold the standard of German virtues and traditions. His alliance with Franz von Sickingen was a manifestation of his dissatisfaction with the German princes and his lack of faith in their ability to play a leading role, as he saw it, in the inevitable break with Rome.

Napoleon is said to have marveled at the inability or the unwillingness of the German princes to put forward arguments stressing national unity as a means of furthering dynastic interests;[12] Ulrich von

York: G.P. Putnam's Sons, 1924, CVIII–CIX, 273–277. References to Velleius Paterculus's *Historiae Romanae* cited hereafter as Velleius Paterculus.

11   'Perhaps,' because the text of Velleius Paterculus had only been discovered in 1515 in Murbach by Beatus Rhenanus; another edition was edited and published in 1516 by Bonifacius Amberbach; the Rhenanus text was published in 1520. There is no concrete evidence that Hutten knew of either of these texts.

12   See Rudolf Rocker, *Nationalism and Culture*, The Rocker Foundation: Los Angeles, 1937, 204–205 Hereafter cited as Rocker.

Hutten would have agreed with him. Hutten's efforts to mobilize the princes by appealing to a sense of national feeling were central to his thoughts about freeing Germany from the dominance of Rome. Having sought the understanding and support of Emperor Maximilian, his successor Charles V, and Archduke Ferdinand, to no avail, Hutten saw the role of the princes as a crucial factor in the struggle for political and economic independence from the Church in Rome. Given his sense of outrage at Germany's exploitation by the Church and his feeling that the time had come for Germans to assert themselves for the survival of the country and the values which, in his mind at least, identified the greatness of the country, Hutten turned to his most effective weapon, his writing, to address the problem; one result was the *Arminius* dialogue.

The dialogue,[13] a form which Hutten adapted from his reading of Lucian's *Mortuorum Dialogi* (*Dialogues of the Dead*), is important in the Reformation period both as a genre and as a mode of discourse.[14] The German rendering of *Mortuorum Dialogi* is *Totengespräche*, conversations between illustrious individuals now residing in the Underworld but discussing aspects of life and character that have bearing on how they lived their earlier lives. The conversation is an exercise in judgment: self-judgment and the judgment of others. The language of the participants has a rhetorical-juridical nature, the spoken language bearing the weight of the discourse, as opposed to dialogue as an aspect of theatrical, dramatic confrontation. Aside from the fact that the dialogue takes place in the Elysian Fields, no attention is given to setting, costume, peripheral activities, or other features that would contribute to a dramatic context. Here one must concentrate on the speaker, the speech itself, and what response the speech elicits from the listeners. To the extent that there is interaction between the participants, it is devoid of overt gestures and expressive only of the most restrained emotional content.[15] It is easy to forget that the

---

13   See Sir Paul Harvey, *The Oxford Companion to Classical Literature*. Oxford: Oxford University Press, 1937 [1989].

14   See Jürgen Kampe, *Problem: "Reformationsdialog" Beiträge zur Dialogforschung*, Band 14, Tübingen: Niemeyer (1997). Hereafter referred to as Kampe.

15   See Kampe, 34–40.

Arminius dialogue was written in Latin, in imitation of Lucian's Greek originals and in keeping with the form, content and, presumably, the intent of the originals. Keeping that in mind, no attempt will be made here to discuss stylistic features, other than to acknowledge that Hutten was in more than one respect a borrower.[16]

The *Arminius* dialogue is representative of forensic rhetoric on a number of levels. In tone, manner of presentation, scope, and resolution, the dialogue is a forensic discourse. The discourse, though at times one-sided, does occur within a *quasi*-courtroom setting, without trappings, but with a structure that defines the proceedings as judicial. Arminius, the principal figure, offers extended examples of courtroom oratory; in fact, his extended monologues comprise the bulk of the dialogue. The proceedings are ostensibly guided by a judge, Minos, in his Greek mythological role, who is assisted by Mercury, a god in his own right but who also has the role, as here, of messenger of the gods.

Arminius is the aggrieved party, the plaintiff, but the ostensible defendants, Alexander, Hannibal, and Scipio, seem to be miscast, since the challenge is not to them but rather to the judgment rendered by Minos. The plaintiff and the defendants, to the extent that the latter are even permitted to defend themselves, are operating *pro se,* i.e., without the benefit of attorneys. There is only one witness, though he is a very important one; his role will be discussed later. Since no physical crime has been committed, there is no need for physical evidence, but the evidence of the historical record becomes an integral part of the proceeding. Cross-examinations, such as they are, elicit detailed responses from Arminius but his challenges to them are for the most part rhetorical questions directed at his opponents or counter-accusations that stifle further dissent. The nature of the Arminius case, i.e., a follow-up to a case that has already been concluded, means that opening and closing arguments are restricted to the plaintiff, Arminius. The cases for the defendants must be gleaned from his comments which are not designed to present the opponents in the best light. Arminius's persuasiveness is a central feature of his oratory and its

---

16   As regards Hutten's borrowings and other less positive attributes, a conscious effort has been made here to avoid the controversial nature of the research of Paul Kalkoff and the sometimes harsh responses to his views.

target is Minos, in this case both judge and jury. Aristotle, in his *Rhetoric*, outlined the role of forensic oratory as it is used here:

> [1356a] Of the modes of persuasion furnished by the spoken word there are three kinds. The first kind depends on the personal character of the speaker; the second on putting the audience into a certain frame of mind; the third on the proof, or apparent proof, provided by the words of the speech itself. Persuasion is achieved by the speaker's personal character when the speech is so spoken as to make us think him credible.[17]

The Aristotelian structures of forensic rhetoric are (a) divisions: accusation and defense; (b) time: the past; and (c) ends: justice and injustice. In *Arminius* the injury, or wrong-doing, is slavery, an injustice involuntarily inflicted upon a people contrary to the unwritten principles and assumptions of general, or natural, law.

Aristotle's view on the universal applicability of principles of justice and injustice is relevant to the judicial nature of the dialogue and the arguments put forth by Arminius. As he says:

> For there really is, as everyone to some extent divines, a natural justice and injustice that is binding on all men, even on those who may have no association or covenant with each other.[18]

The *Arminius* dialogue is in a sense a sequel to Lucian's twelfth dialogue in which Minos is asked to judge the relative distinction of the generals Alexander, Scipio, and Hannibal. The assembled participants in Hutten's dialogue have been increased by two, Mercury and Cornelius Tacitus, Roman historian of the lifestyle and customs of the Germanic barbarians. Just as Lucian identified Hannibal as an African, rather than the Carthaginian, his ethnic, tribal identity, Hutten also identified Arminius by the larger group designation, the German, rather than the Cheruscan. This may seem to be a trivial point except for the general implication it gives to comments about the 'Germans', their behavior, and their innate characteristics. While there is historical evidence to support the claim that Hannibal was fluent in both Greek

---

17   Aristotle, *Rhetoric*, trans. W. Rhys Roberts, New York: Random House, 1954, 1356a, 1–6. Hereafter cited as Aristotle *Rhetoric*.
18   Aristotle *Rhetoric*, 1373b, 7–8.

and Latin, we can only assume that Arminius, given his service to the Roman army, had certain language skills beyond his native language. His comment about the frankness of his speech and the speech habits of Germans, namely, that they avoid flattery when speaking freely and seriously, covers a large segment of socio-cultural history from the early Germanic period to Hutten's sixteenth-century contemporaries. This aspect of Hutten's treatment must be kept in mind in the context of his contention that there was no deterioration of values between ancient Germans and sixteenth-century Germans; this presumed cultural, ethnic continuity covers aspects beyond the moral and ethical nature of Germans.[19] Beyond the issue of whether Arminius could be the best representative of early Germanic as well as sixteenth-century German contemporary values, however, is the question of why Arminius is in the Elysian Fields in the first place. His presence there as a resident general was confirmed by his awareness of the initial judgment of Minos, which awarded the places of military honor to Alexander, Scipio, and Hannibal. In other words, this early Germanic hero, Roman by reward for service, has been incorporated fully into the Classical realm:

> *Arminius.* I neither thought that anyone could fail to see this nor did I doubt that at any time you [Minos] would exercise any other than the highest equity in distributing merit in life, good or bad, as each deserves.

Minos's justification for the exclusion of Arminius from the original judgment is more a comment by Hutten on judicial procedure which, given his experiences with the courts and the imperial authorities in the case of his cousin's murder, could not have been very positive:

> *Minos.* We judge according to that which we are told and we make decisions based on however much anyone has to say in their own behalf. Others we easily pass over, or neglect, as a consequence of the demands of our business, especially those seeking favors. For you can see the difficulty of our business, the burden of the numerous and varied judgments we make, and the limited amount of time left for leisure.

19   Cf. Hutten's essay *Quod ab illa Antiquitus Germanorum claritudine nondum degenerarint nostrates*, Vlri. Ab Hutteni, Eq. Ger. Heroicum. Böcking *Opera*, III, 331–340.

But the more basic reason for neglecting to include Arminius was that nothing about his deeds had been recorded, recalling the criticism of Hutten, Celtis, and Hessus of their countrymen, past and contemporary.

Since we know from the context that a decision by Minos was considered final, Arminius's plea for reconsideration of the verdict would seem to be futile. In the interest of fairness, however, having indulged Arminius thus far, Minos has really no recourse other than to re-hear the case with, so to speak, new evidence that, nevertheless, cannot significantly alter the outcome. It is to the credit of the three generals, Alexander, Scipio, and Hannibal, that there was no objection to this reconsideration.

In the context of the Elysian Fields, i.e., the aspects of time-lessness, perfect happiness, immortality, being favored by the gods, having led a righteous life, etc., the time references in the dialogue and Arminius's obvious unhappiness with his inferior status seem out of place. Part of the disjunctive feeling comes from Hutten's approach and part from the melding of works that served his thematic purpose though they came from very different times and literary contexts.

Hutten's *Arminius* dialogue should be viewed in triangular perspective with Lucian's Dialogue Twelve and Tacitus's *Annales*.[20] The advantage of such a comparison is the light it throws on Hutten's originality, his dependence on his sources, and his view of Arminius as a representative of the Germany for which he, Hutten, was so concerned. This latter dimension is not relevant to the Lucian source, though the arrogance and egotism of the participants comes across with full force in both versions. The basic structure of a judicial decision rendered by an impartial judge has an enhanced mythological focus by the presence of Mercury, the messenger of the gods, in the Underworld setting of the Elysian Fields. To be fair, neither of the texts mentions the Underworld setting but it can be inferred by the

20   Although the *Arminius* text references are to the *Historia* / *Historii* of Tacitus, the relevant passages, as has been acknowledged elsewhere, are to Tacitus's *Annales*.

role assigned to Minos, a legendary figure straddling the historical and mythological worlds.[21]

A major difference between Hutten's *Arminius* and Lucian's twelfth dialogue is the role of Alexander; his pre-eminence as the greatest general is unquestioned by Scipio, who by self-assessment has the rank of second best, and it is not seriously challenged by Hannibal, who is not given a chance for rebuttal argument. However, Hannibal's defense is the one most closely aligned with that of Arminius, since they are both justifying rank on the basis of having risen from an inferior position to one of superiority through sheer force of will and military skill, and both are speaking a language other than their native tongues. Tacitus mentions Arminius's language skills, and we know from Lucian's text, where Hannibal speaks for himself, that the Carthaginian was able to speak Greek. Hannibal's challenge to Alexander, though more personal than Arminius's arguments, is an open acknowledgement of his own inferiority and does not serve his argument well in terms of Alexander's claim of strategic genius. The common denominator for all of the arguments in either version is the art of warfare. Hannibal's criteria, however, are broader in scope, suggesting that those who have risen from obscurity to greatness and dominion over others deserve the highest praise. Their personal effort, the will to power, and the ability to rule over others seem to be, in his view, the ingredients of greatness; Arminius would agree. But while Hannibal found his family situation to be a stepping-stone to his later success, Arminius had to contend with a brother, Flavius, who was firmly committed to the support of the Roman enemy, and a father-in-law and other relatives who could not accept his rise to power and placed loyalty to Rome above family ties. Hannibal's speech has two themes, a historical biographical narrative covering his travels and military encounters from North Africa through Spain and France, ending finally in Italy, near the gates to the city of Rome, and a sharp critique of Alexander. His argument that his successes owed more to a keen intelligence rather than to the blessings of good fortune is uncharacteristic for a hero of his type.

21   See 'Minos,' *Oxford Classical Dictionary*, 692–693.

Alexander relied on the evidence of historical reputation to underline the difference between a king, himself, and a highwayman such as Hannibal. The arrogance of his ambition made the limitations of his inherited kingdom insufficient; only the conquest of the whole world was adequate. Unlike Hannibal, his narrative went beyond the bounds of historical events to include Underworld responses as well. A reference to Charon, the ferryman over the River Styx, contributed to the hyperbole of Alexander's descriptions by indicating that the numbers of dead exceeded his capacity for transport, leaving them no choice but to fashion their own means of entering Hades. He made no claim to divinity, as Hannibal had charged, but left judgments concerning his nature to those who would measure his stature by the scope and significance of his accomplishments. Hannibal's deeds, like those of Arminius, were criticized for being poor examples of legitimate warfare but rather the results of treachery, cunning, and disingenuousness. His boldness and self-assuredness was supported by the voice of Scipio, who selflessly acknowledged Alexander's superiority, deserving premier rank among all generals.

Minos's decision in the Lucian dialogue, being based on the self-representations of the participants, was relatively straightforward and for the most part predictable; such was not the case in the *Arminius* dialogue. The conclusiveness of the previous arguments and Minos's judgment in Lucian's dialogue would seem to preclude the possibility of a sequel that would bring the matter into question. In contrast to the most definitive nature of the conclusion, however, the participants seem almost to welcome another view from a challenger who asked not just to be included but rather demanded for himself the highest rank. Arminius, a Roman citizen and of equestrian rank,[22] provided not only a more robust level of argumentation but also forced the other participants into a more lively defense of their positions. As mentioned earlier, his defense, like the others, was primarily historical but unlike the others it relied principally on the authoritative report of a

---

22   Membership in the equestrian order was open to Roman citizens of means and reputation but not necessarily of good birth; there were thousands of equites throughout the empire. See: 'Equites,' *Oxford Classical Dictionary*, 403–404.

historian, Tacitus, himself a participant in the dialogue. As Aristotle says:

> By *ancient* witnesses I mean the poets and all other notable persons whose judgements are known to all [...] these witnesses are concerned with past events [...] on such questions of *quality* the opinion of detached persons is highly trustworthy. Most trustworthy of all are the *ancient* witnesses, since they cannot be corrupted. (Aristotle *Rhetoric*, 1375b; 1376a.)

In a passage reminiscent of the Boethian *Wheel of Fortune* image,[23] the history-maker, Arminius, and the historian, Tacitus, offer a view of a life in its rise to fame and its downfall into ignominy. Having defeated the Romans and established himself as a ruler at the age of twenty-five, Arminius still remained relatively unknown, according to Tacitus. The fault was not his but rather was due to the arrogance of the Greeks, who only admired Greek accomplishments, and the short-sightedness of the Romans, who always looked with reverence to the past while neglecting the present. This manner of presentation distinguishes Hutten's dialogue from his model in the sense that the record of deeds and accomplishments is kept within the authoritative context of a historical narrative given by the historian himself. Alexander relied on his reputation, circulated by word of mouth or in other forms, while judiciously choosing to enumerate the deeds that he himself felt justified his rank among other military leaders. His response seems at best nonchalant – of the many arguments I might have used, these shall suffice – it speaks perhaps more to the sense of superiority and arrogance of one who had challenged the world and, in his view, had nearly succeeded in making it his own.

Tacitus, as the voice of authority, had confirmation of that role from Mercury, a god whom he worshipped, and from Minos's awareness of his reputation as a fair and just person. These features, added by Hutten, raise the dialogue to the level of a strong vote of confidence in Arminius and the justness of his cause; dissent becomes a non-issue. But the argument itself is less straightforward than the endorsement of Tacitus might imply. Arminius was by Tacitus's

---

23   Boethius, *The Consolation of Philosophy*, Translated by W. V. Cooper, London: J. M. Dent, 1902, *The Temple Classics*, Book II, sect. 25-28.

definition the liberator of Germany, but he was also the tyrant from whom the Germanic tribes, the Cherusci and others, at a certain point had to liberate themselves. As mentioned earlier, Arminius's argument was well served by the comments of Hannibal, who stressed aspects of his own biography that might well be used by Arminius in his own defense. He and Alexander lived full but relatively short lives by comparison with Scipio and Hannibal, but the assumption of great responsibilities at a quite young age was not so atypical.

Arminius's defense of his role as leader brings to light an aspect that makes the Hutten dialogue problematic: the designation of his people as Germans and his country as Germany. The early Germanic period includes ethnic groupings within a tribal culture that occupied a land area that was wild and threatening in many respects and only partially conquered by the Romans. Prior to the eleventh century the Germanic peoples, especially those not yet under Roman rule, had no specific group designation for themselves.[24] From the period of Arminius, ca. 18 B.C.–A.D. 19, we have historical knowledge of the Chatti, Frisii, Chauci, Cherusci, the Suebi, Semnones, Langobardi, the Angli, Hermunduri, Marcomanni, Quadi, the Bastarnae, Goths, Gepidae, Vandals, Suiones, Sitones, and other lesser known tribes. We know that Maroboduus, king of the Marcomanni, was the originator of the first confederation of Germanic tribes, and that he refused to lend his support to the efforts of Arminius to break away from the Romans. Both men had benefitted from Roman service, Roman education, Roman citizenship, and both had become conditioned to and by the Roman way of life. Arminius's efforts to raise an army would have been similar to the process Maroboduus had already accomplished. He sought to bring dispersed and independent Germanic peoples together into a unified military force to face a common enemy. It is not clear that every tribe perceived the threat to the same

---

24   Germans in Roman service would sometimes refer to themselves as *Germani*, the free Germans beyond the Rhine had no collective name for themselves until the eleventh century AD, when the OHG adjective *diutisc,* modern German 'deutsch,' of the people, was used. However, Otfrid von Weissenburg uses the language term *theotisce* for the colloquial language, *Volkssprache*, in the ninth century (868). See also Mertens, 64–77.

degree as did Arminius. He raises the issue himself, indicating that questions were raised whether some tribes were persuaded to support him by the enticement of financial or other rewards. As he said, 'Many considered my situation hopeless and were far from my way of thinking.' It is worth noting that among those who were 'far from [his] way of thinking' were his father-in-law, Segestes, his brother, Flavius, and a relative, Inguiomerus.

Tacitus began his narrative about Arminius, not at the stage of his decision to rebel against his former masters and strike out on his own, but rather at the point at which the Romans, in defeat, have decided to withdraw from Germany. He also includes the subsequent defeat of Maroboduus and Arminius's downfall, both of which occurred seven or eight years after the event for which Arminius was declared Germany's liberator, the defeat of Varus in the Teutoburg Forest. It is worth noting that Tacitus, in his endorsement of Arminius's role, never mentioned this central historic battle. Nevertheless, as an 'ancient' witness, the establishment of his credentials as an historian and someone who knew Germans and German culture became an important part of the dialogue since it had a direct bearing on the veracity of Arminius's self-representation. But while the veracity of his argument may not have been subject to challenge, its logic was not its strong point. There can be no question that the defeat of three legions of Roman soldiers was no mean feat; however, to conflate this event to be synonymous with the defeat of the Roman Empire is questionable. The underlying premise of Arminius's argument is that he who defeated the best must by definition be the best. Arminius balanced these self-aggrandizing comments with expressions of humility, followed by an assertion that combined both humility and arrogance. The suggestion that nothing he would say or do should diminish in any way the fame and glory of others who might have performed similarly heroic deeds is in itself a rhetorical formula for asserting ones own qualities by pretending not to challenge the existence of such qualities in others.[25] Likewise, the assertion that an individual ought to be judged by his merits is

25   Cf. Aristotle *Rhetoric*, 1368a […] comparison should be with famous men; […] it is a noble thing to surpass men who are themselves great […].

inoffensive when the judgment comes from others; self-recommenda-
tion, however, can only be done at the expense of those for whom
similar comparisons might be drawn. Arminius's claim that there was
no ill will underlying his self-serving comments is disingenuous. His
statements about virtue, fame, and conscience ring equally hollow and
formulaic. The egotistical nature of his comments is in keeping with
the foregoing observations, and the emphasis is on the disavowal of
the importance of the views of others, fame, and the preferred reliance
on ones sense of personal responsibility, conscience. The crux of his
argument and the dialogue as a whole lies in the rhetorical assertion
of fairness and humility. The point of the dialogue is to demonstrate
that the deeds of the other generals do not measure up to those of
Arminius, and that when viewed rationally the first place of rank
should be given to him.

All of the self-aggrandizing comments, the expressions of
humility, the pleas for a rational and fair judgment fall into the proper
context when Arminius asks for the forgiveness of the participants in
the discussion, given that his obligation to himself, his sense of his
own worth, precludes giving up his place of prominence to any other,
regardless of that individual's professed merits. He displays humility,
denigration and dismissal of the other candidates, and an assertion of
superiority all rolled into one; the challenge he offers is a bold one:

> Listen to me recite my strengths and virtues, judge them fairly and rationally,
> and you will conclude, as have I, that I am superior to you!

Hutten's dialogue, like those of Lucian, is not a dramatic vehicle
in the sense of the genre that combines speech, gesture, and movement
to illustrate and to develop a plot. His strength is his speech and its
power to present feelings and attitudes without the need for overt
gestures on the part of the speaker. Nevertheless, it is difficult not to
envision the emotional context of Arminius's presentation, not to say
the potential reactions of the listeners. It is equally difficult not to
view Arminius as a self-centered interloper who has inserted himself
into a previously concluded dialogue with the intent of re-examining
an issue that, according to the rules of the Underworld, cannot be
changed. No matter how convincing Arminius's evidence might have

been, Minos's judgment must stand as it was previously rendered: Alexander first, Scipio second, and Hannibal third. One must then ask: what is the ultimate objective of Arminius's argument? Respect? Understanding? Sympathy for his undeserved relegation to an inferior status? All of the above?

At this point, the sixteenth-century context of the *Arminius* dialogue becomes as or more important than the historical context of the actual event on which it was based. Arminius, educated and trained as a Roman soldier, underwent a conversion, or rather a reversion, to his Germanic roots as a Cheruscan leader.[26] This is probably the context that was uppermost in Hutten's mind when he contemplated the plight of Germany in its relationship to the Roman Church. It is important to keep in mind that Hutten's educational, intellectual, and cultural context for a significant part of his life was in fact Roman, in the sense that as a humanist he read, thought, and communicated primarily in Latin; only in the last three years of his life did he begin to communicate in German, at least in writing. The thought process that saw a direct line between the ancient Germanic tribes and late medieval, Early Modern Germans was a basic feature of Hutten's patriotism and his criticism of his German contemporaries.[27] Such a link between present and past is emphasized in his dialogue *Inspicientes,* or *Die Anschauenden* (1520), in which he attributed to his peers, the German knights, an inheritance from their ancestors: military proficiency, respect for ancestral morality, ancient Germanic integrity, and an obligation to defend ancient Germanic customs. The year before (1519), Hutten had discovered an older German text related to the dispute between Heinrich IV and Gregory VII, lending support to his concern about the role of the Papacy in the exploitation of Germany and its restraints on the independence and freedom of the German people. The context of Roman authority being imposed on a people innately disposed to freedom and independence could be super-imposed on the political, cultural situation in A.D. 9 without serious

---

26 This is an assumption; there is no historical evidence to explain why Arminius became so opposed to the Roman presence in Germany.

27 For an enlightening discussion of this topic in the context of Tacitus's *Germania,* see Mertens 37–101.

changes or obvious manipulations. Hutten's plea for ethnic solidarity among Germans, however, while it may have had a counterpart in similar unification efforts among Arminius's tribal culture, was much less successful with his contemporaries, just as similar efforts were only conditionally successful for his prototype, Arminius. Hutten's patriotism – which those discussing him often use in the modern sense without qualification – like Arminius's, was in most respects more an appreciation of ethnic heritage, cultural traditions, and regional landscapes, if the latter can be used to describe a love of country in its broadest sense. He is as unconcerned about regional diversity in sixteenth-century Germany as Arminius was about the tribal and regional differences among his contemporaries. But both have in mind an ideal ethnic, cultural unity, *patria*, that never existed for ancient Germanic tribesmen and was for the most part even at their respective times beyond realization. Despite his contrary argument, Hutten's *patria*, or *Vaterland*, and that of the *patria* he places in the mouth and mind of Arminius were two very different places in terms of either landscape, language, or culture.[28] Perhaps it was the lack of attention to regional diversity, in addition to the fact that he was writing in Latin, which made Hutten's appeal to German patriotism so ineffective among his contemporaries. Recognizing that the problems inherent in superimposing the attitudes and values of one period on an earlier one is also relevant to Hutten's use of the Arminius episode in his dialogue, it is enlightening to consider in this context the thoughts of Christoph Martin Wieland on German patriotism:

> Und es wäre, ungeachtet ihrer Spaltung in so viele größere und kleinere Staaten, und wiewohl das Privat-Interesse unaufhörlich an dem gemeinschaftlichen Bande nagte, eben so unbegreiflich, wie dieses aus so vielen und starken Faden gewebte Band weniger ausgehalten hätte, als es unbegreiflich und ein wahres moralisches und politisches Wunder wäre, wenn ein sehr großer, aber aus äußerst ungleichartigen und schwach zusammenhangenden Teilen bestehender Staatskörper, ohne jene mächtigen innern Kräfte und verbindende Ursachen,

---

28   Cf. Hans Rupprich, Hrsg. Conrad Celtis, *Germania generalis*, In: *Deutsche Literatur in Entwicklungsreihen*, Bd. 2, Humanismus und Renaissance,   Stuttgart, 1935.

von Einem vaterländischen Gemeingeist beseelt, zusammengehalten, und geleitet werden sollte.[29]

Wieland's general comments, based on the experiences of the Greeks, were then expanded and made more specifically relevant to the German situation:

> Ob nun dieser letztere Fall nicht gerade der unsrige sei? ist die erste Frage, die ich allen ehrlichen Teutschen, die sich selbst nicht mit leeren Worten täuschen wollen, sondern denen es um Wahrheit zu tun ist, ans Herz legen möchte. Ich meines Ortes gestehe, daß sich mir starke Zweifel entgegen stellen, wenn ich diese Frage mit Nein beantworten will. Nicht nur mangelt es uns, deucht mich, einahe an allem, was die Nazion mit einem solchen Patriotischen Gemeingeist beseelen könnte: sondern es finden sich auch in unsrer Verfassung und Lage, stark entgegen wirkende Ursachen, welche das Dasein eines solchen Geistes beinahe unmöglich zu machen, oder, falls er auch auf verborgener und unbegreiflicher Weise in unserm Mittel vorhanden wäre, wenigstens seiner Einwirkung zu widerstehen, und seinen Einfluß auf etwas unendlich kleines zu reduzieren scheinen. Wenn es, bei Betrachtung einer so ernsthaften Sache, erlaubt sein muß, die reine Wahrheit frei herauszusagen; wenn es sogar Pflicht ist, einer Nazion nicht mit Tugenden zu schmeicheln, die sie weder besitzt, noch besitzen kann; was sollte uns hindern, frei zu gestehen: daß, wofern sich ja auch hier und da etwas der altgriechischen Vaterlandsliebe ähnliches in den einzelnen Staaten, woraus der große Germanische Körper besteht, regen sollte, nicht nur die Wirkung dieser lebendigen Kraft sehr gering, sondern auch bloß auf den besondern, größern oder kleinern Staat, als dessen unmittelbares Mitglied der angebliche Patriot sich betrachtet, eingeschränkt ist. Es gibt vielleicht, oder vielmehr, es gibt ohne Zweifel Märkische, Sächsische, Bayrische, Württembergische, Hamburgische, Nürnbergische, Frankfurtische Patrioten, usw, aber teutsche Patrioten, die das ganze Teutsche Reich als ihr Vaterland lieben, über alles lieben, bereit sind, nicht etwa bloß seine Erhaltung und Beschützung gegen einen gemeinschaftlichen Feind, sondern auch, wenn die Gefahr vorüber ist, seinem Wohlstand, der Heilung seiner Gebrechen, der Beförderung seiner Aufnahme, seines innerlichen Flors, seines äußerlichen Ansehens, beträchtliche Opfer darzubringen: wo sind sie? Wer zeigt, wer nennt sie uns? Was haben sie bereits gewirkt? und was kann man noch von ihnen erwarten?[30]

29 Christoph Martin Wieland, *Werke*, Bd. 3, Hrsg. Fritz Martini / Reinhard Döhl, München: Carl Hanser Verlag, 1967, 749; Wieland is speaking here of the situation among the ancient Greeks, but the basic assumption applies to other times and national groups as well. Hereafter cited as Wieland.

30 Wieland, 749–750.

It would not do to push the Wieland-Hutten connection too strongly, despite the fact that in later centuries the elevation of Hutten to the level of a national cultural hero became a major aspect of the rise of nationalism in Germany.[31] However, if it is inappropriate to speak of a national consciousness in sixteenth-century Germany, as this study contends, how much more so must it be to attribute such attitudes to the time of Arminius, as Hutten and others seem to have done? At what point does Arminius's defense of his prestige among other generals become less a personal statement and more an expression of a sense of place, an awareness of ethnic identity, a sense of belonging to a cultural phenomenon equivalent to the concept of a Fatherland.[32] Arminius's sense of place, in Hutten's rendition, is of a place that is barren, isolated, inhospitable:

> I had been stationed at one of the farthest outposts in Germany, at such a great distance away, amidst rivers, marshes, and mountains interspersed with places not yet explored by man, and, as you know, separated by the highest mountains of the Alps.

It is perhaps restating the obvious to point out that the 'farthest outpost, at such a great distance away' and 'separated by the highest mountains of the Alps' are distance references from the central place of importance in Arminius's thinking: Rome. The striking feature of his animosity towards Rome, his fervent desire to obliterate all traces of Rome in Germany, is that more than fifteen hundred years later the burden facing Germany, in the view of Hutten, was still the presence of Rome, i.e., the Roman Catholic Church, and a German subser-

---

31 For a broad sketch of these developments, see Wilhelm Kreutz. *Die Deutschen und Ulrich von Hutten: Rezeption von Autor und Werk seit dem 16. Jahrhundert.* Veröffentlichungen des Historischen Instituts der Universität Mannheim. Bd. 8. 1984.

32 The use of this English term to translate *Vaterland*, or *patria*, needs some qualification since, according to the *OED*, the usage occurred first in the seventeenth century. It is being used here to render the concept of love of country, minus the negative connotations modern usage can suggest. German translations of the *Arminius* consistently use the terms *Deutschland* and *Vaterland* for *Germania* and *patria*, the assumption being that the modern terms have the same connotations as the older ones!

vience to Rome that was felt in virtually all walks of life. In the long run, it must be said, Arminius was as unsuccessful in his efforts, as was Hutten. The contradiction, however, which makes the linking of Arminius, Hutten, and German patriotism noteworthy, is the extent to which their failed efforts were no deterrent to their being made models as national heroes. On one level, it may be that the personalities of the two are distinctive enough to warrant elevation to the symbolic status of "national" types. So long as one recognizes and identifies the Arminius personality as a mythic one, borne of a mixture of historical and literary references after the fact, there can be no harm in such a representation. In the case of Hutten, however, who was well-known by some and certainly known at least by reputation by others, the representation hovers between factual activities and idealized wishful thinking, fostered even to some extent by Hutten himself. The heroic image of Hutten is a fabrication that evolved from his outspokenness, his proximity to and involvement in events of historical proportion and import, and the desire of generations after his own to see him in a role that he might have envisioned for himself, that of an Arminius-like German liberator.

Arminius's description of his actions after the defeat of Varus may be described as an example of the will to power.[33] He was persistent in his pursuit of military and political control, he showed himself to be severe when severity was needed and merciful when mercy was more appropriate. He saw some of his actions as expressions of the will of the people and others, his cleansing of the region between the Elbe and the Rhine of Romans, as cultural necessities. By Arminius's own account, the battle against Rome was not an exclusive one but also included Rome's Germanic allies. His victories over the Batavians, the Chatti, and the Frisians, as he described them, helped to eliminate Germanic leaders among Rome's military auxiliaries and were also a means of taking revenge on Germanic troops supporting Rome. The subsequent defeat and flight into exile of Maroboduus, the voluntary and forced abduction of members of his family and relatives, including his pregnant wife, all marked

---

33 For an insightful discussion of 'will to power' and its link to nationalism, see Rocker, chap. 6, 102–114; 518–536.

significant stages in Arminius's campaign against Rome. While his strategic goal, as he stated it, was a unified Germany, his approach towards bringing Germans together was more personal:

> I relied on those who had wives being held in captivity; for nothing causes greater fear and anxiety among the Germans than the thought of being taken captive by ones enemy.

The context of Arminius's campaign and its defined enemy is often distorted by the mythology of ethnic identity and nationalism and neglect of the facts of the narrative, real or imagined. He had already engaged other Germanic tribes, the Batavians, the Chatti, and Frisians, and now he faced Maroboduus and the Marcomanni alongside their allies, the Saxons. It is difficult to know the meaning of unity in this context, since the implication is that the defeat of the enemy entailed, in many respects, the defeat of those for whom one fought to liberate. Arminius's death at the hands of his relatives suggests the fragility of his personal political goals, even though the broader objective, the Roman defeat, was decisively in his favor. The irony of the situation comes through in his own words, as Hutten has him say:

> For me it was never about erecting monuments to myself after having defeated the Romans, nor did I fight for wealth or the acquisition of power and authority.

In modern-day Germany, the Arminius monument near Detmold is a testament to the impact of history, real or imagined,[34] on subsequent generations.[35] The size of the Arminius monument might be said to reflect not only the enormity of the deed for which he has been memorialized but also the arrogance of his pronouncements on his

---

34 This is not meant to suggest that the facts as Arminius [Hutten] gives them are somehow fabricated, but rather to emphasize that the *Arminius* dialogue is a literary work, a mixture of fact and fiction.

35 Detmold, a mid-size city near the eastern edge of the Teutoburg Forest; about 3 miles to the southwest, on the Grotenburg mountain, 1,250 feet high, is Ernst von Bandel's colossal statue, 188 feet tall, of Arminius, the leader of the Cherusci who defeated the Romans there in A.D. 9. The statue is visited by approximately two millions visitors annually.

personal qualities and his right to prominence among generals. It is doubtful that the unity and singleness of purpose among the Germans, for which he took full responsibility, ever existed in the way he described it. Though he claimed not to covet the fame of others and to be free of malice, he nevertheless pointed out the mediocrity of the enemies faced by others and the ineffectiveness of the attacks against them. It was to his advantage to draw clear images of the power and efficiency of the Roman armies and the universal reputation of the Roman Empire, since their defeat must then necessarily have been accomplished by courageous and superior military leadership. While emphasizing masculine virtues over feminine weakness (Alexander), freedom and independence over the yoke of oppression, the pursuit of virtues over acquisition of wealth and power, Hutten's Arminius figure became an idealization of the type of leader he had sought in his own times, one who would be 'victorious in all that [he] pursued, knowing full well that he deserved the highest merit of [his] country, as one who lived a good life in all respects.'

The effectiveness of Arminius's self-representation is echoed by the judgment of Minos who not only endorsed the image Arminius had drawn but also expressed his personal admiration for the great leader and unequivocally ranked him above his previous first choice, Alexander. The fact that Minos's judgments were definitive did not prohibit him from making his preference clear and commanding that others take heed of his choice:

> I hereby order, Mercury, to announce in the forums, the streets, the circuses, at the crossroads, in any places frequented by the gods and men, that Arminius the Cheruscan is the most free, the most victorious, the most German of the Germans, and I decree that he be known as such here and there and by all. By this decree this ranking is thus established and no person shall have any right to dispute it afterwards.

Refuting the meek challenges offered by Alexander, Hannibal, and Scipio, led Arminius to repeat the themes he had established during his original presentation. But by reinforcing his arguments in this way, Hutten created a set of virtues and values that expressed the type of leadership he had urged upon Emperor Maximilian and Emperor Charles V in other writings.

On a broader scale, Hutten used the Arminius context, though not always the figure of Arminius himself, to illustrate his views of Germans and Germany. For example, when Germans confronted adverse situations, such as those existing in the sixteenth century, in Hutten's view, certain prerequisites were necessary: unity and strict obedience to the Emperor. As Arminius said earlier:

> He who attends to the highest matters of state must necessarily have more influence and power over the people he rules [...]. An equivalent act of gratitude on the part of the people, in return for my having restored their freedom and rescued them from an imminent demise, would have been voluntarily to bestow upon me the power of a ruler.

There is an unsettling modernness about Hutten's views on leadership and the German response to it, or the lack of response. The fact that others considered the Germans to be good fighters but not efficient warriors, according to Hutten, was not a reflection on the individual soldiers but rather the fault of their leaders. He saw the lack of a true leader resulting in a people's weakness, a loss of courage, a dissipation of energies and the will to power. But the presence of a strong leader could transform a people; as Hutten expressed it: 'Wenn die Deutschen einmal begreifen, was ihnen not tue, werden sie das erste Volk der Welt sein.' In his view the importance of leadership could not be over-emphasized: there must be one head, one leader to whom all others showed absolute obedience; in war the leader, the general, was more important than the army; Maximilian was the leader by the vote and will of all Germany; He is worthy of this position; so follow him. In his criticism of his German contemporaries, Hutten made points that countered ideas presented in the *Arminius* dialogue. The German definition of freedom, in contrast to Arminius and his comrades, had become a lack of concern for the empire, as the dominant socio-political group, a lack of respect for and disobedience towards the Emperor, and the irrational idea that the German people could be permitted everything without fear of punishment.

In more than one instance, Hutten's Arminius draws attention to his persistent interest in virtue, a quality of character as important as his military skills and leadership qualities. Hutten paralleled this

66

aspect to events in his own day by drawing attention to a major ill imported into Germany by the Roman Church: moral decay and ruin. His description of the situation is important:

> Sehet da die groß Scheune des Erdkreises, in welche zusammengeschleppt wird, was in allen Landen geraubt und genommen worden; in deren Mitte jener unersättliche Kornwurm sitzt, der ungeheure Haufen Frucht verschlingt, umgeben von seinen zahlreichen Mitfressern, die uns zuerst das Blut ausgesogen, dann das Fleisch abgenagt haben, jetzt aber an das Mark gekommen sind, uns die innersten Gebeine zerbrechen und alles, was noch übrig ist, zermalmen. Werden da die Deutschen nicht zu den Waffen greifen? Nicht mit Feuer und Schwert anstürmen? Das sind die Plünderer unseres Vaterlandes, die vormals mit Gier, jetzt mit Frechheit und Wut die weltherrschende Nation berauben, vom Blut und Schweiße des deutschen Volkes schwelgen, aus den Eingeweiden der Armen ihren Wanst füllen und ihre Wollust nähren. Ihnen geben wir Gold; sie halten auf unsere Kosten Pferde, Hunde, Maultiere und – o der Schande! – Lustdirnen und Lustknaben. Mit unserem Gelde pflegen sie ihrer Bosheit, machen sich gute Tage, kleiden sich in Purpur, zäumen ihre Pferde und Maultiere mit Gold, bauen Paläste von lauter Marmor. Als Pfleger der Frömmigkeit versäumen sie diese nicht allein, was doch schon sündlich genug wäre, sondern verachten sie sogar; ja sie verletzen, beflecken und schanden sie. Und während sie früher durch ihr Schöntun uns köderten und durch Lügen, Dichten und Trügen uns Geld abzulocken wussten, greifen sie jetzt zu Schrecken, Drohung und Gewalt, um uns, wie hungrige Wölfe, zu berauben. Und diese müssen wir noch liebkosen; dürfen sie nicht stechen oder rupfen, ja nicht einmal berühren oder antasten. Wann werden wir einmal klug werden und unser Schande, den gemeinen Schaden, rächen? Hat uns davon früher die vermeinte Religion und eine fromme Scheu zurückgehalten, so treibt und zwingt uns dazu jetzt die Not.[36]

Imbedded in these anti-Roman sentiments are the seeds of the nationalism for which Hutten became known and, later, revered. It has its parallel in the anti-Rome position of Arminius, with an additional similarity being that both men, Hutten and Arminius, had to deal with fellow Germans who did not share their sentiments. The latter, as we know, was murdered, the former only suffered exile from his native country.

The role of Minos and his assessment of the presentation by Arminius raises several questions. Why does Minos render a judgment

---

36   Cited here from Strauss, 269–270; see also Böcking, *Opera,* IV, 101ff.

favoring Arminius after having heard only Arminius's self-serving side of the argument? Having known of Arminius and his service beforehand, as he admits, why did Minos render a judgment in favor of Alexander? Since an irrevocable divine judgment had already been adjudicated, why was Arminius's challenge even permitted? The answers are, of course, in the literary nature of the dialogue and in Hutten's all-controlling narrative purpose: to present Arminius as a model hero for all Germans. The approach is all the more surprising in the context of other earlier mythological Germanic heroes, such as Siegfried, Gunther, Hildebrand, Dietrich von Bern, etc. In each case, the image of the mythical figure is not unequivocally positive but rather multi-dimensional, open to interpretation. The Arminius figure is also, historically speaking, not without his faults, but these short-comings play little if any role in the Hutten portrayal. Minos, for example, leaves no doubt where his sympathies lie with respect either to the eloquence of Arminius's presentation or to the physical and mental qualities of the man before him. Recognizing the nobility of Arminius's speech and the goodness of character represented by that speech, Minos went further, however, to attribute to Arminius quali-ties which are purely subjective:

> He was always committed to serving a higher cause, […] his merit derived only from his spirit, his virtue, and his military courage, […] whenever he con-fronted danger it was in the interest of his country, with minimal concessions to vices […].

Minos attested to the unembellished truth of all that Arminius had said and even expressed his admiration for his earlier deeds, all of which brings into question the fairness of the decision-making process. But this is fiction, not history, and Minos is in every respect the voice of Hutten.

Despite its literary nature, the *Arminius* dialogue is more than a literary document; it is programmatic and propagandistic. Its popu-larity in the Early Modern period and the ensuing Enlightenment can be related to this new expression of form and function, in its ability to provide a serious vehicle for ideas and attitudes that spoke directly to an agenda of personalities and programs of action. Such is the emphasis in the judgment of Minos:

Arminius the Cheruscan is the most free, the most victorious, the most German of the Germans [...].

To Hutten's credit, despite the biased portrayal of Arminius, the dialogue raises important issues of ethics and morality relevant to any age. Provoked by the comment of Alexander to the effect that as a king he had always been free, Arminius introduced the concept of freedom as a natural birthright. The idea that people are born free raises the issues of slavery, loyalty, justice and injustice, service and obedience, consent and coercion, and a host of other elements integral to societal existence. For the Romans, Arminius and his fellow Germans were barbarians, even in cases such as Arminius, or Maroboduus, where they had assimilated themselves into Roman society through military and other service. Hutten's view of the contemporary situation does not change this view much. The Germans are still barbarians in the view of the Romans/Italians, but as Hutten adds:

> [...] Wil man aber güte sitten unnd achtung freüntlicher beywonung, auch fleyß der tugent, beständigkeit der gemüt unnd redlichkeit ansehen, so ist dises [die Deutschen] ein wol gesitte nation, und dargegen die Römer mit der allerausser lichsten barbarey verstallt.[37]

His ambivalence towards the Germans is a sub-theme in the *Arminius* dialogue and is perhaps best expressed in the dialogue *Die Anschauenden*.[38] While in *Arminius* the recurring motif is the necessity to wrench unity from the throes of disunity among the Germans, in the dialogue *Die Anschauenden* the Saxons are representatives of the best and worst of German characteristics. Just as Hutten turned to mythology in *Arminius* to emphasize the prowess of the hero in sending countless Romans to their deaths, the evidence for which was registered in the entry of dead souls into Hades, the Saxons are compared to the Centaurs in their conflict with the Lapithen.[39] The contrast between the intellect and the passions would seem to be

---

37 G. Balke, *Huttens Deutsche Schriften, Deutsche National Literatur*, 17/2, *Die Anschauenden*, 295–323; 306 §29. Hereafter cited as Balke.
38 This dialogue will be handled in greater detail later in this study.
39 See Christian Klemm, Hrsg. *Friedrich Kurts Handbuch der Mythologie*, 214–216.

detrimental to Germans, since they are here also being identified with the intemperate wine-drinkers at a banquet, lacking reason:

> [Phaeton] [...] welh ein geselschafft syhe ich da, welche trück, welhe grollen, welh spewen! Da frißt und saufft man unzüchtigklich, überhaufft die gericht, tregt auff das brot mit grossen körben, den tranck in schweren fläschen, schreyet, rufft, singt und heület [...] Diße brasserey mag sich auch wol vergleichen der würtschafft, die ettwan zwey völcker Centhauri und Lapithe mit einander gehabt. [...] daz es yederman verstehe von den Sachsen, Allweg stecken die Sachsen hinder den fläschen![40]

Arminius, too, draws attention to the military prowess of the Saxons in their support of his foe, Maroboduus. The image of the Germans in the *Arminius* dialogue, based exclusively on the representation of the hero, combines physical stamina, strategic and tactical expertise, and inner qualities to round out the profile of the most outstanding general. Hutten's idealized image also characterized those to whom he appealed in *Die Anschauenden*. The link between ancient Germans, the contemporaries of Arminius, and sixteenth-century Germans was, in his view, a commonality of attitudes, interests, abilities, and values. The same characteristics that stood for solidarity and continuity among Germans also distinguished them from their contemporaries in any age. The inappropriate or anachronistic nature of some of Hutten's characterizations of Germans must be viewed in the context of his argument, the assertion of German superiority. The ridiculousness of the idea that Germans had little need for doctors or lawyers pales beside the corollary suggestion that Germans were better off than people who relied on codified laws because the Germans had the advantage of tradition and/or customary law.

This contrast between codified law and customary law is not a practical argument on Hutten's part but rather a poetic exaggeration to emphasize the value of naturalness and heritage. Likewise, the idea that Germans were better at organization and implementation when they were drunk than other people who were sober needs no further comment. There is a curious suggestion, which Hutten endorsed through his speaker, Sol, that the German love of beer and wine was

---

40   Balke 306–307, §32.

somehow linked to their honesty and integrity, that to give up the one was to relinquish the other. The suggestion calls to mind the proverbial expression, *in vino veritas*, but also the characterization at the beginning of the *Arminius* dialogue, 'you must pardon me in advance if my frank manner of speaking should offend you. It is a peculiarity of Germans to avoid flattery when speaking freely and seriously.'

Arminius's self-aggrandizing comments about himself and the cultural references to his people, though we recognize that "Germans" in this context cannot be taken as representative of the cultural group as a whole, reflect two dimensions of thought: Hutten's personal sense of the exclusivity of German-ness, *Deutschtum*, and his humanist sense of the cultural phenomenon of the *translatio imperii ad Teutonicos*.[41] However important these elements may be in assessing Hutten's role in the literary and political life of sixteenth-century Germany, neither can be considered without qualifications. Hutten's concept of German-ness, despite the acclaim of those who see/saw him as the German arch-patriot, was exclusive in the sense that his primary interest was his own class, the imperial knights, the *Reichsritter*. Had he lived longer, there is the reasonable probability that his response to the Peasant rebellion of 1524, for example, would have been the equivalent of Martin Luther's – they have overstepped their boundaries and need to be put in their place. The vagabond years of an impoverished student estranged from his family, the various humiliations at the hands of his patrons, the mental and physical suffering connected with his syphilis, none of the above altered in any way Hutten's belief in the value of his heritage and the destiny of his people. His interest in Arminius was perhaps a reflection of his own experience as a would-be liberator, a disappointed advocate for those to whom the path to freedom and independence was not as straightforward as he perceived it to be. The second aspect, the *translatio imperii ad Teutonicos*, was embedded within the broader concept of humanist historiography, with which Hutten would have to have been

41   For a cogent analysis of this topic as it relates to Germany and England, see Samuel Kliger, The Gothic revival and the German *Translatio, Modern Philology*, Vol. XLV, No. 2, November, 1947, 73–103. Hereafter cited as Kliger.

familiar. The humanists, and especially those writing in Germany, had been largely responsible for introducing into intellectual discourse a different historical perspective that moved definitively away from the dominant medieval historiographical view, salvation history, *Heilsgeschichte*.[42] At the same time the humanists retained some aspects of medieval thought which became standard features of their approach, the *Kaisersidee*: the idea of a strong central ruling authority in the person of the Emperor; the *translatio* concept, which saw the Germans as heirs to the imperial traditions of the Romans;[43] the view of ancient tribal cultures as key elements of ethnic identity, which later became the nucleus of a national feeling that would fuel feelings and attitudes defining patriotism;[44] an idealized view of a Germanic past which many, like Hutten, saw as prologue to the Renaissance humanist cultural view.

A key feature of the Renaissance humanist approach to history and culture, as reflected in German humanists such as Hutten, Celtis, and others, was the notion of a link between the people and the land of their birth, the autochthonous nature of ones ancestors and the values they held. Simon Schama, discussing Tacitus's *Germania* in *Landscape and Memory*,[45] provides the background for this concept as the Roman historian interpreted it. Especially Tacitus's view of the Semnones and their forest rituals strengthened the image of the forest grove as the *initia gentis*, in Schama's words, a place where the race first arose, as if uncoiling, fern-like, from the dark and spongy humus. Schama's vivid imagery is appropriate for the autochthonous context of Hutten's view of German ancestry, which Schama does not discuss, and for those of Conrad Celtis, which he does, briefly. What is missing from the discussions, however, is a more critical view of the myth-based legacy that such attitudes about sylvan simplicity and

---

42   Mertens, 78–84.
43   For a view of the role of Charlemagne's rule as a significant stage in the *Translatio* process, see Kliger, 78ff.
44   For an earlier example of this type of thought, see Otfrid von Weissenburg, *Evangelienbuch*, Vorrede. In: Braune/Ebbinghaus *Althochdeutsches Lesebuch*, 98–100.
45   Simon Schama, *Landscape and Memory*, Toronto: Vintage Books, Canada, 1996. 84. Hereafter cited as Schama.

autochthonous cultural ancestry provided for Germans of subsequent centuries. Schama approaches the subject with candor at one point, pointing out the differing fortunes of the progenitors of such attitudes, Tacitus in his *Germania*, and those of the country itself:

> By the conclusion of the Thirty Years War in 1648, there had been twenty-six editions of the *Germania* and Germany lay in shattered fragments. Its only power was the Holy Roman Empire, once again tied inseparably to the Roman church militant. Its landscape which had given such cheer to humanists of Conrad Celtis's generation, was a destitute ruin: depopulated and burnt-over; a wilderness traipsed by pathetic caravans of destitute vagrants and brutalized by marauders. (Schama, 101)

The line of continuity from Tacitus to Celtis to Herder, as Schama describes it, is culturally enlightening, and his emphasis on the graphic representations of the forest mania and other manifestations of patriotic feeling from the sixteenth century on gives proper scope to the dimensions of the various guises of German national feeling. In the context of German-ness being rooted in the soil, Schama's description of the original plan for an Arminius / Hermann statue designed by the architect Karl-Friedrich Schinkel is illustrative:

> For Hermann, leaning on his sword, was to be mounted on a pedestal of un-fashioned rock, the whole statue emerging, supernaturally, from the treetops of the oakwoods that surrounded it. (Schama, 109)

Though Schinkel lost out to Ernst von Bandel for the final successful design, the mythical underpinnings of both representations bridged the cultural gap between the nineteenth century, the perceptions of the early Germanic culture of Arminius, and the various literary, religious, and political views of the ensuing periods. Tacitus's Arminius had become Hermann[46] and subsequently became the prototype as well of the Emperors Maximilian, Charles V, and Wilhelm I. A direct line of cultural continuity was drawn between the Battle of the Teutoburg Forest in A.D. 9 and the decisive defeat of the French at Sedan and

---

46   There have been assertions that Luther was the first to use the Germanized name, Hermann, for Arminius; for an important comment on this development, which started probably with Aventinus, see Mertens 37–101.

Metz, celebrated in true Germanic fashion in 1875 with the dedication of the *Hermannsdenkmal* in Detmold.[47] These images and the underlying mystical, mythical currents that link them are all part of a mentality that persisted in German culture for centuries. The cultural phenomenon described by Georges Dumézil as a "pre-established congruence between past and present" is present in Hutten's expression of a continuity between *Germanic* values and *German* values in his *Quod ab illa antiquitus Germanorum claritudine nondum degenerarint nostrates*. Such a mindset, while it does not require a full correspondence between then, *tunc*, and now, *nunc*, does suggest that the linkage, even with variations, is significant and culturally affirming.

> Tunc cum tempus erat, gerere arma, et cogere gentes expugnare urbes, regumque; infringere fastas, fecimus agregie, motisque indulsimus armis, Nunc placidas artes, pacemque; admittere curis est opus, atque animos tranquillum advertere in usum.[48]

David Friedrich Strauss suggested that Hutten's attitude reflected an historical perspective – for which Strauss unfortunately gave no source – which viewed the course of human history as a flow of periods alternating between war and peace. The former, characterized by violence, aggressiveness, the assertion of might as the guarantor of right, and the latter as a period of tranquility, development of creative forces, the positive achievements of humanistic studies, arts, philosophy, and a concern for peace and harmony. As a humanist, Hutten probably did envision the latter as a theoretical framework and general goal of the educational and creative endeavors of a community of scholars and public intellectuals. On the other hand, the period of Hutten's life, from the late fifteenth through the first two decades or so of the sixteenth century, was a time of intellectual ferment, social change, and political intrigue, not to mention the wars in Italy in which Hutten himself was peripherally involved.[49]

One could argue, as Hutten seems to be doing, that there was a greater sense of continuity between the real conditions in Hutten's

47   Shama, 112.
48   Böcking *Opera* III, 331.
49   Strauss, 55.

time and those of his Arminius figure: a time of prosperity, social dissent, and the perception that Germans were being stifled in their progress and creativity by the yoke of Roman oppression, i.e., first the Empire then the Church. Arminius's freedom of the mind, his independence of the will, for example, seems more appropriate to the humanist thought of Hutten than the mentality of a Germanic barbarian. One must keep in mind, however, that Arminius was in only a limited way, a fully Germanic individual. Much is made of the fact that he had been educated in Rome, was quite familiar with Roman society, and had adapted to and become part of the Roman way of life. Having achieved citizenship and equestrian status were not trivial milestones along the way for a non-Roman. His comments on freedom are of interest:

> What right does anyone have to take away from others one of the benefits of nature: freedom?

Freedom, or *libertas,* as a natural right inherent in ones humanity, was so defined even by the Romans.[50] Arminius does not seem to be talking about his situation as a military leader within the Roman army with authority over auxiliary troops, as we understand the role of someone such as he.[51] His comments about freedom and injustice are in the context of freedom and its opposite, slavery. His concern is for oppression, the conditions of life imposed on a subservient people by dominant, inconsiderate masters. He also implies that the situation came about at the hands of a superior force, one that did not hesitate to use violence to impose its will on a conquered people. Arminius does not resort to specifics to describe the exact events by which he and his people lost their freedom to the Romans, but it is clear that he sees their situation as an unnatural constraint on their exercise of their human rights. His counter to Alexander's charge of disloyalty to his superiors is in line with his depiction of himself as a man of virtue.

---

50   Orlando Patterson, *Freedom*: Vol. I, *Freedom in the Making of Western Culture*, 220. Hereafter cited as Patterson.

51   Arminius's father, Sigimer, a prince among the Cheruscans, had been taken captive by the Romans and had made a military career in the Roman army, commanding Cheruscan auxiliary troops; Arminius had a similar career.

Among the qualities generally considered to be characteristic of a virtuous man, loyalty was prominent, along with integrity, trustworthiness, and self-control.[52]

> And if it is a crime against nature to enslave a free man, as I believe, then to have respect for that gift of nature, freedom, cannot also be a crime. In the end, loyalty is that which we give when we ought to.

Arminius's defensive argument is not only an endorsement of personal freedom as a natural right but also of civic freedom which, in his view, when ignored by a tyrant such as Varus called for acts of civic rebellion, his 'crime of conscience.' The notion of equality before the law and the acceptance of the legal structure of authority are part of his view of things as they ought to be.[53] The most confusing aspect about Arminius's comments at this point is the legal structure to which he refers. Quintilius Varus's rule in Germany was by all accounts irresponsibly negligent,[54] and Arminius's objections to that rule and the violent actions he undertook are being described as a defense of the common laws and rights of the country. Either he is speaking in defense of Rome, being in that sense more Roman than the Roman, or he is addressing himself to a country and a body of laws which at that time did not exist. He disputed the point that he had shown disloyalty to his superiors – it was not that I failed to render loyalty to legitimate rulers – but suggested rather that his actions were those of anyone faced with the injustices of a vicious tyrant.

Arminius's comments in his own defense provide a rich contrast to the sixteenth-century situation for which his rebellious, heroic role

---

52   Patterson, 221.
53   Velleius Paterculus talks about the mendacious Germans who, in his view, created false allegations culminating in lawsuits to be brought before Quintilius Varus, and were then grateful for Roman justice to settle the disputes. [...] *At illi* [the Germans] *natumque mendacio genus, simulantes fictas litium series et nunc provocantes alter alterum in iurgia, nunc agentes gratias quod ea Romana iustitia finiret feritasque sua novitate incognitae disciplinae mitesceret et solita armis discerni iure terminarentur* [...]. Velleius Paterculus, 299.
54   Velleius Paterculus makes the critical comment that Varus thought of himself as an administrator rather than a general commanding an army in occupied territory. Ibid, 298–299.

had become the primary model. There can be no doubt, however, that the context of his comments is that of slavery and freedom, oppression and liberation from oppression. Even the description by Tacitus, *haud dubie liberator Germaniae*, suggests that the Germans had the social status of slaves, as Arminius says, 'those who were decreed to be slaves.' By no stretch of the imagination can the German situation with respect to the Roman Catholic Church in the sixteenth century, or any other century, be described as slavery in the social sense. On the figurative level, however, and in the sense of being burdened and oppressed by a set of obligations that had been imposed from without, the German situation was tantamount to a state of social injustice that affected people at all levels of the society. The attitude of the Church leaders towards the Germans, it might be said, was similar to the view of Germans that Velleius Paterculus attributed to Varus, that they were human only in appearance.[55]

The set of circumstances that motivated Arminius to take the actions he did arose from a sense of the injustices he saw around him and a feeling of obligation to act on behalf of his fellow Germanic tribesmen. Underlying this sensitivity, however, was a mentality more akin to an educated, aristocratic Roman than a Germanic warrior. To express pride in a life devoted to the pursuit of virtue seems more appropriate for a humanist, someone committed to the principles of ancient Greece and Rome, than a Germanic warrior:

> The pursuit of virtue was always the highest calling for me, not the desire for fame, or greed [...]. I devoted my entire life to the pursuit of the highest virtues [...].

Arminius's monolithic view of Germany, undifferentiated by any specific tribal identifications and regional characteristics, is anachronistic and as idealistic as was his view of the merit he deserved from an ungrateful people, i.e., the family members responsible for his death.

In contrast to the historical narrative in which Arminius enumerated his valorous deeds and justified his inclusion in the ranks of the excellent generals, the latter, extended defensive narratives build on a

---

55   Velleus Paterculus, 297.

complex of concepts that form a background for the actions described in the former; the juxtaposition of slavery and freedom, virtuous actions over against the treachery of relatives, the pursuit of virtue as opposed to actions to seek fame and glory. The Latin words *iugum* and *servitus,* both suggestive of a loss of personal freedom, are central to Arminius's comments in the second part of the dialogue, and they also serve to highlight Alexander's view of the distinction between himself and Arminius. Herein lies a distinction which Arminius did not accept, namely, the difference of *once* having been a slave and *always* having been free. In his view, freedom is a natural condition which is not compromised by a temporary enslavement. Even if, under certain conditions, he says, I had been forced to accept the conditions of slavery, nothing prevents me from throwing off that yoke once the opportune situation presented itself. Alexander's retort as regards faith, or loyalty, *At fidem dederas*, raises a question of the context within which the two men are speaking. Since there can be no question of linking slavery and loyalty, or giving ones word on an issue when one is in a condition of servitude, the context of Alexander's comment must be that of the concept of virtue. Virtue, as Arminius defined the concept, is relevant to the aristocratic values of a certain class of Romans. Despite the fact that he cannot be included in the social class that might have held such values, Arminius declared the pursuit of virtue to be an end in itself and an important part of his life. A general catalogue of virtues for his time would have included, among a series of qualities, self-control, determination, loyalty, trust-worthiness, integrity, etc.[56] While Alexander's comment is extraneous to the issue of slavery, it is integral to the concept of virtue and Arminius's personal integrity. As a Germanic and Roman military officer, Arminius seems to be caught between two codes of conduct. On the one hand, as Roman citizen of equestrian rank, he is bound to his Roman superiors by an explicit or implicit oath of loyalty; on the other, however, as a Germanic warrior with links to his tribe, the Cheruscans, and ethnically to other tribes as well, he seems to feel an obligation to be concerned about the personal freedom of those to

---

56   For a general discussion of virtue, *virtus*, in the context of freedom and slavery, see Patterson, 221.

whom he has a blood relation. The irony of Arminius's noble sentiments on behalf of his people is that his efforts elicited actions that
countered the virtues he espoused.

Even by Germanic standards, a violent act pitting blood relatives
against relatives would have been viewed as reprehensible. Unfortunately, we lack concrete information as regards the motivation for
the act, except *invidia* and the fact that it was described as a crime, or
outrageous deed, *facinus*. The contrast between Arminius's virtuous
behavior and the criminal behavior of his relatives, *domestica invidia,
et propinquorum dolo facinus patrante,* is worth noting because it
draws attention to the broader social context, in which virtuous
behavior was a measure of the man,[57] and the more personal, private
context of a man's behavior among those closest to him, those most
aware of his aims and objectives. It is interesting that the nature of
Arminius's fall is not an aspect that differentiates him from his
competitors but rather one that links him to them. The issue of tyranny
and the murder of tyrants, justified or unjustified, is a subject to which
all of the men participating in this dialogue can relate. Scipio's
criticism of disloyalty and viciousness on Arminius's part is as easily
parried as Hannibal's charge of excessive ambition. By reference to
two important examples, Tarquinius Superbus and Julius Caesar,
Arminius aligned himself with crucial stages in Roman history and
with acts which could be construed as necessary expressions of
patriotism.[58] Scipio's use of the word *perfidia,* a deliberate breach of
faith, calculated violation of trust, treachery, which by all accounts is
an accurate description of Arminius's actions against the Romans, is
not effective. Arminius's defense against the charge is facile:

> the most treacherous are those who, having observed changes of fortune, make
> corresponding, accommodating changes in their loyalties.

---

57 Keeping in mind that the original meaning of *virtus* included manliness,
    strength, courage and bravery.
58 Tarquinius Superbus was, in legend, the son or grandson of Tarquinius Priscus
    and son-in-law of Servius Tullius. Tarquin supposedly murdered Tullius and
    established an absolute despotism–hence his name Superbus, the proud.

Despite the fine tuning of his argument, it is difficult to see why Arminius's actions would not qualify as perfidious, waiting as he did for an opportune moment to rebel against the Romans. On a positive level, however, Arminius's actions demonstrated patience, an independence of the will, and a calculation of actions that would guarantee optimum success.[59]

> My mind was devoted to this one ambition, to be prepared, should the occasion present itself, to free my fellow Germans who were bound by the yoke of servitude. Until the day when I was able to act, I kept my intentions hidden within and my desire for freedom.

Despite the self-serving nature of his arguments, Arminius deftly defended himself against charges of going back on his word (Alexander), disloyalty towards his superiors (Scipio), and power-hungry ambition (Hannibal), in each instance presenting his actions as expressions of love of country and empathy with his countrymen.

Hannibal's questioning of the compatibility of love of country and a desire to rule ones countrymen or liberation from one oppressive situation only to be subjected to another elicits an enlightening response from Arminius as regards the will to power. His description of his rise to power is an unapologetic endorsement of the emergence of the natural leader, one whose inner makeup, his virtue, is manifested by his actions. Such a person takes the envy of others for granted. His prerogative to lead and rule, also a natural gift that conferred upon him superiority over others, was also taken for granted. In fact, had he not assumed the power as a matter of right, as the people's liberator, he suggested, they should have given him power over them voluntarily. Having brought the people together under the rule of the fatherland, *sub patrium regnum collecturus*, was synonymous with being under the rule of Arminius!

From a modern perspective, it seems almost a commonplace to suggest that a person bearing the greater responsibility deserved and needed greater powers. In A.D. 9, the sixteenth century, or in subsequent periods, however, when Arminius, whose role as a cultural hero

---

59   For a modern literary example of independence of the will in a master-slave situation see, Berthold Brecht. *Maßnahmen gegen die Gewalt.*

had taken on special meaning for certain segments of German society, the implications were ominous. It should be noted in this context that liberators who anticipate the gratitude of the people being liberated are often disappointed. As Arminius pointed out, he was neither the first nor would he be the last to suffer such a fate.

Chapter Four
Hutten in Literary Contexts

Ulrich von Hutten was crowned Poet Laureate by Emperor Maximilian on 12 July 1517. His literary efforts, at this time all in Latin, had brought him to the attention of fellow humanists and students of humanistic studies at various universities in Germany and Italy. The recognition, coming at age twenty-nine, might have brought with it an assurance of academic success at the professorial level or beneficial appointments in government service. Unfortunately, Hutten was able only to a limited degree to capitalize on his accomplishment. His literary productivity, extending through the period 1506–1520, fell into three broad categories: poetry of various types, formal and informal epistolary writings,[1] and dialogues. Prior to 1520, he wrote exclusively in Latin; in that year, however, he began to translate his Latin works into German and produced a few works originally in German in an effort to attract a broader audience. Some assessments of Hutten's literary skills often give the impression that his German translations of his own works were stylistically equal to his Latin originals; most will agree that they were not.[2] The variety of his literary output included, to cite just a few examples, the extended narrative complaint against his treatment at the hands of the Lötz family in Greifswald, the dialogues *Nemo* (1510) and *Arminius* (published posthumously, 1529), a poetics treatise *De arte versificandi* (1511) which served later as a textbook at various universities, a series of epigrams dedicated to Emperor Maximilian (1519), a number of the letters in the second part of the *Epistolae obscurorum virorum*, and a significant number of poems, letters, and political treatises. The first edition of his collected

---

1   For the purpose of this discussion, given the role letters played in Hutten's contacts with humanists and others, all letters are viewed as important parts of Hutten's literary output, but only a select few will be examined analytically.

2   This study will examine assessments of Hutten in past and current histories of literature to illustrate this point.

works, *Opera poetica Hutteni postum*, was prepared by his friend Eobanus Hessus (Straßburg, 1538).

Efforts to clarify the literary role and contribution of Ulrich von Hutten in the context of a German literary tradition have been complicated by the ambiguous nature of his personal and professional lives, i.e., his strong commitment to humanistic studies and the power of the written word, in Latin, coupled with an equally strong and committed devotion to the liberation of German society from what he saw to be debilitating subservience to the Roman Catholic Church. The disjunction between Hutten's preferred language, Latin, and his message, the desire for a stronger, independent Germany, formed a sub-text underlying most of his writings prior to 1520, when he undertook to remove the disjunction by translating his works into German. But, as has been pointed out, efforts to incorporate Hutten into German *literary* history cannot be made without including a host of qualifiers and, ultimately, an acknowledgement that his patriotic fervor, though expressed in literary forms, overwhelmed any literary objectives he may have had. Gustav Balke's comment as regards Hutten's writing styles is pertinent, suggesting that Hutten's best works were in Latin and that he was unable to show in his German a commensurate level of enthusiasm and independent style:

> Der deutschen Literatugeschichte gehört Huttens Wirken nur zum geringsten Teile an; denn sein Bestes schrieb er lateinisch. In seinen deutschen Dichtungen ringt er mit der Sprache, und nur selten gelingt es ihm, dieselbe seiner Begeisterung dienstbar zu machen. Seine deutsche Prosa liegt ganz im Banne des Lateinischen. Die Satzfügung in den Poesien ist von der lateinischen Syntax beeinflußt. Auf Rechnung der lateinischen Metrik ist es zu setzen, wenn sich in den Dichtungen der Zusammenstoß eines auslautenden *e* mit einem anlautendem Vokal so selten findet. Die klassische Form des Dialoges wurde durch ihn in die Flugschriftenliteratur der Reformation eingeführt und zu einer geläufigen, volkstümlichen, schriftstellerischen Gattung erhoben. Er erreichte es, daß die Literatur aus der Studierstube des Gelehrten heraustrat, daß der, welcher dem Volke etwas zu sagen hatte, volkstümlich schrieb. So wurzelt denn für

die deutsche Literatur Huttens Verdienst vornehmlich darin, daß er sich als Deutsche fühlte, daß er für Deutschlands Größe, Deutschlands Ruhm stritt.[3]

Here, as is so often the case both with his critics and apologists, it appears that Hutten's service to German literature was not literary at all but rather his increasing awareness of his own ethnic identity and the patriotic nature of his efforts to use words to raise the consciousness of his fellow countrymen.

Wilhelm Kreutz's study of the reception of Hutten and his works since the sixteenth century emphasizes the Latin-German duality alluded to above and in the Balke comment, and it is, to date, the most comprehensive and balanced analysis of these larger aspects of Hutten's role and reputation. His insights as regards the transition from the confessional dominance of the Hutten image in the sixteenth century to the political, revolutionary, nationalistic image of later centuries are illuminating not only for an understanding of Hutten's place but also for an appreciation of changing social and political attitudes in German society over the same time period. However, as valuable as Kreutz's examination of the Hutten image is, he makes no claim to provide in-depth analyses of any of Hutten's works. While this study also does not claim to offer close readings of *all* of Hutten's major works but rather concentrates on the *Arminius* dialogue, in the interest of context an effort will be made in passing to look at other works, recognizing that a general familiarity with some of Hutten's works may exist among German readers but a general unfamiliarity, not to say ignorance, of his works is the norm for most scholars in disciplines other than German literature. Since the *Arminius* translation and the analysis comprise a central part of this study, this chapter will attempt to place Hutten's Latin works and some translated later into German into a broader literary context.

Kreutz's study, a slightly revised dissertation (1984), considers Hutten's works from the standpoint of, among several aspects, their general tone, their relevance to contemporary audiences, and their

---

3   Gustav Balke, Hrsg., *Thomas Murner. Die Deutschen Dichtungen des Ulrich v. Hutten,* In: *Deutsche Nationalliteratur*, Bd.17/2.Darmstadt: Wissenschaftliche Buchgesellschaft, 1967.

reception in later periods. The study has an excellent bibliography, two tables charting reception patterns, but an index only of names, making it very difficult to tell which of Hutten's works are discussed. Nevertheless, if one's objective is to develop an assessment of Hutten's literary role, Kreutz's approach can be very useful. For example, a review of Table 1: *Die zeitgenössische Rezeption Ulrichs von Hutten*, provides short-titles for forty-eight works printed between the years 1510–1523, the year of Hutten's death. Hutten's *Febris I*, written in 1518, was printed twelve times in the following year, seven in the Latin version and five in German translation. If the number of printings is used as a measure of popularity, this work ranks as number one. The high point came in 1521 with publication of thirty-six works, all but two in Latin. Kreutz's tabular survey shows a link between contemporary events and reader interest: Hutten's text *In pepericornum exclamatio* (1511), a response to the Pfefferkorn-Reuchlin controversy, was printed twice in 1514 (Latin), once in 1515 (Latin), and five times in German (4, 1514; 1, 1521). The Latin dialogues were equally popular: *Nemo II* (1515–1518) had eight printings (6, 1518; 2, 1519); *Aula* (1518) eight Latin printings between 1518 and 1521 (3, 3, 1, 1); *Phalarismus* (1517) six printings between 1517 and 1520 (4, 1, 1). Two works with direct thematic links to the Reformation controversies, *Trias Romana*, a Hutten version based on an anonymous original,[4] and *Klag über den lutherischen Brand* (1520), appeared only in German, the former in six printings (5, 1519; 1, 1520) and the latter in seven, all in 1521. Since the *Arminius* dialogue, written between 1516–1519, was published posthumously, it does not appear in this table. Table 2, however, *Die postume Huttenrezeption vom 16. bis in die erste Hälfte des 18. Jahrhunderts*, which does consider posthumous publications, is divided into two sections, *16. und frühes 17. Jh.*, *17. und erste Hälfte 18. Jh.*, showing that the *Arminius* appeared four times as an independent publication, four times as part of a collection in the sixteenth century and early seventeenth centuries, and twice in collections published in the seventeenth

---

4   Kreutz indicates that while Hutten's reliance on the German 'Triaden' published in Mainz by Schöffer in 1519 is now accepted in Hutten scholarship, the authorship of the original work is still uncertain. Kreutz, Rezeption, 319, note 'c.'

and first half of the eighteenth century; it was mentioned three times in the bibliographic entries of works during this same period.[5] During his relatively short life and for some time after his death, Hutten's ideological identification was linked to the confessional camps arising from the Reformation.[6] Some Protestants saw him as a co-revolutionary with, if not precursor of, Luther; Catholics viewed him unequivocally as an instigator and proponent of anti-Catholicism. In 1776, two initiatives aimed at identifying and popularizing illustrious figures from the sixteenth century had the subsidiary effect of reviving knowledge of Hutten and his writings and creating for him a role as hero of the German people. Initially, as discussed earlier in this study, Christoph Martin Wieland published his 'Nachricht von Ulrich von Hutten' in the *Teutscher Merkur* (1776) as part of his series on outstanding men of the sixteenth century.[7] On the impetus of Wieland's study, Johann Gottfried Herder wrote an essay which contributed greatly to the renewed esteem for Hutten as a writer and German patriot.[8] The importance of these essays and their impact on Hutten reception, as documented and analyzed by Wilhelm Kreutz, is beyond question. While one may not quibble about the facts of the matter, there may be room for speculation about the intent behind the essays. Wieland's stated intention of reviving the reputations of German writers who had been undeservedly neglected is both reasonable, given the personalities involved, and justified. Herder's response is equally justifiable but seems to go beyond the interests of literary history to enter into the realm of cultural and national pride.

---

5   The Arminius dialogue was used in school instruction in Germany from the sixteenth century on.

6   This stage of Hutten's literary role and reception in Germany is treated thoroughly and objectively in Kreutz's Kapitel II, 'Märtyrer der deutschen Freiheit: Die Popularisierung Ulrichs von Hutten am Ende des 18. und in der ersten Hälfte des 19. Jahrhunderts,' 63–126.

7   *Wielands sämmtliche Werke*, Bd. 35, Leipzig, 1858, 250–261. [*Der Teutsche Merkur*, Jahrgang 1776, Heft I, 174–185]. Hereafter cited as Wieland Werke. See also Kreutz Rezeption, 63–64.

8   Johann Gottfried Herder, *Werke in zehn Bänden*, Bd. 2, *Schriften zur Aesthetik und Literatur*, 1767–1781, Hrsg. Günter E. Grimm. 609–629.

Intentionally or not, these essays marked the beginning of a nationalistic, patriotic view of Hutten as the ideological standard-bearer of an earlier period who had given voice to ideas and attitudes of a new age and beyond. His emergence as the representative of an age owed much to the changing attitudes in Germany nurtured by the Enlightenment and to a reassessment of the sixteenth century as a time of great patriotism. The latter impression was due primarily to the impact of Goethe's play *Götz von Berlichingen* and its historical links to the personalities of Hutten's life and times, most notably Franz von Sickingen, a brother-in-law of the historical Götz.

From a literary perspective with strong social implications, the linkage of Hutten and the *Geniezeit,* or *Sturm und Drang* period, represented an awareness of a state of mind which did reflect some of his cultural attitudes. His emphasis on freedom – *deutsche Freiheit* – for example, may not match exactly the concepts of freedom and nature promoted by Rousseau and later the *Sturm und Drang* poets, but the liberating force behind his Arminius-figure and his respect for ancient German civilization were nevertheless congenial to the *Sturm und Drang* mentality. The regard for Arminius as a type of noble savage in Germanic-Roman garb and the assertion that Germanic-German values had been consistently uniform from the ancient period to the sixteenth century are views that could only be sustained from the perspective of an illusion of an inherently noble spirit that survived time and change. It should be noted, however, that this linkage of Hutten and the *Sturm und Drang* is not a natural one, since only scholars of Early Modern Germany were more than generally familiar with Hutten or his works.[9] This phenomenon raises the question of how a relatively unknown writer became a symbol of national pride, national identity, and German virtues? Kreutz deals at length with this unlikely scenario, suggesting that what was known about Hutten's life, accurate or inaccurate, overshadowed the little that was known about his works and their literary value.[10] A striking feature of the Hutten image-building process is the manner in which contemporary events or events of the recent past were used to encompass elements

9   Kreutz Rezeption, 123.
10   Kreutz, 123.

only remotely related to the real personality. In other words, an existing image of Hutten, in some respects already distorted, was adapted to new realities which required even further distortions. The historical framework for this process was the Reformation, the image of Martin Luther, and the Peasants' War (1524); Hutten's link to each of these was tenuous at best. He voiced enthusiastic support for Luther but was not at all interested in the confessional ideologies motivating the Reformation. He endorsed and admired Luther's approach to and rapport with the common people, but he was unable to emulate him in his own writings, even after he began to write in German or to translate his own works into German. His revolutionary spirit could have been used to energize the social awareness of the peasantry, but he was relatively uninterested in the plight of those outside his class and, regrettably, died before the peasant uprising took place.[11] Connecting Hutten to these phenomena required an emphasis on sympathetic attitudes and potential effectiveness while neglecting the historical reality. Nevertheless, Hutten began to be seen in various postures relevant to the eighteenth century, for example, as a sixteenth century Mirabeau,[12] a nobleman with revolutionary ideas and a strong sense of national identity.[13] The developing image was not entirely fabricated but rather was based to a large extent on attitudes and associations as opposed to aggressive actions, except where the actions represented a response to injustice or victimization. Hutten's view of political authorities fell into two categories: respectful, devoted subservience to Emperor Maximilian, his grandsons Charles V and the Archduke Ferdinand I; visceral dislike of Duke Ulrich of Württemberg, whose personal and political affairs led to Hutten's characterization of him as a despotic, adulterous murderer whose actions were an insult to the Hutten family, the knight class, the imperial government, and the German people. The vigorous opposition

11 Regrettable in the sense that we can never know how he might have reacted to the turn of events; Luther's response, however, is known to us, and it was negative and dismissive.
12 Honoré-Gabriel Riqueti, comte de Mirabeau (1749–1791),French politician and orator, one of the most notable figures in the National Assembly that governed France during the early phases of the French Revolution.
13 Kreutz Rezeption, 101. citing Karl Herzog, *Ersch-Gruber Enzyklopädie.*

to tyranny and despotism made it easy for Hutten to develop arguments that encompassed, on one level, outrage at the personal tragedy of the murder of his cousin, Johann von Hutten by Duke Ulrich and, on another level, the discontent and revolutionary zeal spawned, in his view, by the abusive, exploitative authoritarian role of the Catholic Church. The Hutten who saw the controversies surrounding Martin Luther at one point as 'monk's quarrels' was the same Hutten who began to see the revolutionary potential of the Reformation without endorsing in any effective way the religious doctrines underlying it.[14] The seven printings of his German text *Klag über den lutherischen Brand* (1520) may be interpreted as a spirited defense of Luther's writings, but the text is more general in tone and accusatory of the Church's behavior in areas that had become typical of reform criticisms: the greed and luxury of the Papal and priestly lifestyle, indulgences, intolerance of other views, and the drain on German financial resources. Luther is mentioned twice in the 131-line poem and his writings are referred to in the most general way.[15] A modest action on Hutten's part, but it reflected an attitude that touched a nerve among the reading public, affirming the notion that here, at least, words spoke louder than actions.

From the last decade of the eighteenth to the middle of the nineteenth century attitudes congenial to Hutten's views gained popularity and drew the perceived Hutten persona more and more into the spotlight of radical political thought. As Kreutz points out, the complex of attitudes found in various writers to support and perpetuate the new Hutten image encompassed a variety of mindsets from social, political, and religious realms: a particularly German sense of respectability, 'teutschem Biedersinn', hatred of the Papacy, anti-despotism, national spirit, a cult of patriotism rooted in Pietism, 'geprägt von einem tief im Pietismus wurzelnden patriotischen Gefühlskult', and

---

14 Hutten's affinity for Luther's revolutionary spirit soon gave way to a recognition of the irreconcilable disparity of their approaches; see Bernstein, 93–96.

15 Hutten, Deutsche Schriften, 'Klag über den lutherischen Brand'; see also, Ernst Joseph Herman Münch, *Des teutschen Ritters Ulrich von Hutten sämmtliche Werke*, Bd. 5, 'Teutsch Requiem oder Klag über den Lutherischen Brand zu Mainz', Berlin: G. Reimer Verlag, 1825. 43–50.

the picturesque façade of the romantic world of the knight, the 'Ritterromantik'.[16] A further perplexing aspect of the effort to popularize Hutten's image lay in the lack of interest in making his works available to a broader reading public. Once again we are confronted by the contradiction of a man whose ideas and image might have been more effective earlier had he written more in German than in Latin.[17] Several translations of Hutten's Latin works that did appear in the early years of the nineteenth century were thematically relevant to the political implications of the Napoleonic era for Germany and to his view of himself: the polemical writings against Duke Ulrich of Württemberg (1801), a letter to Willibald Pirckheimer in which Hutten expresses his unsuitability for the quiet life of the scholar (1801), the controversial exchange with Erasmus (1813), and the *Arminius* dialogue (1815).[18] Of these works, the Pirckheimer letter and the *Arminius* dialogue are of interest to a broader understanding of his self-image and his sense of Germany's image, past and future.

In some respects, Hutten was not a man of his times, if we take that characterization to mean that his attitudes, ideas, and ideals were reflective of a consensus among his peers. From the perspective of social criticism, Sebastian Brant, Thomas Murner, Erasmus, or Conrad Celtis all provided greater insights into the socio-cultural behavior of various classes of Germans and more incisive critiques of the times than does Hutten.[19] Murner, for example, appointed *poeta laureatus* by Emperor Maximilian in 1506, when Hutten was just beginning his

16 Kreutz Rezeption, 90. The sources for the various phrases are not clearly cited, but it seems that Kreutz is drawing primarily from Leonhard Wächter's *Sagen der Vorzeit*, Bd. 4, Berlin 1790.

17 Kreutz Rezeption, 283, footnote 433, citing an assessment by F. Bouterweck, *Geschichte der deutschen Poesie und Beredsamkeit*, Bd, 9/10, Göttingen, 1812, 443.

18 Kreutz Rezeption, 92 for a fuller assessment of the impact of these early publications on the popular reception of Hutten in the nineteenth century and their importance for the bibliographic/biographic knowledge of him and his works.

19 Sebastian Brant (1457–1521), *Das Narrenschiff* (1494), Thomas Murner (1475–1537) *Narrenbeschwörung* (1512), Desiderius Erasmus (1469–1536) *Encomium moriae* (1509), Conrad Celtis (1459–1508) *Oratio*, Antrittsvorlesung (1492) University of Ingolstadt.

exodus from Fulda, was responsible, so far as we know, for the only contemporary German translation of the Hutten syphilis tract *De Guaiaci medicina et morbo Gallico*.[20] With the exception of Celtis, whose inaugural lecture at the University of Ingolstadt, as discussed earlier, drew attention to the shortcomings of contemporary German students in their knowledge of German history and to the poor image of Germany among scholars and educated people in other lands, a nationalistic sensitivity in the manner of Hutten is not evident. Had Hutten's works been better known, there might have been a more receptive audience for his thoughts in the aftermath of the Thirty years War (1618–1648), just as there was during the changing political and philosophical outlook of the eighteenth century, and in support of the expression of increasingly nationalistic feelings in the nineteenth century. Among the participants of the *Burschenschaften* movement and those who played active roles in the revolution of 1848, for example, Hutten's ideas, or rather what people perceived his ideas to be, found fertile soil. By the same token, some of the ideas in his *Arminius* dialogue are far more compatible with German attitudes in the 1930s than those of the 1530s. It is not surprising that the emerging image of Hutten, the so-called 'Märtyrer der deutschen Freiheit', nurtured by his support of the Reformation and perpetuated by Protestant Pietism, should come into its own in the first half of the nineteenth century, a time when German honor, independence and the collective abstract concept 'Deutschtum' were steadily gaining popularity in certain circles. The ideals of the Burschenschaften movement, liberty, honor, unity, may not have been in every sense identical to those of Hutten, but in a general way the underlying essence, 'das deutsche Wesen', was the same. This broader view of German-ness and the continuity of German virtues was a subject of interest for Hutten. Having one foot in the literary camp of German humanists and the other, however tenuously, in the world of German-Italian imperial politics, Hutten was sensitive to the contrast. While the former was active and healthy, the latter, in his view, seemed to be on the decline, thanks primarily to

---

20   *De Guaiaci medicina et morbo Gallico*, 1519, dedicated to Albrecht of Mainz. German trans. by Thomas Murner, Aug. 1519, followed by French and English versions. See Benzing, 65–72; Böcking *Opera*, V, 397–497.

Rome in the broadest sense and the Catholic Church more specifically. As he did with most issues of concern, Hutten addressed this
troubling situation in writing. His approach was to look back to what
he saw as the wholesome ancient Germanic past and analytically to
verify its continuity with the sixteenth century present. The objective
was to compare contemporary Germans, i.e., sixteenth century Germans, with their Germanic ancestors to show that no degeneration of
values had taken place.

However, a broader process was taking place that not only fits
the context for the mentality of the *Arminius* dialogue but also ex-
plains in part the increasing interest in and respect for Hutten as writer
and thinker. As Kreutz pointed out, the early nineteenth century in
Germany was in a certain sense a culminating point for a process of
secularization that brought Protestantism, Pietism, and Nationalism
together;[21] Hutten's popularity formed a sidebar to this process.[22] This
was also a time when, for some, the past offered more heroic personalities than the present. In the same sense that Hutten had taken
pride in the virtues of his ancient Germanic ancestors,[23] so did the
nationalists of the early nineteenth century see the sixteenth century
as a time of heroism in the effort to restore German freedom from
oppressive political and cultural forces. In greater measure than during
his lifetime, Hutten was seen now as the counterpart in spirit to Martin
Luther, and the Reformation had become a stage in a broader cultural
revolution. The problematic aspect of this patriotic perspective is the
lack of attention given to the Peasants' War (1524) as an element in
the fight for freedom and justice in sixteenth century Germany, and
admittedly, the impact of Hutten's early death (1523) on his potential
role must be considered. Equally curious is the extent to which the
isolated, exiled Hutten had become a fully honored member of a new
political pantheon that included, among others, Friedrich Ludwig

---

21 Hajo Holborn groups Protestantism, Humanism, and Nationalism. See in this
    study, Introduction, 18.
22 Kreutz Rezeption, 93; especially notes 446, 447.
23 Kreutz Rezeption, 94. Kreutz cites a segment from Ernst Münch's foreword to
    his edition of Hutten's *Ausgewählte Werke*, 3 Bde. Leipzig, 1822–23, which
    contains the phrase, [...] jedes Teutsche Herz, in dem das Blut besserer Väter
    noch wallet.'

Jahn, Ernst Moritz Arndt, Karl Freiherr vom und zum Stein, Johann Joseph Görres, and Gerhard von Scharnhorst.[24] The most strident voice of dissent as regards Hutten's value as a writer and significant thinker seems to have been that of Gottfried Arnold (1666–1714), whose own life as a dissident and unconventional personality, despite his ability later in life to function effectively as a pastor and to express deeply religious convictions in hymns, did not make him sympathetic to Hutten's actions or ideas. Without much concern for the accuracy of his criticisms and accusations against Hutten, Arnold saw him as a potentially corrupting influence on Luther and, together with Franz von Sickingen, representative of the violent dissent that showed a lack of understanding of Luther's convictions. Arnold apparently saw Hutten as a vengeful, blood-thirsty person whose efforts would have been far more harmful to the Reformation had it not been for restraint on Luther's part. This judgment gives far too much credit to both men. Arnold's linkage of Hutten and the Peasant War is based purely on a coincidence of stylistic similarities in articles in support of the peasants and some of Hutten's vituperative writings.[25]

The negativism of Arnold was hardly representative of the consensus of scholarly opinion, though the Catholic viewpoint as represented by Cochläus, equally negative, found imitators in both the sixteenth and the seventeenth centuries. Kreutz provides a detailed record of the influence of Cochläus's views on Catholic writers of subsequent generations,[26] The evidence of a more positive change in the scholarly and literary attitudes about Hutten rests in two camps: Latin pedagogy, as represented by the publication of Hutten's *Ars versificandi* by Melanchthon in the sixteenth century and Gottsched in the eighteenth, and Protestant polemic, as found in Jacob Burckhard's *Commentarius*, three volumes of selected works and a literary assessment of Hutten which, like Cochläus's negative view, became the

---

24 As mentioned in the introduction, Hutten joins Scharnhorst as persona behind a 'named' division of the Wehrmacht in WWII.

25 Kreutz Rezeption, 49f.

26 Kreutz Rezeption, 'Das katholische Huttenbild des Cochläus und seiner Nachfolger,' 42–50.

prototype of positive views of Hutten, his writings, and his legacy.[27] However, as Kreutz points out, this legacy is in itself problematic, being based on productive misunderstandings – produktiven Mißverständnissen – and fatal misinterpretations of the national writer Ulrich von Hutten.[28] The fact remains that despite the efforts to turn Hutten into a hero for all of the German people, his image was still being cultivated by and for the intellectual élite, or more specifically the scholarly academic community. The vehicles for bringing him to the attention of the reading and thinking public were collections of his Latin and, to a lesser degree, his German works, reviews of these collections, analyses of selected works, and entries in general works about the literature of the period. Even the designation of Hutten as a co-revolutionary or forerunner, precursor of Luther did not change the fact that most people, though they may have heard his name, were unfamiliar with the works in which his ideas found concrete expression.[29] Nevertheless, by the mid-eighteenth century Hutten's image had improved considerably and his readership, the well-educated, now had more information about his life and improved access to his works.[30] This same readership provided fertile ground for the development of nationalistic attitudes, at first in the abstract and later in more concrete initiatives. The convergence of humanistic and nationalistic feelings and attitudes grew from small, isolated movements of like-minded individuals to broader initiatives culminating in the 1848 revolutions. To suggest, however, that Ulrich von Hutten, the person or the writer, played any significant role in these events, other than vague propagandistic references to his interest in a strong emperor, his ideas about German freedom, and the identification of him as a progenitor of the Reformation, would be to overstate the case and, perhaps, to exaggerate his value as a German cultural icon.

Any attempt to explain the emergence of Hutten as a figure of national importance would be incomplete, as mentioned earlier, with-

27   Jacob Burckhard, *De Ulrici de Hutten fatis ac meritis commentarius*, 3 Bde. Wolfenbüttel, 1717–1723.
28   Kreutz Rezeption, 55.
29   Kreutz Rezeption, 52.
30   Kreutz Rezeption, 59.

out consideration of the role of Johann Gottfried Herder.[31] Herder's prominence calls for a closer examination of his view of Hutten and the impact of his views on subsequent interpretations. The connection between Herder's Hutten essay and Wieland's efforts to commemorate personalities such as Hutten has already been discussed. Wieland's connection to the *Arminius* dialogue, however, has not. Christoph Martin Wieland (1733–1813), early on came to the attention of the Swiss critic Bodmer in the period 1750–1752; Wieland had sent him four stanzas of an heroic epic, 'Hermann', a narrative poem about the Germanic hero, Arminius. It appears, coincidentally, that another writer, Christoph Freiherr von Schönaich, was writing an epic poem, *Hermann, oder das befreyte Deutschland,* subsequently translated into English as *Arminius, or Germany Freed,* which was sent to Gottsched for approval. The similarity of the two efforts led to some confusion as regards which work belonged to whom.[32] The note given in the *Allgemeine Deutsche Biographie* entry for Wieland suggests that this work was not published until 1882, which seems to be in error.[33]

In 1793 Herder published his Hutten essay again with a few minor changes in the text but with seven extensive footnotes.[34] The opening lines give the impression of a lack of sincerity. His admitted embarrassment at having waited so long to attempt to acknowledge Hutten, though perhaps sincere, seems forced and perfunctory. The basic features of a romanticized Hutten image emerge through a sketch of his early life marked by abstract contrasts: Hutten's flight from the lazy, peaceful lifestyle of the Fulda monks was instigated by

31   For a more detailed treatment of this aspect of Hutten reception, see Kreutz Rezeption, Chapter II, 63–76.

32   See V. Stockley, *German Literature as known in England 1750–1830*, Port Washington, NY: Kennikat Press, 1929, 15; 38; 105. The work dates from 1764, and of the translation Stockley says '[it] shows at least great industry, for the poem is a long one in twelve books. But as English it could not be much worse, being often incomprehensible. It is obviously the work of a foreigner.'

33   Cf. Review by Lessing: [Christoph Martin Wieland:] Ankündigung einer Dunciade für die Deutschen. Nebst dem verbesserten Hermann. Sero sapiunt Phryges. Frankfurt und Leipzig, 1755. In 8vo. auf 61/2 Bogen.

34   Johann Gottfried Herder, *Sämtliche Werke*, ed. Bernhard Suphan, Vol. 16, Hildesheim: Georg Olms Verlagsbuchhandlung, 1967, Part VI, Denkmal Ulrichs von Hutten, 273–297. Hereafter cited as Herder Suphan (page/section).

the whisperings of his 'Genius', abandoning the monkish life was choosing the good for the sake of goodness, but, in Herder's view, the darkness of the monastic life, i.e., religion, had overcome the light of reason. The slavery of a life oppressed by the Church had suppressed the spirit of freedom in an independent Germany; these were the forces that were stifling the life and breath of Hutten's fiery spirit.[35] For Herder, initially, the noble spirit of Hutten found its final resting place on a small island in Lake Constance (Bodensee), which later in the essay he corrected to *Ufnort* [sic], a small island in Lake Zürich.[36] Despite the allusion to the unenlightened control of religion, the religious tone prevails in the call to pilgrimage for young Germans to the grave of Hutten, Germany's forgotten hero whose life had been a 'mirror of the times' (Spiegel aller Zeiten). Herder's admiring hyperbole never quite rings true, though it always relates to a factual aspect of Hutten's life. If we assume that his 'Societät der Wissenschaften' refers to the humanistic solidarities, for example, those associated with the name of Conrad Celtis, then we grasp the hyperbolic dimensions of his comment that Hutten accomplished more in his brief life than many a society over eons.[37] Herder's reputation at the time of this essay served two purposes, one positive, one less so. On the one hand, his stature lent authority to the endorsement of Hutten as a writer of importance; on the other, the inaccuracy of some of his comments led to critical assessments by others that were, unfortunately, not corrected for years. For example, we now know that Hutten's contribution to the *Epistolae obscurorum virorum*, as valuable as it was, was not the major part of that work, nor was his talent necessarily superior to that of Crotus Rubianus, author of the first part and, we assume, responsible for encouraging Hutten's participation on the second part. It is also questionable whether the *Epistolae*, what-

35 Herder Suphan 273–74, sect. 330, 331.
36 Herder Suphan 274, Unter solchen Hohnsprechungen liegt nun der Edle bei einem armen Pfarrer auf einer kleinen Insel im Bodensee [...] und starb auch dort [...]. Herder Suphan 291; [...] er starb End' Augusts 1523 im 36 Jahr seines Alters. Ufnort heisst die kleine Insel im Zürchersee [...].
37 Herder Suphan 275, sect. 332.

ever Hutten's contribution, should be considered the 'heroic work of his life', [das] 'Heldenwerk seines Leben'.

Herder's assessment of Hutten is marked by a more general view of the role of providence in our lives, the impact of youthful connections and circumstances:

> Morgenröte des Lebens, Jugendeindrücke, frühe Freunde, Situationen von Jugendhaß und Jugendliebe – sie machen meistens den Anklang unsrer Bestimmung. Sie weben das Grundgewebe, in welches spätere Schicksale und reifere Vernunft uns den Einschlag geben. (Herder Suphan 275/ 334)

There is a fateful aspect to the view that ones outlook on life is conditioned by the events and experiences of early childhood, the dawn of ones life, that ones youthful hatreds and loves become determinative influences in the attitudes developed later in life. The belief that our destinies, our mature reasoning, are threads of a basic tapestry woven in the early years, is perhaps true, but not a very comforting thought. The logical consequence of this line of reasoning, as it applies to Hutten, is that the pains and frustrations of his youth were reflected in the dashed hopes and unfulfilled dreams of his mature years, brief as his life was. Likewise, the ideals of freedom and independence nurtured in him early on in various ways and by various individuals would be the same ideals that sustained his belief in the mission of liberating Germany from the yoke of Roman Catholic oppression and abuse. It would seem that Hutten's precocious talent was a blessing and a curse. The mentality that distinguished him from many of his peers, at least on the political level, as a progressive, independent-minded thinker, also alienated him from many of his peers, including Martin Luther, as a radical revolutionary whose penchant for violence was unacceptable.

Herder's view of Hutten traveling to Italy first as a soldier in the army of Emperor Maximilian is romantic but inaccurate, and his deduction that the exposure to syphilis came at this time is unreliable. In fact, given the likelihood of a certain incubation period, it is highly unlikely that the two events are so closely connected. But the romanticism of his narrative is impressive: there in Padua he [Hutten] was bitten on the foot by a serpent whose poison he carried with him for the remainder of his life.[38] Herder's defense of Hutten's malady is sympathetic and deservedly so. As he points out, syphilis was a disease of almost epidemic proportions in the sixteenth century and one could contract it quite innocently – certainly on one level of reasoning – and be condemned to lifelong suffering because no cure was then known.[39] Hutten's contribution in this regard, i.e., his efforts to find a cure and his treatise on the subject, has probably not been given due credit. Both his public expression of gratitude to the Fuggers, responsible for the import of Guaiac trees into Germany, source of the resin *Guaici medicinam,*[40] and his treatise *de morbo Gallico* dedicated to Archbishop and Prince Elector Albrecht von Mainz, are indicative of his interest in protecting others from the pain and suffering he was experiencing. Herder is correct in seeing in these literary efforts a sense of Hutten's patriotic pride, his concern for the health of fellow Germans, and his desire for the intellectual enlightenment of those who may have been in a position to affect the general welfare of others.

Herder's literary judgments placed Hutten in the artistic traditions of Greece, describing his works as epigrams, or *Sinngedichte,*[41] linking his image-making skills to those of Daedalus, comparing his travels throughout Germany to the odyssey of Ulysses and his oratorical style to that of Demosthenes.[42] This image of Hutten as the

---

38 Herder Suphan 276/335. 'Und hier [in Padua] hing sich die Schlange [...] an seinen Fuß, deren Gift er zeitlebens mit sich trug [...].'
39 Henry VIII, king of England, would also succumb to the disease, January 28, 1547.
40 Cf. lignum vitae (Guaiacum officinale), a Caribbean tree with very hard, dense, and durable wood used in making the bushings for ships' screws and for mallets. The wood contained gum guaiac, a resin that had been used medicinally since the fifteenth century as a specific, but ineffective, cure for syphilis.
41 Lessing described the epigram as a poem which, like an inscription, draws our attention and curiosity towards an individual object and holds us more or less to that object until both are satisfied. Expectation and enlightenment, or eluci dation, are the essential parts of an epigram; the former, like a riddle, gives tension by means of an apparent contradiction, while the latter provides a surprising interpretation of the meaning. Thus the German name Sinngedicht created by Philipp von Zesen (1649) as substitute for epigram.
42 Herder Suphan 279, sect.340.

German *Demosthenes* who wanted to be more than Demosthenes, whose invectives against Duke Ulrich of Württemberg were, heart and soul, like the orations of Demosthenes, who later became 'unser' Demosthenes, suggests the extent to which Herder contributed to the perception of Hutten as a German hero whose protestations on the political level like those for his murdered cousin, lamentably, would go unheard.[43] Herder was also complimentary about Hutten's Latin abilities, suggesting that he far exceeded the scholars committed to imitating Ciceronian style but rather was able to incorporate the sounds and actions of his personal experiences into his literary style. Whether one agrees with Herder's assessments or not, it is interesting to consider the process of bringing a writer from literary obscurity into the mainstream of literary traditions more than two hundred years after his death.

Nowhere is the superstructure of Herder's literary assessment of Hutten clearer than in his effusive comments about the *Epistolae obscurorum virorum* (1516–17), which he described as a national satire filled with spirit, fire, wit, and extremely specific, pertinent, truthful details.[44] Now, with the benefit of scholarly research and interpretation, we can be more accurate and objective about the role of Crotus Rubeanus, whom Herder saw as someone who had merely helped Hutten, whose laudable and substantial contribution to the second book of letters hardly warrants awarding him sole authorship rights for the work as a whole.[45] That the European popularity of the *Epistolae* was due in large part to the fact that they were written in Latin, did not hinder Herder from seeing something especially German in them, something that made their essence, *die feinsten Spitzen des Salzes drin*, inaccessible to foreigners. It was this inde-finable *Teutschlatein* and an unfamiliarity with monastic customs that justified designating the *Epistolae* as a National, i.e., German satire. In

---

43   Herder Suphan 279, sect. 342.
44   Herder Suphan 280, sect. 342. [...] eine National satyre voll Geist, Feuer, Witz und äußerst genauer, treffender Detailwahrheit.
45   Herder Suphan 279, 342. [E]r schrieb die Epistolas [sic] obscurorum virorum. Daß Crotus daran Teil gehabt, ist unleugbar; sie aber deswegen, weil Crotus mitgeholfen, dem Hutten absprechen zu wollen, ist so töricht, als sie gar Erasmus zuzuschreiben [...].

order to accept this judgment, one must ignore the roles of contemporary works such as Brant's *Das Narrenschiff* (1494) and Murner's *Die Narrenbeschwörung* (1512), both of which are excellent examples of satire, both written in German, and both taking issue with the current follies of the Church and the society in sixteenth century Germany. The popularity of the former was only enhanced by its later translation and publication as *Stultifera navis* by Jacob Locher, which served as the base text for subsequent translations into English (1507f), French (1497f), and Dutch (1500).[46]

Aside from likening Hutten's publication of a German translation of Lorenzo Valla's exposure of the *Donation of Constantine* as a forgery to a prank by Till Eulenspiegel, another popular literary work contemporary with Hutten,[47] Herder's outline of Hutten's claims to fame also represent the frustrations of his personal and political life. Hutten paved the way for Luther, but they never met; he admired Erasmus, who admired Hutten's writings, but they never became friends; he was friendly with Pirckheimer, but rejected Pirckheimer's advice to pursue the contemplative life of a scholar; he was in contact on various levels with religious and political leaders, but his efforts, despite the *poeta laureatus* honor from Maximilian and earlier financial support from Archbishop Albrecht, went mostly unrewarded. Herder expressed Hutten's predicament well in a litany of frustration:

> Hutten hatte keinen Beschützer. Albert [Erzbischof Albrecht von Mainz] konnte und dorfte es nicht sein: zum Erzherzog Ferdinand schrie Hutten laut, aber vergebens; noch lauter an Kaiser Karl, an die ganze Teutsche Nation; aber vergebens. Er hatte Herz genug an Kaiser Karls Hof nach den Niederlanden selbst zu gehen, aber umsonst: er fand kein Gehör [...]. (Herder Suphan 283, sect. 350)

---

46 Henry and Mary Garland, eds., *The Oxford Companion to German Literature*, 3rd ed by Mary Garland, Oxford: Oxford University Press, 1997. Hereafter cited as Garland.

47 Hermann Bote, *Ein kurtzweilig Lesen von Dyl Ulenspiegel geboren uß dem Land zuo Brunßwick. Wie er sein Leben vollbracht hat. XCVI seiner Geschichten.* (1510–1511) This is the oldest surviving version; the Eulenspiegel archive in Bamberg reports approximately 1100 versions and adaptations. Garland, 827.

He had no protector, his efforts to find imperial support were futile, even seeking patronage and support at court was all for nothing; despite the strength and eloquence of his arguments, he found no hearing among those in a position to help. This German Demosthenes, as Herder put it, with so many apparent advantages, greatness, truth, freedom, noble heritage, reputation, patriotism, was forced to cope with financial need, modest professional roles, and, because of his strong reliance on Latin, a limited literary impact.

The sensitivity and mentality of Franz von Sickingen was as important for Hutten at this stage of his life as those of Eitelwolf von Stein had been during his time in Fulda. The difference, as Herder pointed out, lay in the circumstances of Hutten's personal life. In Fulda, everything lay before him, despite the uncertainty of his financial situation, the as yet unproven value of his intellect and his literary talents, and the innocence of youth that left him open to possibilities of unimagined scope and potential. At the time of his refuge in Sickingen's castle and the developing friendship with a man whose class and interests mirrored Hutten's own, Hutten's life was essentially behind him in the sense that the political revolutionary deeds for which Sickingen was known were beyond Hutten's capabilities. His was, in the truest sense, a life of the mind, dedicated to informing and educating Sickingen, translating and publishing his Latin works in German, creating new works in Latin, and addressing himself more vigorously to the issues with which he had come to be identified. It is within the circumstances of these final years that the tragedy of Hutten becomes clear: a loud and strident voice in support of freedom from the tyranny of the Church, a passionate spokesperson for patriotic values, a strong and sincere proponent of the virtues of family, class and privilege in German society, Hutten's voice had found few echoes among the very people he sought to influence. He had experienced rejection by some of his closest friends on points of substance, he had seen respected Humanists, also friends, reject his call for support of the Lutheran Reformation, and he had realized that his German writings, despite local circulation and popularity, had not achieved the objectives of either a call to arms or a heightened national self-awareness on the part of his fellow Germans. Being exiled physically from Germany, emotionally and personally exiled by the efforts of

Erasmus in Switzerland, and exiled ideologically and symbolically by only being able to find refuge and support from Zwingli, a Luther opponent, in the isolation of a domicile on the island of Ufenau in Lake Zürich, Hutten's life came to a sad and penurious end.

Kreutz attributed the slightly more objective tone of the revised essay to a change in the relationship between Herder and Wieland, in whose journal, *Teutscher Merkur*, the original essay appeared.[48] The distinctions can be subtle; for example, one might infer that Hutten's *Nemo*, or Niemand, referred to his personal estimation of his lot in life, as Herder's original essay suggested,[49] but a more cautious formulation in the revised essay makes it more a matter for interpretation.[50] The final judgment, however, remains in both versions: [Hutten] began his life as a nobody and remained such to a certain extent throughout his life:

'Beim ersten Auftritt war er ein Niemand und ist gewissermassen Zeitlebens ein Niemand geblieben.'[51]

The contradiction between the *Nemo*/Niemand judgment and the context of making Hutten into a German hero speaks directly to the image-making process inherent in Herder's essays. While it is true that Hutten traveled to Italy and that he was a soldier in Maximilian's army, it is not true that this was his first trip or that he was truly a soldier in the conventional sense. As mentioned earlier, Hutten arrived in Italy in pursuit of humanistic studies, became involved with French and Swiss troops near Pavia, suffered imprisonment and humiliation at the hands of both groups, and, in despair that his life would get better, composed an epitaph for himself. Only later, having been released from prison, bereft of all his possessions, destitute, and in pain from his syphilis, Hutten became a soldier but essentially a non-combatant because of his physical limitations. Herder stressed those elements that fit the context, the patriotism, support for the imperial initiative

---

48   Kreutz Rezeption, 73.
49   Herder Hutten, 612; [...] 'und freilich für ihn eine üble Ahndung.'
50   Herder *Denkmal Ulrichs von Hutten*, [...] *und wenn man deuten wollte*, für ihn eine üble Ahndung. [my emphasis] 277, sect. 338.
51   Ibid.

against the Venetians, animosity towards the French, but he does not mention the Swiss who mistreated Hutten as badly as did the French. Though he emphasizes the importance of judging a literary work according to the standards and values of its own time, Herder moves away from the literary to make the point that Hutten's nationalistic attitudes towards the French, were they to be translated from Latin into German, could also satisfy eighteenth century contemporaries.[52] Herder's opinion that a people cannot change their national characteristics may not be directly attributable to Hutten but does seem to reflect his feeling in some respects. In his poem 'Die Bewerber um die Herrschaft über Italien', as Italia complains to Apollo about her three suitors, the Venetians, the French, and the Germans, Apollo suggests that she choose: the Venetians are full of deceit, the Germans are full of wine, and the French are filled with arrogance, pride; the Venetians will always be treacherous, the French always arrogant, but the Germans will not always be drunk, so choose!

Changes in Herder's thought in the process of rehabilitating Hutten in the eyes of the scholarly German public are instructive. Hutten's literary, intellectual contributions which earlier had done more for Germany than learned societies had done for eons, has now done more than many a society in centuries had been permitted to do or was able to do, '[...] als manche Societät in Jahrhunderten thun dorfte oder thun mochte'.[53] Still a hyperbolic statement, and still one that raises the question of what exactly Herder felt Hutten had done that others had not done? In the 1776 version of his essay, his admonishing criticism of Germany in its response, or lack of response, to Hutten, was followed by the plea that young people make Hutten's grave a pilgrimage goal and that they view his life as a mirror of all times. In the 1793 version, the pilgrimage idea remains but Hutten's life has become a reflection of various times (sei euch ein Spiegel mehrerer Zeiten). The difference between 'aller Zeiten' and

---

52 Herder Suphan 276, note (b); Manche von diesen [Huttens Gedichte] sind so charakteristisch, als ob sie zu unserer Zeit gemacht wären, und würden vielen Lesern in einer guten Übersetzung wohl tun. Die Nationen bleiben sich immer gleich bis ans Ende der Tage.'

53 Herder *Denkmal Ulrichs von Hutten*, 265/333.

'mehrerer Zeiten' may be subtle, and the idea of making a pilgrimage to a site which was then as now unknown may be puzzling,[54] but what is striking in the 1793 version is the omission of the criticism of Germans and Germany. Herder's comments about the *Epistolae obscurorum virorum* also underwent subtle changes from the 1776 to the 1793 version: Hutten's reaction to the Reuchlin critics is in both cases disgust and revulsion, but the critics are at first *Geschmeiss*, a term from the hunting idiom which can range in meaning from 'vermin' to the 'waste material from animals'; in the second version they have become simply a mob, *Brut*, whose actions, in Herder's view, provided the material for Hutten's *epistolis*[sic], for the 'Heldenwerk seines Lebens'. It is noteworthy that Hutten's reaction in the 1793 version is merely displeasure, annoyance (Unmut), and the *epistolis* [sic] is now a bold work with future potential, 'das künftige Heldengedicht'. The categorization of the *Epistolae obscurorum virorum* as a Heldengedicht is obviously not a genre classification, as that term is usually meant, but rather a comment on the heroic nature of the spirit underlying the work and its challenge to the spiritual authorities of Hutten's time. It is questionable whether anyone today would consider the work heroic or that it could be seen as the high-point of Hutten's entire literary output. The lack of familiarity with Hutten's works, even in Herder's time, and the seeming unawareness of the principal role of Crotus Rubeanus in the *Epistolae* underline the artificial nature of the image Herder is propagating. Herder's appeal to 'Mother Germany,' is equally stilted and hollow and seems incongruous with the strongly masculine image Hutten invokes in his appeals to the emperor and his fellow countrymen on behalf of the 'Fatherland'. The maternal image does not play a very strong role in Hutten's writings, though he did apparently entertain thoughts of marriage and the ideal wife at one time without, however, any serious action to develop this part of his life.

---

54 As mentioned earlier, Herder's reference to Hutten's last refuge as an island in Lake Constance (der Bodensee), corrected towards the end of the essay to Ufenau island in Lake Zürich, is common to both versions.

Despite his efforts to characterize Hutten as a warm and sensitive person, as reflected in his style,[55] Herder is forced to acknowledge that both Luther and Melancthon overtly expressed a level of displeasure, even trepidation when it came to Hutten.[56] The attitude of Erasmus, justified or not in avoiding personal contact with Hutten in Basel, accords with that of others such as Reuchlin, Crotus Rubeanus, even Eobanus Hessus, who, though admiring Hutten's wit, literary style, and commitment to humanistic values, still found it difficult to reconcile this admiration with his calls for violent political action and, with the exception of Hessus, his unequivocal rejection of Catholicism. Wilhelm Kreutz summarizes the matter of Herder's view of Hutten succinctly and effectively:

> Herder stilisierte den deutschen *Nationalschriftsteller*, dessen Werke keiner kenne, zum Symbol der fehlenden nationalen Identität der Deutschen und fand in ihm – wie der unterlegte geschichtsphilosophische Figuralismus des *verlorenen Sohnes* unterstreicht – das Vorbild für das generationelle Selbstverständnis des Sturm und Drang.[57]

Kreutz also points out the imbalance between the general awareness of Hutten's suffering, futile effort, and ultimate exile from Germany as a model for political dissidents, and the rather limited familiarity with his literary works among the public and even the more specialized German literary scholars. It is worth noting that the Hutten image propagated by Herder is less enthusiastically endorsed by subsequent literary scholars, who offer more objective assessments of the limited role Hutten's Latin works could play in an overall judgment and the limited value of the small group of German works when compared with his vernacular language contemporaries.

For Wilhelm Scherer, for example, Hutten was introduced only in the context of those for and against Luther. His literary contribution, also linked to the Reformation, was that of raising the dialogue form of literary discourse to the level of an independent genre in

---

55   Herder Suphan 280, note (d); 281 note (e).
56   Herder Suphan 282–283, note (f).
57   Kreutz Rezeption, 123.

German literature.[58] Scherer's sketch runs about a page and a half and recounts mainly the types of writing Hutten favored and provides brief summaries of some of the better known works. The few lines he included about the posthumous *Arminius* dialogue placed it in the context of the influence of the newly discovered texts of Tacitus and Velleius Paterculus in the early sixteenth century.

Twentieth-century assessments, while more comprehensive in their treatment of Hutten's literary accomplishments, are also quite divided in their judgments concerning the prevalence of his role as a culturally significant political figure supporting the Protestant Reformation over his contribution to sixteenth-century German literature. Richard Zoozmann, for example, in his 1905 edition of Hutten's *Gesprächbüchlein,*[59] referred to the writer's sharp sword [of wit] (a frequently used attribute), his healthy powers of observation, his penchant for coming to the point and always striking the nail on the head. Hutten's prose and poetry, in his view, possessed a nobility and forcefulness that never failed to convince or to awaken passion. He saw Hutten's aggressive personality as on the one hand more urbane than Luther's and on the other more conciliatory. Despite evidence to the contrary, Zoozmann saw Hutten's personality as congenial and endearing.[60] His characterization of Hutten reached a hyperbolic level when the image of the sharp witty sword was combined with the 'accurately wielded scourge of the satirical poet glowing with holy anger – die stets trefflicher geschwungene Geißel eines in heiligem Zorne lodernden satirischen Dichters'. (Zoozmann, *vii*). Zoozmann's flowery language extended even to Hutten's long bout with syphilis:

> Um diese Zeit ungefähr war es, daß der junge Steckelberger den Leichtsinn einer süßen Stunde mit einem für sein ganzes Leben anhaltenden bitteren Nachgeschmack büßen sollte. (Zoozmann, vxi)

58 Wilhelm Scherer. *Geschichte der deutschen Literatur von den Anfängen bis zu Goethes Tod.* 1883, 320.
59 Richard Zoozmann. *Gesprächbüchlein Ulrichs von Hutten.* Angermanns Bibliothek für Bibliophilen, Bd. 4. Dresden: Hugo Angermann. 1905. Hereafter referred to as Zoozmann.
60 Strauss reported comments from Mutianus Rufus, Camerarius, Erasmus and others who found Hutten decidedly uncongenial.

Indeed, the 'frivolousness of a sweet hour paid for with a bitter after-taste that lasted a lifetime' was a fact of his personal and literary life for which Hutten paid penance many times over.[61] The first of Hutten's works referred to by Zoozmann, the *Querelae,* is a written grievance against the Lötz family which Zoozmann admits does not deserve an outstanding place judged on its literary merits.[62] Its importance may be more informational than literary, though the individual poems do show how Hutten was able to deal with a personally painful and frustrating event, after the fact, in a broader moralistic context. But even this view is problematic since the *Querelae* are biased, representing the complaint of someone who felt he had been the victim of an injustice; there is no record of the Lötz side of the disagreement. But, as with so many incidents involving Hutten, details are sparse.[63] The *Querelae,* a two-part collection of ten elegies each, provides an outline of the incident involving the friendly, generous reception and the subsequent angry, bitter rejection of Hutten by the Lötz family, father and son; it also includes a variety of other kinds of information. Some of the elegies are dedicated to individuals who may or may not have been connected with the incident; Elegy IV of the second book, for example, is devoted to praise for Egbert Harlem, professor in Rostock, who provided refuge and support for Hutten after the ordeal of being robbed and beaten, probably at the hands of the Lötz's hired men.

Zoozmann drew attention to Hutten's interest in the technical aspects of writing, which led to the development of a handbook on

61   It is interesting to note that syphilis, which by some assessments had reached epidemic proportions in sixteenth century Europe was nationalized in a sense, being called the 'French sickness' [Franzosenkrankheit]; for the French those suffering with the disease were the Spanish Fire people [Spanischfeuerleut], while for others it was the 'Nordic Plague' [Nordische Pest] or 'Italian Leprosy' [Italienischer Aussatz]. Zoozmann, xvi.

62   *Ulrichi Hutteni equestris ordinis poetae in Wedegum Loetz Consulem Gripesualdensem in Pomerania et filium eius Henningum Vtr. Juris doctorem Querelarum libri duo pro insigni quadam iniuria sibi ab illis facta.* Joannes Hanaw, 1510. Zoozmann, xx.

63   Zoozmann acknowledges the difficulty of placing blame in this matter: 'Auf wessen Seite der größere Teil der Schuld lag, ist nicht klar zu ersehen.' Zoozmann, xviii.

poetics which he dedicated to his friends the Ostend brothers and which found widespread reception later.[64] He skipped the Latin poems Hutten wrote in Vienna, except to say that the scholars there were enchanted by them, and he concentrated on the epigrams and satires composed in Pavia. Hutten's elegant Latin style, according to Zoozmann, revealed his efforts to break away from the stiff mythological symbols that had become crutches in the poems of other humanist poets. His poems showed a degree of gracefulness and perfection of form uncharacteristic of a German poet writing in Latin.[65] Hutten's literary talents, in Zoozmann's view, came to the forefront after his reading of the *Epistolae obscurorum virorum*, which he received in Bologna shortly after their publication in 1516. Since the letters were probably sent to Hutten by his friend, and the author of the *Epistolae*, Crotus Rubeanus, Zoozmann may be right in suggesting that reading them was not a pleasant experience for Hutten.[66] His description of Hutten's response, however, and his assessment of Hutten's contribution may be open to question:

> So verfasste er in der ersten Glut der Begeisterung, in genialer Schnelligkeit eine Anzahl dergleichen Briefe, die 1517 als zweiter Teil erschienen und den ersten Teil weit in den Schatten stellten. (Zoozmann, xxiv)[67]

There can be no doubt that Hutten set about contributing to the defense of Reuchlin with great enthusiasm, though it may not have been as immediate as Zoozmann suggests. His evaluation of the comparative skills of Hutten and Crotus Rubeanus may also have been tainted by the fact that Crotus ultimately remained with the Old Church rather than becoming an ardent Luther supporter. Acknowledging that Crotus was indeed the principal author of the first part of the *Epistolae*, Zoozmann qualified his acknowledgement by doubting

---

64 Ulrici Hutteni, *De arte versificandi liber unus heroico carmine ad Jo. Et Alex. Osthenios Pomeranos equites*, 1511.
65 Zoozmann, xxi.
66 'Diese Epistolae [...] hatte Hutten kaum mit wachsendem Behagen gelesen' [...] Zoozmann, xxiv.
67 The first volume of *Epistolae obscurorum virorum* was a joint effort led by Crotus Rubeanus and it appeared in 1514–1515; volume two, which appeared in 1516–1517, is attributed by Zoozmann largely to Ulrich von Hutten.

that Crotus had the skill to have matched the writing in the second part attributed to Hutten:

> [...] doch dessen Urheberschaft [im ersten Teil] ist dem Crotus Rubeanus nicht abzusprechen, der nicht die Gabe für die Bedienung eines so schweren Geschützes leidenschaftlicher Invektiven besaß, wie sie Hutten im zweiten Teile zeigt. (Zoozmann, xxiv)

Zoozmann felt that Crotus's, slightly wounding pin-pricks and superficial ridicule showed a lack of understanding of the seriousness of the matter as exhibited by Hutten:

> [...] weil es ihm mit der Sache der Aufklärung nicht ebenso heiliger Ernst wie Hutten war. Auch zeigte sich darin schon jetzt jene Charaktereigenschaft, die den späteren Abfall des Crotus von der Sache der Reformation erklärt. (Zoozmann, xxiv)

Zoozmann was somewhat more objective when he acknowledged the strangeness of Hutten's writing in German, which he made more palatable by continuing to write in Latin:

> Hutten hatte Ende 1520 Deutsch zu schreiben begonnen, eine Arbeit, die ihm zuerst von statten ging und die er sich dadurch versüßte, daß er gleichzeitig neue lateinische Dialoge ausarbeitete. (Zoozmann, xxv)

One can gloss over Zoozmann's unqualified endorsements of Hutten's nationalistic feelings, it is more difficult, however, to ignore his assessment of Hutten's literary influences. It is a matter of opinion that Hutten's use of thematic triads in his *Vadiscus* was a model (*Vorbild*) for Luther's style in the two treatises of 1520,[68] but it is an overstatement to suggest that Hutten cultivated the vernacular literature of his time period or that he set the tone for political discussion in the second half of the sixteenth century. Such an assessment is as unfair to Hutten as it is to contemporary writers, such as Sebastian Brant, Nikodemus Frischlin, Thomas Murner, Willibald Pirckheimer, and a number of other fifteenth and sixteenth century German writers.

---

68   DeBoor/Newald, *Geschichte der deutschen Literatur*, IV/1, 725 'Einzelheiten aus Huttens Publikationen übernahm Luther in seine Programmschrift *An den christlichen Adel deutscher Nation*' (1520). Hereafter cited as DeBoor/Newald.

More recent criticism emphasized the gap between the Neo-Latin writings of the German Renaissance humanists such as Hutten and the vernacular literatures, suggesting the difficulty today of making aesthetic judgments about such writings or of seeking to see in them any definitive measure of the sensitivity or insightful approaches by which we assess modern literature.

> Ein Zugang zu dieser gemeineuropäischen neulateinischen Literatur vom Standpunkt des ästhetischen Genusses ist heute kaum mehr möglich. Man wird der neulateinischen Lyrik etwa nicht gerecht, wenn man in erster Linie subjektive Offenbarungen des Innenlebens sucht. Man kann die neulateinische Literatur aber in ihrer historischen Bedeutung erfassen. Diese liegt in ihrer breiten und langdauernden Existenz und durch diese bedingt in ihrer Vermittlerrolle zu den volkssprachigen Literaturen. (DeBoor/Newald, IV/1, 460)

In one view, Hutten's self-centeredness, his use of literary vehicles to vent his anger, and his plea for justice are also characteristics that moved him away from the mere imitation of the style and forms of the Latin humanists.[69]

The humanist context and the influences of classical Latin writers also served as the basis for Stammler's assessment of Hutten in *Von der Mystik zum Barock*.[70] Given the typical humanist views of issues and personalities of the time, there was a basic contradiction in Hutten's humanist credentials and his revolutionary style and inclinations. As Stammler pointed out, the humanists were essentially pragmatists on social issues, preferring to weigh the good against the bad, the old versus the new, supporting Erasmus over Luther, without committing themselves to the support of either side as an absolute solution.[71] Hutten's convictions, however, were often couched in absolute terms with little patience or understanding for alternative points of view. Stammler, like others, saw Hutten's major contribution

---

69 DeBoor/Newald, IV/1, 615ff.
70 Wolfgang Stammler. *Von der Mystik zum Barock*. Stuttgart:J.B. Metzler'sche Verlagsbuchhandlung, 1927. Hereafter cited as Stammler.
71 Stammler, 42; 75. Stammler states, for example, that during the period 1517–1520 the name of Luther does not occur at all in humanist correspondence, and that for them the Leipzig disputation was more a case of Eck versus Erasmus than Eck versus Luther.

to be the establishment of the dialogue as a German genre, a conscious imitation of the dialogues of Lucian, which he had gotten to know during his studies in Italy.

Die Einkleidung des *Totengesprächs* bevorzugt er, Personifikationen und Allegorien von Abstrakta legt er gern eine Gedanken in den Mund, die antiken Götter stattet er mit stark menschlichen Zügen aus. Hutten [übernimmt] noch allerlei von dem Erbe des älteren Dialogs. Eine Person steht im Mittelpunkt, die anderen sind mehr oder weniger Nebenfiguren, geben nur kurze Antworten oder stellen Fragen, um das Thema in Fluß zu bringen. Dieses wird von den Hauptfiguren in rhetorischem Schwung, mit humanistisch gefeilten Sätzen durchgeführt; der Autor selbst verrät sich als der eigentliche Spieler. [...]die Figuren sind vielfach noch Masken, die mechanisch auf das Stichwort den Mund öffnen und ihre Rolle herunterplappern; noch ist die mimische Umformung nicht genügend gelungen. Hutten nämlich war mehr Redner als Dichter, vor allem kein Dramatiker. Die Macht des Wortes soll bei ihm des Ausschlag geben, dagegen will er nicht durch die Charakteristik seiner Figuren Wirkung ausüben.[72]

Stammler's judgment about Hutten introduced elements that added another dimension to the highly laudatory view of Herder. While emphasizing the isolating effect of Hutten's having held on so long to ancient rhetorical traditions and the Latin language, Stammler acknowledged the localizing impact Hutten achieved by finally writing in German or translating his earlier works into German. What is new, however, is the suggestion that Hutten's motives for supporting Luther and even for his association with Franz von Sickingen may have been less than forthright, more egotistical.

Neuere Forschungen zeigen, daß [...] bei seinem Eintreten für Luther und vor allem in seinem Bündnis mit Sickingen *unlautere Motive mit eine Rolle gespielt haben* [emphasis added] und [daß] er nicht mehr als der landläufige romantisch verklärte, ideale Vorkämpfer des Deutschtums erscheinen kann.[73]

Ultimately, however, Stammler stressed Hutten's popular appeal, despite Luther's rejection of his political revolutionary impulses, his efforts at raising the level of polemical writing, and his call for

72   Stammler, 106–111.
73   Stammler, 110–111.

energizing the best virtues of the German people, their loyalty, their religiosity, and their courage.[74]

The tendency towards a divided opinion of Hutten as literary figure and social revolutionary persisted in modern criticism. From a cultural, historical perspective Hutten was generally given positive reviews; however, the literary assessments were not equally supportive. The assessment of Hutten's role in the second part of the *Epistolae obscurorum virorum* in the DeBoor/Newald literary history is strikingly pointed:

> Der zweite Teil der *Dunkelmännerbriefe* ist kein originales Werk mehr, sondern eine Fortsetzung des ersten. Hutten halt sich an die Grundidee und Konzeption des Werkes, aber er besitzt viel weniger poetische Kraft als Crotus. Er bringt Fortsetzungen, Ausfuhrungen, Weiterdichtungen, Ergänzungen, Umformungen. Er verfugt aber nicht uber die Naivität des Crotus, er ist greller, übertreibt die Motivik und Verbreitert die Anlage. Crotus nahm die Obskuren nicht tragisch, Hutten nimmt sie bitter ernst; nicht selten mißversteht er seine Vorlage. Crotus war Genremaler und Idylliker und arbeitete mit indirekter mimischer Satire, Hutten arbeitet mit direkter Satire und tendenzioser Polemik.[75]

According to this assessment, to paraphrase further, Hutten lacked creative imagination and the talent effectively to structure a presentation; he was a fighter, an extreme idealist. He was also unable to treat his material as it needed to be, as direct satire suitable for a brief pamphlet format. Maintaining the external form of the first part of the *Epistolae,* made the second part seem less an organic extension than a mechanical add-on, resulting in an apparent mismatch between the form and the content. Describing Hutten as a 'politischer Tagesschriftsteller,' not especially complimentary, would today be tantamount to calling him a political hack.

Aside from the literary critical assessments of Hutten, which run the gamut from unbridled praise to moderate admiration to less charitable views of his talents and intellectual insights, his life inspired independent literary works, and at least one theme, the liberating exploits of the Germanic hero Arminius, found dramatic expression if not popular acclaim at the hands of modern writers. As a response to

74   Stammler, 292.
75   DeBoor/Newald, IV/1, 715

the increasing tensions between France and Germany in the early nineteenth century, several writers emerged in the course of that century as inheritors and purveyors of the spirit attached to the life and persona of Ulrich von Hutten: Heinrich von Kleist (drama, *Die Hermannsschlacht,* 1808–09), Gottfried Keller (poem, *Ufenau,* 1858), Conrad Ferdinand Meyer (epic poem, *Huttens Letzte Tage,* 1871), and Christian Dietrich Grabbe (drama, *Die Hermannsschlacht,* 1836). Only Meyer can be said to have been influenced by a direct personal interest in Hutten's life, details of which he apparently drew largely from the Strauss biography.[76]

Zürich, located at the northwest end of Lake Zürich, is in close proximity to Ulrich von Hutten's final resting place, the island of Ufenau, and the city has ties to three Swiss citizens with personal and literary connections to Ulrich von Hutten: Huldrich Zwingli, Gottfried Keller, and Conrad Ferdinand Meyer.[77] The reformer Zwingli, a contemporary of Hutten, older by four years, provided a refuge for Hutten following his exile from Germany and his ultimate rejection by Erasmus at Basel. Though we may never know what brought the two men together, beyond Christian charity and humaneness, there are superficial, circumstantial ties that are of interest. Both men, for example, had ties to Venice and France: Hutten, as a student in Italy during the Venetian war against Maximilian's forces and the unfortunate imprisonments he endured from both the Swiss and the French; Zwingli, who sought support from Venice and France to further the Reformation movement and who died in the second war of Kappel in 1531, while serving as chaplain to the Zürich forces,. Both men were admirers of and correspondents with Erasmus. Each had an interest in Martin Luther, Hutten's being supportive but having had no personal contact, Zwingli's more confrontational and ultimately

76 Acknowledgement is made of the numerous works having to do directly or indirectly with the heroic figure, Arminius, but only those of Kleist, Keller, and Meyer will be considered here.

77 An interesting example of confusing Hutten and Arminius is found in Paul Vitz's *Sigmund Freud's Christian Unconscious:* "Set in the past [C. F. Meyer's] poem (Huttens Letzte Tage) is centered on Ulrich von Hutten (1488–1523), an historical figure well known as a soldier who fought against Rome for German political and religious freedom. 97–98.

114

unsatisfactory. Having risen from humble origins, Zwingli was well educated, theologically well read, and competent in the Classical languages and Hebrew. Hutten, despite close connections and experience at various universities, never obtained an academic degree but was respected as a humanist scholar and lecturer, had no deep interest in theology, and, apart from concern about the abuses of the Roman Church, seems to have had no personal interest in religion.

The connections to Keller and Meyer are both literary. Meyer's long poem *Huttens Letzte Tage*, written in 1871, has been described as his first literary success and a poem of permanent importance. He is said to have described it himself as his first work, though not literally so, and it appeared in fifteen editions during his lifetime.[78] The seventy-one poems were originally grouped into eight sections with thematic titles, the first being *Ufenau* (later, *Die Landung*), Hutten's arrival at the small island in Lake Zürich, and the last, *Das Sterben* (later, the more poetic, *Die Abfahrt*), Hutten's farewell to a rather sad and disappointing life. Subsequently, Meyer made substantive revisions and emendations to the various editions, resulting in distinctive titles for each of the seventy-one poems, chronicling various stages of Hutten's personal and literary life. The extended poem of rhyming couplets is a first-rate literary effort that contributed much to the heroic, patriotic image of Hutten at a time when German national feeling was at a highpoint.

Gottfried Keller's poem 'Ufenau' (1858), though more modest in tone and in literary quality, is, nevertheless, noteworthy in several respects: more than three and a half centuries after Hutten's birth and death, students from his land of exile are making a festive pilgrimage to the island where he finally came to rest; Keller's image is an idealized version of the Hutten who came to Ufenau shortly before his death; and there is only a hint of the isolation and despair Hutten had to have been experiencing after being legally exiled from his homeland. In fact, contrary to the specifically German patriotic images with which Hutten came to be associated, Keller portrayed him as a refugee

---

78 Henry and Mary Garland, *The Oxford Companion to German Literature*, 3rd ed. Oxford: Oxford University Press, 1997, 408. This entry places Ufenau incorrectly in Lake Constance.

from the Holy Roman Empire. In a certain sense, this is probably a more accurate view, since Hutten never questioned the authoritarian nature of imperial political structure, except to challenge the role of the princes, and with perhaps unwarranted confidence transferred his allegiance from one emperor to another in the hope of finding a man who would be a rallying point for German patriots.

Keller's retrospective view of Hutten is instructive as regards image-making, which is not to say that that was his objective in this poem; the rehabilitation of Hutten as a patriotic icon was well under way by the mid-nineteenth century. Like most images used to evoke strong emotions, Keller's depiction of Hutten emphasizes broad abstract features that are only peripherally and superficially linked to the reality of the physical entity at the heart of the image. Hutten as a free and bold knight, a unique example, is an image of someone Hutten himself may have wished to be but, probably to his great disappointment, never was. Having been driven away from the homeland of the Holy Roman Empire while bearing one of the empire's most illustrious honorific symbols, the *poeta laureatus* designation, Hutten's physical description, as Keller saw it, reflected the real situation, paled by anger and sorrow, while his unflagging, bright inner spirit shone forth through the metaphorical 'windows to the soul', his eyes.

The sixteenth-century imperial knight, a social class that was losing its status even during Hutten's lifetime and despite his efforts, was not the image Keller chose for Hutten but rather the more traditional and heroic cultural image from the Middle Ages. Sword in hand, he valiantly approached the island where waves lovingly kissed the shore, embracing it not in terms of the modern concept 'Liebe' but rather the medieval love concept, 'Minne,' as anachronistic for Keller's time as it would have been for Hutten's. His rhetorical greeting, 'sei mir gegrüßt!', addressed apparently to the spirit of the place, and the image of the despair and resignation of a broken, dying man contrasts greatly with the literary image of the medieval hero returning to the jubilantly welcoming society from which he, for a variety of reasons, may have been absent. But the isolation of Hutten's final exile cannot be subdued even by poetry, nor can the image of defeat be dispelled by that of a strong mental state enlivened as if intoxicated

116

by the headiness of young wine. Keller's Hutten has become a shadowy spirit, committed to the grave after years of struggle and suffering but equally committed to the rightness of his actions when alive, and prepared, were he to be given another chance, to do it all again the same way. Hutten had described himself as an Odysseus, a restless wanderer over stormy seas, an image Keller also used. The sense of resignation and acceptance that Keller's Hutten exhibits, his sense of the ephemeral nature of pain and the trivial nature of concern, may well have been the case at the end of Hutten's life, but they do not describe the painful and crippling effects of the syphilis that plagued him for all of his adult life. Keller did, however, capture an emotional state that must have been equally painful for Hutten, the recognition that the many good friends he had, and to whom he showed good friendship as well, abandoned him at the time he needed them most. The abandonment was not only emotional, but in the cases of Reuchlin, Crotus Rubeanus, and others, it was ideological as well. Keller's message from Hutten to the Swiss students recommended persistence and perseverance even in the face of struggle and suffering, for such conditions bring out the heroism of the human spirit. The context of Keller's poem is important; written ten years after the adoption of a Swiss constitution (1848) and during a decade when tensions between Switzerland and Prussia over Neuchatel were heating up and ultimately resolved in Switzerland's favor, the poem was a paean to a man whose values were admirable in the abstract but hardly compatible with the widely accepted Swiss neutrality position. The religious and ethnic diversity so characteristic of Switzerland stood in contrast to the homogeneous ethnic chauvinism of Hutten. This opposition between political reality and artistic sentiment made Keller's poem much less forceful and less creatively important than Meyer's epic narrative.

Meyer's long poem on Hutten's final days is placed even by its title in the realm of the imaginative. It was fitting that he turned to the symbolism of ancient Greece to describe Hutten's final refuge. The wandering Odysseus coming home to Ithaca, the peaceful paradise of Ufenau, are images that Hutten may have used himself, but they overlay a basic truth, his awareness of alienation and isolation as his lot in life. On Ufenau, as in other places of residence, he was a stranger: 'Ich bleibe Gast auf Erden immerfort.' Hutten remained a guest in his own land. Compared to Odysseus, whose adventurous tales of cunning and deception did not detract from his reputation as heroic figure and leader, Hutten was a stranger with a cause but without divine guidance or protection.

The mythological motifs are linked effectively to the localized images of a journey coming to its end. It seems somewhat redundant to mention Charon and the river Styx after the introductory scenes of Hutten in the company of a lone ferryman (*Schiffer, Schaffner, Ferge = poet*. Fährmann). The little church, the lone reception committee of a priest-physician-pastor, the dark-green harbor shadowed by a somber but majestic oak tree, dominant as if guarding the peace and tranquility of the place, a scene uncharacteristic of Hutten's life though appropriate for his death. Contrasts are pervasive; a simple inquiry as to the number of island inhabitants comes across as if it were a request for a military report: 'Wie stark, Pfarrer, ist die Besatzung hier?' The reply emphasizes the isolation: only Hutten, the priest-physician, and the ferryman who, one assumes, comes and goes as required. A small room in a modest hut with a low entryway contrasts with the openness of the surroundings, one shore nearby, the other further away, and an abundance of healing mountain air to be inhaled vigorously as one would quaff a cooling drink. The optimism of the priest-physician as regards Hutten's chances of healing and recovery is tempered by Hutten's own less enthusiastic response, 'Ich glaub's. So oder So!'

Hutten's slumber on the first night is a seamless mixture of dream and reality, the isolation of Ufenau and the familiar congeniality of Schloss Steckelberg, the family castle. The acoustic link between the quite different milieus was the sound of the bells of the grazing herds. Meyer's romanticized image of Hutten's departure from the ancestral home twenty years earlier, *mit leichtem Wanderbündel*, is chronologically accurate, but it doesn't convey the level of anxiety an eleven year old must have been experiencing as he is separated from his family for the first time. The atmosphere of the small chamber in which he now finds himself was also a combination of fantasy and practical reality. Sorting out his 'Siebensachen' – the odds and ends of his personal possessions – reveals the level of privation he has come to accept: the clothes he is wearing, a razor, and a quill. But Hutten's real state of impoverishment posed no constraints to Meyer's idealized image of him. The pen and the sword – Schwert und Feder – are the pillars of the idealized Hutten's life. It is a stretch to see Hutten's hand as 'schwertgewohnt', used to handling a sword, and the idea of the feud, *Fehde*, either by pen or sword, is more reminiscent of his friend, Franz von Sickingen, than of Hutten. The action, however, is truer to the Hutten of record, a tireless writer who used his pen to attack his enemies as an arrow flies into the ranks of an enemy army, 'wie der Pfeil in Feindes Heer'. The potential for harm inflicted by his devastating criticisms became greater over time, as Hutten's argumentative skills increased, and Meyer represented the change well by the image of the arrow transformed into a spear, a longer, more forceful, and potentially more damaging weapon. The generalized target, the lies of the priests, was only a part of the broad spectrum of laments and complaints Hutten registered in his writings. His legacies, those of sword and pen, are handled differently: when the arm has become too weak to wield the sword, there is the hope that another will emerge to take it up and carry on the fight; but Hutten's pen can be of no practical use to any successor except as an enduring symbol of his ideas and literary efforts. Such ideas will not only continue to be useful, even as he lies decaying in his grave, but they will be doubly as effective over time.

Hutten's concern for his physical well-being was a constant issue in his adult life, but the toll taken by the syphilis that plagued him throughout was felt both physically and mentally. The formulation of the dilemma, as posed by Meyer, is a good illustration of the way in which the one may influence the other. The passion of the heart, expressed in a variety of polemical treatises, was unaffected by the various cures attempted to relieve the pain and suffering of the syphilis. Subjecting the physical body to a regimen of fasting and iso-lation in hot, dark, humid rooms was of no consequence, Meyer suggests, if the soul continued to break the fast and assert its need for spiritual energy to maintain the fight. The answer was for Hutten to forget he was Hutten. Hutten's response to this diagnosis and sug-gested program of healing was the recognition that this was a sickness unto death, for to forget who he was and what he stood for was to become, like the subject of his early dialogues, *Nemo*, a nobody:

> Freund, was du mir verschreibst, ist wundervoll: Nicht leben soll ich, wenn ich leben soll! (Meyer, HLTage, V)

The sense of trust and resignation is reinforced by a school activity ostensibly dating back to the Fulda days: the pupils drew a sundial and then were challenged by the abbot to find the two words that summarized its symbolic significance. Hutten's startling discovery, during the night, of the phrase '*Ultima latet*' – the final hour is hidden – was as spiritually enlightening for the young boy as it was emotionally uplifting, the dawning of first fame, as Meyer described it. But the nature of the fame was open to question. In his section XX, 'Jacta est alea', Meyer presents the argument from the perspective of Hutten's father whose concern was clear: to attack the Church is crazy, and who knows how such an adventure will end. Bad enough to be a poet, Meyer has him say, but to be declared a heretic is far worse. Such a distinction had significance not only for the principal figure, but also for his immediate and extended family:

> Wenn nur in Holzschnitt du und Kupferstich den Lorbeer trägst – was anders kümmert dich? [...] du hast ein schlechtes Herz. (Meyer, HLTage, XX)

The coldness of Hutten's response, as Meyer formulated it, directed at both father and mother, gave substance to the isolated martyr complex suggested by the transformation of the laurel wreath of the *poeta laureatus* into a crown of thorns:

> Ich selber trage [...] einen schlichten Dornenkranz. Wozu der Lorbeer? (Meyer, HLTage, XX)

But does the imperial decree make one a poet? Without bringing Hutten's talent as a writer into question, Meyer does seem to be making a distinction concerning Hutten which modern critics have also made: *Dichter* versus *Verseschmied?* Meyer has Hutten himself endorse the latter, the wordsmith, as the fairer description, but as a wordsmith addressing the things that matter he is still fulfilling a useful role:

> Ich bin ein Verseschmied! So nenn' ich mich! Am Feuer meines Zornes
> Schmiedet' ich Rüstung und Waffen zu des Tags bedarf und wahrlich,meine
> Schwerter schneiden scharf! (Meyer, HLTage, XXViii)

Meyer also incorporates the *translatio imperii* concept into the thinking of his image of Hutten, suggesting a coexistence of the two:

> Den ersten Turnk dem heil'gen röm'schen Reich! Möcht' es ein weltlich
> deutsches sein zugleich! (Meyer, HLTage, XXIX)

This political, historical reference seems much more compatible with the historical Hutten than the following agrarian motif based on a Zwingli reminiscence. Since we know so little about Hutten's relationship to Zwingli, it is probably impossible to tell whether the anecdote is apocryphal or not. Nevertheless, the Zwingli who sheds tears of joy at the sight of agrarian activities, the planting of grain which will produce, as his father pointed out, the bread God has provided, represents an image that one would not easily associate with Ulrich von Hutten.

Meyer's extended narrative blends in with Keller's short poem by saluting the students who have come to honor Hutten, the exception being that the Hutten of Meyer's work is still alive and able, from a concealed vantage point, to enjoy the paean to himself. Emphasizing Hutten's academic service as an unrewarded producer of books, the students acknowledged his double service to the nation, one whose loyalty needed to be appreciated and honored. The patriotic sense embedded in such sentiments and the subsequent references to the need for unity among German-speaking citizens of the empire takes on a sinister tone as the argument moves towards its logical conclusion:

> Geduld! Es kommt der Tag, da wird gespannt ein einig Zelt ob allem deutschen
> Land! Geduld! Wir stehen einst um ein Panier, und wer uns scheiden will, den
> morden wir! Geduld! Was langsam reift, das altert spät! Wann andre welken,
> werden wir ein Staat. (Meyer, HLTage, XXXvi)

Meyer's words, Hutten's thoughts. Here, and in the blacksmith anecdote, Hutten's sympathies are well represented. The triple anvil strikes from a larger-than-life blacksmith at midnight in the Black Forest

121

form a context for Hutten's loyalties: first, to bind the Devil in Hell where he belongs; second, to bind the enemies of the empire that they may not advance to challenge it; and third, to forge a sense of loyalty and renewal of the old imperial crown.

Meyer's romanticized, idealized image of Hutten manages, nevertheless, to create contexts in which the spirit of the historical Hutten appears with believable contours. Even towards the end, the 'scientific,' negative diagnosis of Paracelsus (1493–1541), who was a contemporary of Hutten and author of a detailed description of Hutten's nemesis, syphilis, and the hallucinatory appearance and poignant fading away of the spirit of Franz von Sickingen, seem to be plausible if improbable events. What does not ring true, however, are the several sections devoted to Hutten's pious Christian reminiscences and his identification with the suffering Christ:

> Denn als ein Christ und Ritter lieg' ich hier [...] Fernab die Welt. Im Reiche meines Blick, an nackter Wand allein das Kruzifix. An hellen Tagen lieb' in Hof und Saal Ich nicht das Bild des Schmerzes und der Qual; Doch Qual und Schmerz ist auch ein Irdisch Teil, Das wußte Christund schuf am Kreutz das Heil. Je länger ich's betrachte, wird die Last mir abgenommen um Die Hälfte fast, denn statt des einen leiden unser zwei: Mein Dorngekrönter Bruder steht mir bei. (Meyer, HLTage, LXvi)

Meyer's Hutten, the Christian Humanist, sought solace in the words of two polar figures, St. Paul and Socrates:

> 'Es ängstet sich, es sehnt sich allezeit / Die Kreatur in ihrer Endlichkeit.' Was wartet unser, wann des Erdeseins unruhig Licht erlischt – von zweien eins: Für sel'gen Wandel ein bequemer Raum? Ein ungekränkter Schlummer ohne Traum?

The positive statement of the former – the anxiety linked to recognition of ones finiteness, one's mortality – is countered nicely by the inquisitory uncertainty of the latter – so what happens to us once the light of mortality has been extinguished? But despite the certainty of the one, he says, it can't hurt to place some stock in the other – a comfortable space where one can slumber without dreaming.

Ending as it began, arrival and departure by boat, the work has Hutten acknowledge his gratitude to his host and his recognition of the isolation and confinement of the body along with the freedom of the spirit and the soul. His lack of anxiety at impending death, belies the quotation from St Paul. In fact, the enthusiasm of his greeting to the approaching ferryman upon his return provides a parallel to the 'Sei mir gegrüßt' greeting upon his arrival. The paleness of the land of the spirits, the tall, stark figure of the ferryman, stand in contrast to the greenness of the island prison he now will leave behind. The freedom of action and thought so sought after in Hutten's life, now seem to be the attainable objectives of his death:

> Bin ich ein Sklave, der sich fesseln läßt? Gib frei! Gib frei! Zurück! Ich spring' ins Boot [...] Fährmann, Ich kenne dich! Du bist – der Tod.

The enthusiasm and aggressiveness of Hutten's life, so often frustrated by life events, are now made manifest by his eager jump into the arriving boat and the recognition that the ferryman is a well-known, and perhaps longed-for figure, death.

Heinrich von Kleist's drama *Die Hermannsschlacht* (1808) has no overt connection to Ulrich von Hutten except for the similarity of its themes and the central aspects of Hutten's life: oppression, ethnic chauvinism, the quest for liberation, deep-seated hatred for the oppressor. Kleist's Arminius figure also has little in common with the Germanic tribal hero as portrayed by Hutten, though throughout he refers to himself as the Cheruscan and arbitrarily interchanges Cheruscans and Germans as the tribal identifier. The most striking feature of Kleist's portrayal, however, is the unequivocal boldness of his sense of treachery. Kleist's Arminius is a user, a manipulator, someone who plays lightly with the truth and always seems to have only his own best interests at heart. The patriotic rhetoric remains superficial and uncomfortably insincere, given the consensus opinion that Kleist's objective was to incite patriotic fervor among Germans against Napoleon and France. But while Kleist's *Hermann* may be similar in spirit to Hutten's *Arminius*, Kleist's patriotism, as one might anticipate, is not a direct parallel to Hutten's ethnic chauvinism.

Given that the links between Kleist's play and Hutten's dialogue are at best indirect, the viability of the thematic material over the two hundred years separating the two writers deserves comment.[79] The strongest impressions that arise from Kleist's characterizations are the uncertainties of the Germanic leaders as to Hermann's ultimate intentions, the ambivalent view of the Romans, Varus and Ventidius, and the crass, self-serving treachery and viciousness of Hermann and his wife, Thusnelda. Kleist has the advantage over Hutten in the representation of this latter aspect because the nineteenth century drama could sustain developments of plot and motivation which the sixteenth-century dialogue could not. Aspects which Hutten could only allude to, the treachery of Arminius, for example, could be openly and graphically illustrated in Kleist's play. Likewise, the judgment of Arminius's actions, so openly and positively endorsed by Hutten's attitude and expressed openly in the opinion of the judge, Minos, remain provocatively open to speculation in Kleist's drama *Die Hermannsschlacht*. Despite the fact that both versions of Arminius's actions draw upon the Germanic past, some aspects of the characterizations fit plausibly into the respective representations while others do not. Kleist's Hermann underlines his independence and self-reliance by a statement that would have been alien to the Germanic Arminius, '[...] verknüpft mit niemand, als nur meinem Gott', modernized to something like 'between me and my God' or responsible only to myself and God. On the other hand, however, the statement does support Hermann's treacherous actions, which on various levels seem only designed to reap the greatest advantage for himself. The idea that Germany was completely lost is also a plausibly sustainable view for early nineteenth-century Germany but hardly possible for Hutten's Arminius. The comparison of the innate qualities of Germans and Italians has a chauvinistic quality also seen in Hutten:

> Ich glaub, der Deutsch' erfreut sich einer größern Anlage, der Italier doch hat seine mindre in diesem Augenblicke mehr entwickelt.

A double-edged comment that acknowledges the Roman-Italian accomplishments while implying that, under similar conditions of freedom

---

79   For reasons of time and space, the Arminius drama of Daniel Caspar von Lohenstein has not been considered here.

and self-determination, Germans could have accomplished as much if not more. The political applicability of such a view was expressed in the same spirit:

> [Wenn] unter einem Königsszepter, jemals die ganze Menschheit sich vereint, so läßt, daß es ein Deutscher führt, sich denken, ein Britt', ein Gallier, oder wer ihr wollt; Doch nimmer jener Latier, beim Himmel! der keine andre Volksnatur Verstehen kann und ehren, als nur seine.

– a sentiment reminiscent of the lines about the Greeks, attributed to Tacitus in Hutten's *Arminius* dialogue:

> [...] being much celebrated in the songs of the barbarians, Arminius was unknown in the annals of the Greeks, which only admired its own [...].

Kleist, like Hutten earlier, saw the problematic Germany–Rome relationship as the prototype for subsequent difficulties, be it sixteenth-century Germany and the Roman Catholic Church or nineteenth-century Germany and Napoleon. The differences in their views, however, are not insignificant. In early 1809, Kleist, in the face of German regions firmly in support of Napoleon and a Prussia that was not in a position to offer substantial opposition to him, looked rather to Austria for support of his patriotic views. His reception by the Austrians was less than enthusiastic, and the euphoria surrounding the French defeat at Aspern-Essling in May 1809 was quickly dispelled after the decisive French victory in the Battle of Wagram two months later. Kleist took refuge in Prague, but the changes in the military-political realities made the appearance of his patriotic play, *Die Hermannsschlacht*, highly unlikely. Kleist's response to the political environment helped to illuminate the nature of his political views in *Die Hermannsschlacht*. The difference in his patriotic attitudes and those of Hutten are expressed in his comments concerning Austria in an article entitled *Über die Rettung Österreichs*. To wage war for prominence and distinction, for independence, to preserve an imperial crown, Kleist suggests, is to do so for lower, subordinate purposes; the true objectives should be God, freedom, law, and morality.[80]

---

80 Curt Hohoff, *Kleist*, Rowohlt Monographien, Hamburg: 1958, 92. Hereafter cited as Hohoff Kleist.

Zuvörderst muß die Regierung von Österreich sich überzeugen, daß der Krieg den sie führt, weder für den Glanz, noch für die Unabhängigkeit, noch selbst für das Dasein ihres Thrones geführt werde, welches, so wie die Sache liegt, lauter niedere und untergeordnete Zwecke sind, sondern für Gott, Freiheit, Gesetz und Sittlichkeit, für die Besserung einer höchst gesunkenen und entarteten Generation, kurz für Güter, die über jede Schätzung erhaben sind, und die um jeden Preis, gleichviel welchen, gegen den Feind, der sie angreift, verteidigt werden müssen. (Hohoff Kleist, 92)

While Hutten's anger extended to Rome, as the embodiment of the Catholic Church and more specifically the papacy, Kleist saw his enemy in a more limited sense, Napoleon, the emperor, rather than France as a country, its people, its culture, its literature. At the same time, his catalogue of virtues that underlay the patriotic concept was much broader than Huttens: God, the Fatherland, the Emperor, Freedom, Love and Loyalty, Beauty, Knowledge, and Art. This is not to say that Hutten had no regard for these concepts but rather that they were not integral parts of his patriotic sense as embodied in the *Arminius* dialogue and other writings. As Curt Hohoff points out, Kleist was very sensitive to political realities; the emperor and empire were not idealized concepts but realities upon which the contemporary situation depended, for better or for worse.[81] The liberation of Germany, if it was to be successful, depended on real personalities who could translate ideas and ideals into actions. This attitude may account for the fact that the *Hermannsschlacht* drama offers much more in the way of concrete plans, discrete actions, political intrigues, misdirections and manipulations, than long impassioned speeches about the virtues of patriotism. Hutten's *Arminius*, however, was the embodiment of ideas and ideals which he hoped to see manifested in the actions of Maximilian and later Charles V but which, to his disappointment, never were expressed in the forms he so desired. Kleist's Hermann-Arminius was a mythical background figure with no claims to historical accuracy in the dramatic representation.[82] Hohoff has made the case in point:

81   Hohoff Kleist, 94
82   Hohoff Kleist, 94

Die Personen der *Hermannsschlacht* heißen Napoleon (Varus), Hermann (Österreich) als Befreier, Marbod (Norddeutschland) als Zögerer, Die Verbündeten des Varus (Fust, Gueltar, vor allem Aristan) sind die mit Napoleon verbündeten Fürsten des Rheinbundes, Bayern und Sachsen.[83]

It would be easy to over-emphasize the effectiveness of Kleist's presentation of the oppressor-oppressed theme in a drama as compared with Hutten's in a dialogue; the contemporary political conditions and the modes of presentation were very different. Nevertheless, the thematic implications are important for an understanding of the roles that both literary works may have played in the development of a patriotic consciousness in Germany in their respective periods and for subsequent generations. As Kleist's Hermann suggests that to fight for freedom is to put everything on the line, to risk all for the prime objective: uproot wives and children, melt down one's precious metals, sell off or pawn one's jewelry, lay waste one's lands, kill off the herds, and burn the houses; this is the sacrifice one must make. When his leaders respond that these are the very things they believed they were defending, Hermann replies: 'Nun denn, ich glaubte, eure Freiheit wär's' – I thought we were fighting for our freedom. Hermann makes it clear, and this can also be said of Hutten's Arminius, that the task was to make ones personal hatred for an enemy become a hatred shared by ones people as well. To be unable to realize this task would be tantamount to failure, 'So scheitert meine ganze Unternehmung!' Kleist was able to do with his dramatization what Hutten could never have accomplished in his dialogue: to provide a strong and plausible motivation for unity among the Germanic tribes. While Hutten's Arminius paid lip service to the necessity of unity – a goal which Maroboduus, his later opponent, had already begun in a limited sense – Kleist's Hermann took more drastic action, sending each of the tribes a piece of the body of a young virgin ravaged and killed by Roman soldiers.[84] The collaborative effort and

83   Hohoff Kleist, 94
84   Hohoff Kleist, 98. Kleist makes reference to Judges 19:29; When he had entered his house, he took a knife, and grasping his concubine he cut her into twelve pieces, limb by limb, and sent her throughout all the territory of Israel. Then he commanded the men whom he sent, saying, "Thus shall you say to all

promised alliance between Hermann and Marbod is a far cry from the animosity between the historical Arminius and Maroboduus, who became a victim of the inter-tribal struggles, as did Arminius himself.

The difficulty of translating patriotic concepts from an earlier age to one's contemporary period has already been mentioned. Such a transference of values becomes especially problematic when the ensuing periods have experienced significant cultural developments. The concern in Hutten's case also involved his use of Latin. The *patria* of Hutten's *Arminius*, rendered also as *Germania*, had they been actually used by the ninth-century Germanic-Roman warrior, would not have had the connotations of either 'Fatherland' or 'Deutschland.' At the next level, what Hutten heard in the term *patria* and conceptualized for himself as 'Fatherland' and 'Deutschland' was also something very different from Kleist's renderings of the same terms. Hohoff addressed this issue in his discussion of Kleist's personal life and his literary persona. The movement from an ego-bound consciousness, *Ichbefangen*, to a broader sense of belonging to a community, was reflected in his use of the term 'Vaterland':

> Hier [in der *Hermannsschlacht*] heißt das Vaterland Deutschland, im *Prinzen von Homburg*, wird es Preußen heißen. Nicht als ob sich Kleist innerhalb eines Jahres von einem deutschen auf ein preußisches Vaterland zurückgezogen hätte. Beide Länder sind im ganzen der gedichteten Motive Sinnbilder für ein Größeres, für ein Gemeinwesen, wo der Mensch nicht allein ist, nicht mehr vor dem Chaos steht. Deutschland oder Preußen sind dichterische Orte, wo die Freiheit des Menschen einen Sinn hat.[85]

This conceptual ambiguity is also evident in Kleist's Hermann, to whom August had promised 'die Oberherrschaft in *Germanien*', once Marbod had been eliminated, but who also expressed the hope that Marbod, while in the role of '*Deutschlands* Oberherrscher', would take responsibility of ridding *Das Vaterland* of the tyrannical oppressors [emphasis added]. Hutten's 'Germania' or 'Deutschland' is not an idealized concept, an idealized literary construct of his creative

the Israelites, 'Has such a thing ever happened since the day that the Israelites came up from the land of Egypt until this day? Consider it, take counsel, and speak out.' See also Judges 20: 6.

85   Hohoff Kleist, 98.

imagination, it is rather all to real, an embodiment of all that he felt he and his people could realize, given opportunity and effort. The reality of this image is perhaps one of the reasons why Hutten's contemporaries found his arguments and actions unpalatable. His political world was as real as the religious world of Martin Luther, the difference being that Hutten's success would have depended on overt political actions which he accepted as revolutionary but which others were reluctant to condone. It is also perhaps the irony of Hutten's literary impact that later generations would see in his *Arminius* idealized, ideological themes and motifs that would support the dreams of Germans for whom the political realities fell short of their imagined political potentialities.

The tone of the final statements of Hutten's *Arminius* and Kleist's *Hermannsschlacht* is important. In the former case, as throughout the dialogue, the thought centers on Arminius as one whose reputation, how others saw him, was central to his concept of who he was, even in the Afterlife:

> *Minos.* Enough; this ends the matter. It is clear that no one among you was immune to treachery and deceit despite your excellent virtues. But it is truly necessary now for those who have become acquainted with Arminius, his nobility and inborn qualities, to acknowledge him and admire him. Henceforth, German, it is fitting that your honor increase, and it is our obligation and my command that we never forget your virtues. Now, go, Mercury, and with those who accompany you immediately announce my judgment. Return, all of you. to the places from which you have come.

Arminius's self-representation tipped the scales in his favor, despite the existing reputations of his competitors and the arguments they raised in opposition to him. Hutten attributes to Arminius excellent virtues, nobility, inborn qualities, and the right to be acknowledged by his peers and admired, one must assume, by all who hear of him in the future. While the historical record may raise doubts about some aspects of these attributions, there can be no doubt that Hutten saw Arminius as such a figure, a Germanic heroic role model for his sixteenth-century contemporaries.

Kleist's Hermann, following the defeat of Varus and the swift, unremorseful execution of a Germanic prince who had allied himself with Varus, makes his ends clear, in a tone that may have suited Hutten's Arminius, had Hutten intended to use his dialogue in a different way:

> *Hermann*: Führet ihn hinweg! Was kann er sagen, das ich nicht schon weiß? (Aristan wird abgeführt.) Ihr aber kommt, ihr wackern Söhne Teuts, und laßt, im Hain der stillen Eichen, Wodan für das Geschenk des Siegs uns danken! Uns bleibt der Rhein noch schleunig zu ereilen, damit vorerst der Römer keiner von der Germania heilgem Grund entschlüpfe: Und dann – nach Rom selbst mutig aufzubrechen! Wir oder unsre Enkel, meine Brüder! Denn eh doch, seh ich ein, erschwingt der Kreis der Welt vor dieser Mordbrut keine Ruhe, als bis das Raubnest ganz zerstört, und nichts, als eine schwarze Fahne, von seinem öden Trümmerhaufen weht!

The implications are ominous: now that we have destroyed our enemies, all that remains is a black flag rising from the ashes, an omen of further troubles to come. Hermann has apparently heard all the arguments for the superiority of Rome, the inferiority of the Germanic tribes, and the necessity of convenient alliances to benefit both groups. It would seem that Hermann is more of a Germanic warrior-leader than the Romanized Arminius, for his animosities cannot be appeased by alliances, honors, tributes, and spoils. He seems set on nothing less than the destruction of Rome, and it is this objective that he bequeaths to his followers – Wir oder unsre Enkel, meine Brüder! – we or our grandsons, my brothers. The grimness of his vision of the future was matched by his self-serving treachery, his vicious revenge upon those who opposed him, and his willingness to ignore the lines of blood and ethnicity when it suited his purposes.

Chapter Five
Hutten in Cultural and Political Contexts

Hutten's travels in the years between 1505 and 1512–13 were physically challenging, intellectually formative, and moving in a line that seemed to have an implicit destination: Italy. The intermediate stopover in Vienna is also understandable in the context of his general educational and intellectual interests. Humanistic studies had already found a favorable environment in the city as a consequence of Conrad Celtis, the preeminent humanist, having responded to Emperor Maximilian's invitation to take up residence there and to create another of his solidarities, the fraternal, intellectual, and in Vienna, residential societies that included a number of Hutten's friends and supporters. What is less certain about this period is the reason he left Vienna after such a short stay. David Friedrich Strauss, who does not hesitate to speculate about Hutten's motivations,[1] took his lead from Böcking and suggested a possible reason based on a letter of the *Epistolae obscurorum virorum*, the literary satire for which Hutten had some responsibility.[2] The anecdote concerned Johann Heckmann who was in fact Rector of the University of Vienna during Hutten's time there. We are clearly in the realm of fiction, however, as regards the student in the anecdote who, lacking a degree of any kind, wanted to lecture on metrics and poetics but is refused permission, for obvious reasons, and threatened with imprisonment for reasons that are not altogether clear. Given Hutten's debilitating and depressing experiences in the foregoing weeks and months, it is difficult to imagine him being so arrogant as to pursue such a course at a university with an active group of humanists with degrees and license to offer approved courses. As disparate and perhaps peripheral as these elements may

---

1   Strauss, 56. Strauss recounts a story which may or may not be based on Hutten's experience in Vienna.

2   Hutten is often cited as the 'author' of the *Epistolae*; he is in fact responsible only for a significant portion of the second volume.

seem, taken together with his previous disappointments and the probable uncertainty of his situation in Vienna, the premature departure does suggest something about the possible state of Hutten's mind. The realization that his educational program was not progressing in a disciplined manner, his late but committed acquiescence to his father's wish that he study law, his humanist interest in learning Greek, and his vision of an imperial Germany free from outside influence, all pointed to the confluence of the personal and the political that would characterize his life from this stage forward. His ties to his family and his sense of self were perhaps stronger now than at any time previous to his departure from Fulda. Ethnic identity had become more important to him, and his sense of a personal political mission was clearer than it had ever been. However, his success was constrained by the premature progressiveness of his ideas and the recurring fever and crippling pain of syphilis.

The awakening of Hutten's political sensibility seems almost coincidental.[3] Not long after beginning his law studies in Pavia, the military situation after the Battle of Ravenna (1512) brought Swiss troops in against the occupying French troops. As improbable as it may seem, Hutten became a pawn in the midst of these opposing forces. While it is not clear what overt expression, if any, Hutten's support for Emperor Maximilian may have found, it is reasonably certain that given his physical limitations,[4] the most effective would have been literary.[5] On the one hand, he saw the emperor as a symbol of the continuity of German custom and tradition; on the other, he saw him as the German leader who should not have to tolerate insults from Venetians or any other foreigners. The former view was expressed in an essay stressing the continuity of values in German culture,[6] the

3   The following observations are based generally on the outline of Hutten's activities as presented by Strauss and reiterated by Balke, Bernstein, and others cited earlier.

4   Hutten's syphilis had at this time crippled him and gave him considerable pain. Strauss, 57.

5   There is no evidence, however, that the Emperor was in any way influenced by Hutten's appeals.

6   *Quod Germania nec virtutibus nec ducibus ab primoribus degeneraverit, Heroicum*; also appeared later under the title *Quod ab illa antiquitus Ger-*

latter in another essay dedicated to Emperor Maximilian, subsequently published by Vadian as a pamphlet.[7] Two aspects of these responses stand out: the intensity of Hutten's interest in the current status of German–Italian political relations, and the sense of confidence required to make a personal appeal to the Emperor in the hope, one must assume, that he would take notice. The initial signs of modesty and self-effacement that introduced the latter work are formulaic, though they may also indicate a sensitivity to the audacity of his undertaking, a personal appeal to the Emperor encouraging military action against the Venetians. Hutten charged that the Venetians had insulted the name and the honor of the Emperor, but he also made clear that his defensive response on the Emperor's behalf was to be a literary one.[8] In fact, Hutten's initial contacts with military forces in Italy border on the ridiculous. First he was a prisoner of the French, suspected of being a supporter of the Emperor, then he was imprisoned by the Swiss, suspected of being sympathetic to the French. There is a sense of the pessimism and despair he felt while imprisoned by the French in the epitaph he composed for himself:

> Der, zum Jammer gezeugt, ein unglückseliges Leben / Lebte, von Übeln zu Land, Übeln zu Wasser verfolgt, / Hier liegt Huttens Gebein. Ihm, der nichts Arges verschuldet, Wurde vom gallischem Schwert grausam das Leben geraubt. War vom Geschock ihm bestimmt, nur Unglücksjahre zu schauen, Ach, dann war es erwünscht, daß er so zeitig erlag. Er, von Gefahren umringt, wich nicht vom Dienste der Musen, Und so gut ers vermocht, sprach er im Liede sich aus.[9]

But he did not die at the hands of the French, instead he found himself a victim of the Swiss. Once again the ridiculousness of Hutten's situation and a sense of the value the Swiss placed on him as a prisoner of war are underlined by the fact that, impoverished as he

---

manorum claritudine nondum degenerarint nostrates, Ulr. De Hutten eq. heroicum. See Böcking Opera, III, 331–340.

7   Ad divum Maximilianum Caesa. Aug. F.P. bello in Venetos euntem Ulrici Hutteni eq. Exhortatio [...] Mense Januario, Anno 1512. Böcking Opera, III, 123–158.

8   Ibid.

9   Strauss, 57–58; Böcking Opera I, 26

was, the Swiss accepted the little he had in exchange for his freedom.[10] The Hutten who arrived shortly afterwards in Bologna was a very sick man, his financial resources had been reduced to a minimum, and the bad memories of two unjust imprisonments were fresh in his mind. In a sense, Hutten's subsequent military service could be seen as an effort at revenge, a compensation for his previous mistreatment by enemy soldiers, or as an act of desperation by a man who had lost practically all of his material resources; the latter is probably more accurate. However one chooses to view it, his real service at this time was not on the battlefield but rather in his literary output, the epigrams dedicated to Emperor Maximilian.[11] The epigrams are chronologically linked to Hutten's experiences and observations during his various involvements with German–Italian–French–Swiss military and political relations. The titles of the epigrams chronicle realistically and symbolically his view of an imperial Germany beset by challenges from two undeserving powers, the Venetians and the French. The tone is set by the first poem about Emperor Maximilian:

Von dem Adler
Seht den gewaltigen Aar, der jetzt unblutig und friedsam / Tag' und Jahre sich halb schlafend in Ruhe gewiegt. / Aber es greif ihn einer nur an und störe die Rast ihm: Sterben will ich, wofern der sich nicht übel getan. Nimmer ist dies ja ein Schlaf, aus dem kein Erwachen es gäbe; Oft schon hat er, gereizt, auf aus der Ruh sich gerafft; Und wenn kühn er vom oben sich schwingt in die offenen Lüfte, Wehe, wie breitet er dann Schrecken und Furcht um sich her!

The sleeping giant, in this case, the imperial eagle, portrayed as a lover of peace, is a stranger to violence, but also a terrible foe for any who would wake him from his rest. The mistake of his enemy would be to take his peaceful slumber for a deep sleep from which he could not be awakened. For once awakened, the terror and fear he would engender would engulf all around him. The poem 'Vom Kaiser und den Venezianern' counters the imagery of the powerful imperial eagle with that of the Venetian frogs, crawling up croaking from

10   Ibid.
11   *Ulrici de Hutten eq. Germ. Ad Caesarem Maximilianum Epigrammatum liber unus.* Böcking *Opera*, III, 205–268.

the marshes of Venice to claim the dry land for themselves but being driven back by the sharp talons of the bird of Zeus, Emperor Maximilian and his army. 'Auf die Franzosen, als sie dem Kaiser die Flucht andichteten' shifts the focus from the Venetians to the French, the rooster so arrogant as to challenge the eagle. The political–military alliance of France and Venice against Maximilian was doomed to failure, in Hutten's epigrammatical view, but it provided the basis for a witty commentary that also shows Hutten's capacity for criticism of his fellow Germans:

> Drei umwerben mich jetzt – Italia klagts dem Apollo – Widrige Freier zumal: Venedig, der Deutsche, der Franke; Der voll Trug, der andre voll Wein, der dritte voll Hochmut. Muß es denn sein, so bedenke mich doch mit erträglichem Joche. Stets treulos, erwidert der Gott, ist Venedig; der Franke stets hoch-mütig; der Deutsche nicht immer betrunken: so wähle![12]

Hutten's epigrams dedicated to Maximilian were based on personal observations on the political situation and events in Italy in 1511–12. While the primary motivation seems to have been the confrontation between Italians and Germans, followed by a desire to encourage Maximilian's military venture against the Venetians, the underlying attitude went beyond the contemporary situation to suggest a sense of cultural continuity and a respect for and obedience to imperial authority reminiscent of medieval rather than sixteenth-century views. Unfortunately, his trust in his peers, the knights, and in an idealized image of Maximilian and later his successor, Charles V, proved to be unwarranted and disappointingly naïve. However, his personal vicissitudes notwithstanding, Hutten's world view at the time arose from a mentality based on germanic tradition, a sense of tit-for-tat justice, and the solidarity of like-minded individuals, in this case, both his social peers and his intellectual peers, the humanists. At no time was this structure challenged more than in the Reuchlin affair and, later, in the incidents surrounding the Hutten family and Duke Ulrich of Württemberg. Hutten's sense of loyalty to a cause and to individuals found expression in three different arenas but with equal intensity. His ethnic allegiance to the emperor, his humanistic solidarity with Reuchlin, and

12   Strauss, 62.

his personal love and fealty towards the unjustly treated members of his family were all of a piece and drew forth the full effect of his eloquence, emotions, and literary skills.

Despite the political content of Hutten's literary activities at this time and the personal implications that German–Venetian–French relations had for him, his interests and concerns represented a very small part of a much larger picture. As early as 1495, Maximilian had been an ally of Venice in the Holy League against the French. At home, he met the resistance of the princes to a strong centralized power, but he failed in his attempt to bring the Swiss under his authority (1499, Peace of Basel). His efforts to contain the French were thwarted again when they regained control of Milan. Continued problems at home led to the establishment of the Reichsregiment, which threatened to remove Maximilian from power but failed. Subsequent military successes and political maneuverings did increase Maximilian's prestige and financial resources but did not give him what he wanted, namely, the ceremonial confirmation and coronation, bestowing upon him the title of emperor along with his recognition as German king. Venice was a major obstacle in this process, denying Maximilian passage to Rome to be crowned in the traditional manner by the Pope. Maximilian now found it advantageous to join with France, Spain, and the Pope in the League of Cambrai. Once again, however, the domestic politics of Germany disadvantaged Maximilian abroad, leaving him unable to maintain his part in the League. Having been persuaded to refuse the office of Pope for himself, an offer resulting from schism within the Church, Maximilian shifted his allegiances once more, allying with Spain, England, and the Pope against France. Despite a French defeat (1513) by the Swiss, France ultimately gained control of Milan and the Venetians were awarded Verona. These developments ended Maximilian's military efforts in central Italy. In 1519, his grandson, Charles V, became Emperor.[13]

13   This material has been condensed from various sources. See Norman Davies, *A History of Europe*, 524–525; 545; Thomas Brady, Heiko Obermann, James Tracy, eds. *Handbook of European History, 1400–1600, Late Middle Ages, Renaissance, and Reformation*, Vol. I: Structures and Assertions, The Art of War, 'European Warfare in the Sixteenth Century', 547–552.

Hutten's imprisonments, first by the Swiss and then the French, do not rank even as footnotes to these broader European events, except as the adventures of a young man who happened to be in the wrong places at the wrong times. His images of Germany and Germany's political prestige in the person of the Emperor were at odds with the political realities of the period. Unlike Maximilian who saw his vision of the continuity of the medieval Roman Empire of the German nation become more complicated and elusive because of political and economic necessities, Hutten was able to maintain a literary vision of German culture and virtues which, in his view, had remained consistent through the centuries. His essay on the subject was framed not in the form of a question but rather an assertion: (version 1) *Quod Germania nec virtutibus nec ducibus ab primoribus degeneraverit, Heroicum*; (version 2) *Quod ab illa antiquitus Germanorum claritudine nondum degenerarint nostrates, Ulrich De Hutten, eq. Heroicum.* Namely, that the differences between his own time and that of the ancient Germans were differences of both culture and activism but with a continuity of values and virtues.[14] Whereas the earlier times saw violent means as a way of life, justifying assault on cities and the overthrow of kings, the present was dedicated to peaceful pursuits, the cultivation of the arts in various forms to facilitate the understanding of society and the universe. Despite his recognition of the value of humanistic studies in the development of a civilized society, Hutten had no qualms about encouraging Maximilian to wage war against the Venetians, nor does he refrain from images of violent overthrow and conquest in his view of the struggle of Germany against its avowed enemies, Venice and France.

The combination of revolutionary and reactionary attitudes in the same person also suggests how he could be so attractive to some and so repulsive to others. His patriotic fervor was grounded on the one hand in a wish for the future independence of Germany from the exploitative relations with the Catholic Church and greater political independence within the empire, while on the other it saw the realization of such wishes as being dependent on the core of

14   For an in-depth treatment of this attitude and other pertinent observations, see Mertens as cited earlier.

ancient Germanic values and traditions underlying his personal view of German-ness. This strongly positive view of Germany's ancient past coupled with harsh criticisms of his contemporaries, a recurring theme in Hutten's writings, echoed Conrad Celtis's criticism of Germans in his inaugural lecture at the University of Ingolstadt, October, 1492.[15]

> Tollite veterem illam apud Graecos, Latinos et Hebraeos scriptores Germanorum infamiam, qua illi nobis temulentiam, immanitatem, crudelitatem et, si quid aliud, quod bestiae et insaniae proximum est, ascribunt.[16]

Celtis lamented the bad reputation Germans had been given by writers in various cultures – Greek, Latin, i.e., Roman, and Hebrew – and the consequent attributes that resulted: drunkenness, lack of discipline, ferocity, and other traits that were more characteristic of animals or madmen. Both Celtis and Hutten recognized the value to Germans – especially young Germans – of looking to the ancient past, but not in the traditional humanist manner – to discover the glory of Greece and Rome as manifested in literature and history – but rather to discover for themselves the virtues of the *German* past. The lament was not only that students were ignorant of the history of Greece and Rome but more importantly that their knowledge of German history was lacking. The thematic similarity of Celtis's concerns and Hutten's later appeals is important enough to discuss in detail.

Celtis's Germany, like Hutten's, was a Germany of the distant past with clearly definable geographic features, a central place in the European context, and one whose customs, passions, and attitudes, they felt, ought still to play an important role in contemporary life.[17] For both men it was not a matter of whether or not Germans had performed memorable deeds or not but rather that there were no skill-

---

15   Celtis *Oratio*, sect. 7.
16   For an on-line German translation see Joachim Gruber, Bibliotheca Augustana, *Conrad Celtis, Oratio in gymnasio in Ingelstadio publice recitata*, 1492. Textus et editio digitalis:, Translatio germanice, 2001, http://www.fh-augsburg.de. Hereafter cited as *Oratio* Gruber.
17   For complete text see Hans Rupprich, Hrsg., *Conrad Celtis Germania generalis, Deutsche Literatur in Entwicklungsreihen*, Bd. 2, Humanismus und Renaissance, Stuttgart, 1935.

ful, competent historians, or storytellers, who might have recorded those deeds for posterity.[18] While this may have been a criticism with some validity coming from Celtis, it was more on the order of a generalized lament on Hutten's part since, strictly speaking, there had been creditable efforts by Germans to write and defend their own history that were contemporary with his complaint.[19] Celtis's astonishment that the Greeks and Romans had shown such a great interest in Germans and Germany has its counterpart in Hutten's *Arminius* where the star witness's testimony to the German general's greatness was relegated to Tacitus, a Roman. The leitmotifs of this part of Celtis's *Oratio* are the words 'shame' – *pudori* and its variant forms – directed at the students and their lack of knowledge about Germany, and 'amazement' or 'astonishment' – *mirum, miraculum* – forms which he used to express his own feelings about their shortcomings and the laudable contributions of non-Germans to the writing or recording of German history. Hutten became the type of student to whom Celtis had addressed his program of humanistic studies. Such studies, and a grounding in personal virtue, were in Celtis's view the path to social esteem and reputation, immortal fame, and good fortune.[20] Despite Hutten's commitment to these values, he failed to achieve the public successes Celtis had outlined. From a more personal perspective, however, he can be said to have used his eloquence in ways that Celtis would have approved.[21] Both shared a sense of the injustice suffered by Germans and Germany at the hands of neighboring peoples for whom the enviable deeds of Germans, primarily military, were either ignored or used against them. They saw the handling of this cultural, historical information as either distortions of the truth or outright fabrications.[22] Celtis's appeal to the Germans' loss of self-respect has the ring of Hutten's later criticism.[23] Likewise, the scorn for the princes, their lack of education, their luxurious lifestyles and love of

---

18   Hutten's use of these themes and others has been discussed in various places in this study.
19   See Mertens, 80–96.
20   Celtis *Oratio*, chap. 2, sect. 2.
21   Celtis *Oratio*, 4, 8.
22   Celtis *Oratio*, 5, 13–15.
23   Celtis *Oratio*, 6, 2–3.

money, all caused Celtis to suggest that it might be better to be living a rough life in the forest, like their Germanic ancestors did, than to succumb to the ruinous life of greed and excess common to the contemporary princes.[24] The immortal fame that Celtis recommended to young German students – using the examples of St. Jerome and St. Augustine – could only be achieved through the study of both Greek and Latin. The personal and professional benefits would come only after long, wakeful nights, diligent study, and familiarity with foreign regions, or study abroad, not through a wasteful, purposeless lifestyle of gluttony, gambling, and whoring.[25] In a more practical vein, but still emphasizing the value of language skills and wisdom, Celtis attributed the moral, intellectual, and political success of past, current, and future empires to the encouragement of civilizing humanistic studies and the honor shown to those who teach them.[26] Celtis's concluding words embodied the literary efforts to which Hutten devoted himself but it is arguable whether his efforts brought immortality or fame and honor to his Fatherland.[27] One of the premises of this study is that, Hutten's intentions notwithstanding, the love of native landscape and the idealization of its people and their cultural attributes can over time lead to an insularity of feeling and belief that can be detrimental to those with whom one feels no particular kinship. The cosmopolitanism of the humanists, which Hutten must also have shared to some extent, had no part in his message once he decided that ethnicity and identity were more important than any commitment to letters. This change in values was reflected to a certain extent in his decision to begin writing in German and translating earlier works into German. It is worth noting that this decision, an effort on Hutten's part to seek the comfort and support of a linguistic if not ideological community, was far less beneficial to him than his earlier solidarity with the attitudes, ideas, and modes of expression of his fellow humanists. Whereas earlier his participation in the humanist confraternity could take for granted a certain harmony of ideas and

24 Celtis *Oratio*, 8.
25 Celtis *Oratio*, 9, 11–12.
26 Celtis *Oratio*, 10, 1–2.
27 Celtis *Oratio*, 10, 16.

attitudes, bound by a common intellectual interest, the new approach – new at least for Hutten – held no such guarantees. For even like-minded Germans did not necessarily share the patriotic fervor so evident in Hutten's writings. It was perhaps this unwarranted assumption, that those who speak my language will share my loves, my hopes, my ideals, that set such limitations on his patriotic, ultimately self-serving efforts. In this latter respect, Hutten's abandonment of efforts to gain the support of the princes and his alliance with Franz von Sickingen are but preliminary steps to his alienation and isolation from the very audience he sought to influence by presenting his ideas in German instead of Latin.

Hutten's introduction to the *Gesprächbüchlin*,[28] dedicated to his friend and patron Franz von Sickingen, emphasized the importance of friendship and identified Sickingen as a well-known, courageous, sincere advisor to an emperor, a trusted and comforting friend. By reference to the proverb 'A friend in need is a friend indeed' – In nöten erkennt man den freünd – Hutten suggested that this and other such proverbs came into being out of necessity, or, as a concretization in proverbial form of beliefs that had come to be affirmed in their validity by human experiences over time. To call a person 'friend' is not possible, Hutten suggested, without first having had the time and opportunity to deal closely with that person in a situation of emergency or need, to have come to know that person intimately and in external matters, to have had opportunity to test and be tested. It is a blessing from God to have had such opportunities, to have found someone whom one can call 'friend' without reservations or qualifications. Hutten's personal situation of having faced physical challenges, attacks on his honor, the loss of his financial resources, made survival dependent on the kindness of friends. As he indicated, not friends who were there with comforting words, but rather friends who were prepared to act in concrete and helpful ways – 'nit als offt geschicht mit tröstlichen worten, sonder hilfftragender that' – that is to say, someone like Franz von Sickingen. The value of this situation

---

28 Heinz Mettke, Hrsg., *Ulrich von Hutten. Deutsche Schriften*, Bd. I. Leipzig: VEB Bibliographisches Institut. 1972. Hereafter cited by page number immediately after the excerpt.

was also supported by a proverb, namely, that a good friend is a gift from Heaven. Although fair weather friends were a more common phenomenon in the society than true friends, one must be careful that they not be rejected out of hand. Hutten's comparison of the two types of friendship was drawn from medicine: physicians saw a difference between food that is only sweet and tasty and other foods that may be not only sweet and tasty but also healthful and restorative. Of the two types, the healthy and restorative would of course be preferable. This reasoning underlay the friendship with Franz von Sickingen, someone who had not been swayed by what others had said about Hutten but rather by what he had come to know of him through personal experience. Sickingen's regard for the truth and his sensitivity to Hutten's sufferings, physical and mental, formed the foundation of their friendship. It is important to keep in mind that this was a time when Hutten was finding fewer places of refuge and fewer friends on whom he could rely. The more vigorous and antagonistic his writings, the more isolated he became from the very people, family and friends, whom he might have expected to be most supportive. A recognition of his situation made it quite reasonable to view Sickingen's support and offer of a place of refuge to be a place of last resort for him – his 'Herberge der Gerechtigkeit' – a place where an interest in justice would prevail.

It is difficult to know what Hutten's concept of justice encompassed at this point, but given the personal injustices he had suffered at the hands of the Lötze family, his imprisonments and mistreatment at the hands of the Swiss and the French, and, finally, the egregious miscarriage of justice experienced by his family in the matter of Duke Ulrich of Württemberg, it is easy to see how he may have become cynical about justice and the possibility of a just society. Sickingen's hospitality and generosity, even as expressions of human kindness, must also have seemed to Hutten like a life-line extended at a time of great despair.

Hutten's mission at this point in his life – and Sickingen agreed that it was both an honorable and sincere mission – was to bring a lamentable socio-political situation in Germany to the attention of educated Germans. This mission had two important aspects: first, that educated Germans, learning the truth, would be willing and able to bring about change; secondly, that the Germany of Hutten's concern was in fact a nation, not in the sense of a political entity with a centralized government, but rather that of a people who shared common customs, common origins, a unique history, and a common language. The latter aspect was a point of some import to Hutten, who after years of couching his ideas in fluent Latin treatises, letters, and poems, came to realize the value of addressing his people in their native language. Hutten described his appearance on the political scene in Germany – in self-important terms – as the emergence of a joyful sun, dispelling the clouds of inclement weather.

Despite the reality of the social and political situations underlying Hutten's concerns, an understanding of his approach depends much on reading the symbolic, metaphorical nature of his language. The *Gesprächbüchlin*, a German version of *Inspicientes*, 'Die Anschauenden,' was prepared by Hutten – as he said, hastily, 'eylendts', and with relative ease, 'on grösseren fleiß' – as a New Year's gift for Franz von Sickingen. Fortunately, since Hutten dated the dedication, it seems that the reason for haste was to have the gift ready by New Year's Eve of 1521 for presentation at Sickingen's castle, Schloss Ebernburg, on the following day (*Geben zů Ebernburgk vff den heyligen newen jars abent jm jar nach Christi geburt M CCCCC vnd einvndzweintzigsten*). The gift was symbolically significant: a new version of the dialogue at the beginning of a new year to a man who represented, for Hutten at least, a new direction for political activism, and from a man who felt he had been given a new lease on life.

The preface to the reader emphasizes a basic theme: truth versus deception; the idea of renewal is important here also. Truth has been reborn, and deception, or deceit, has lost its appeal. The phrase 'hat der btrugk sein schein verlorn' underlines the misleading aspect of appearances which because of their appeal lead people to neglect the underlying truth. The removal of the deceptive façade exposes the truth, presents it anew and makes the creators of the deceit suspect to discerning observers. The popular response to this new initiative should be to praise and honor God and to pay no further heed to the lies that have been told in order to suppress the truth. The suppression of truth was an act, or a variety of acts, which brought certain benefits to many while fostering discontent and frustration among others. The

143

objects of this criticism were the priests, conventionally described as lazy. Pious Germans were entreated to observe the differences between the messages of the priests and the truth, and between God, who is eternal, and the Pope, who will die just like any other person. The entreaty and the subsequent warning to pious Germans of the need to come together to take advice on how best to cope with the years of deception and manipulation are but a prelude to the essential message, i.e., Hutten's commitment to the truth and his determination to pursue it at all costs:

> So will ich auch geloben, das von warheit ich wil nymer lan, das sol mir bitten ab kein man. Auch schafft zůstillen mich kein wer, kein bann, kein acht, wie vast vnd seer man mich darmit zůschrecken meynt. (Mettke, 7)

In essence, the pursuit of truth had become a life's goal from which neither weapons, nor the threats of banishment and accusations of outlawry could dissuade him.

Hutten's reader is left in no doubt as to his definition of truth and his identification of the greatest abuser of truth and reliability. His most important adversary was the Pope and the arrogance of office that had enabled him to see himself as God's supreme arbiter of Truth in this world. The suggestion that even a child could see the lack of truth and the obvious manipulation in Papal words and actions is in essence a backhanded criticism of those who respected papal prerogatives. In Hutten's view, papal authority had over time gone beyond the bounds of sophisticated issues of purely theological interest and had now become matters of concern that even a child would recognize as ill-advised. His concern was not just substantive but rather sought through humor to illuminate the manipulations and machinations of a Pope whose arrogance had not only widened the gulf between himself and his followers but had increased his desire to consume all:

> Als ob er meynt der Sonnen schein, vnd ander ding am himel hoch zůzyehen vnder bäpstlich joch. (Mettke, 154)

The concern for truth and the political context of papal actions did not preclude the creation of a narrative vehicle that was a poetic fiction drawn from the mythological realm.[29] Hutten seems to have considered the dialogue *Die Anschauenden* to be somewhat more creative than the others in the *Gesprächbüchlin*.[30] As such, the dialogue participants were well-known figures from Classical mythology, father and son, setting up a structure for a dialogue that was critical and didactic at the same time. The dialogue begins with Sol (Apollo/ Phoebus) in conversation with Phaeton, his inexperienced, curious son whose adventure trying to replace his father ended in near catastrophe for the earth and, depending on the version, death for him:

> [Phaeton] [...] seinen vatter gebetten hat, jn lassen den Sonnen wagen einen tag auß regieren. Der jm das erlaubt. Dieweil er aber, den wagen vnd die pferd nit zů regieren wisszte, irreth er am himel, für zů nider, vnd zündet das gantz erdtreich an. Darumb jn Jupiter, als er das ersah, mit dem tonder niderschlůg, vnd in Pad – ist ein wasser in Italien – warff. Da ward er, als etzliche gedicht haben, zů einem schwanen; als aber Lucianus sagt, ist er in der Sonnen reich, von seinem vatter zů einem regierer vnd gubernator gesetzt, vnd nun mer ein vnsterblicher gott worden. Dißes hat alles seinen sonderen verstandt. Aber hye würt Phaeton, der Sonnen fůrman genennt. (Mettke, 155)

The proverbial sources Hutten added to this narrative are in some instances obscure but seem to have some connection to characterizations that served his theme. The son of the earth – whose origins are so obscure that he does not know the identities of his father or mother – may be relevant to the figure of Phaeton, who spends a certain amount of time searching for his real father. The connection of this 'proverbial' source to Hutten's objective is not nearly as pertinent, it would seem, as the references to the centaurs and the Lapiths, both associated with the type of behavior that is used to characterize Germans. The centaurs, whose creation is also linked, literally, to

29 This view is held despite Barbara Könneker's assertion that in order to take up a position as regards contemporary political events Hutten dispensed with poetic or fictional trappings. Barbara Könneker. In: *Literaturlexikon: Autoren und Werke deutscher Sprache*. Hrsg. von Walter Killy. Berlin: Directmedia, 2000.

30 The 'others' refers to the three other dialogues translated into German that comprised the *Gesprächbüchlin*: *Feber das Erst, Feber das Ander, Wadiscus, oder die Römische Dreifaltigkeit, Inspicientes*, all published in 1521.

cloudy beginnings are described as being by nature lustful, fond of drink, intemperate, and sexually promiscuous.[31] Hutten's reference to the proverbial 'centaurish' behavior, derived from the mythological story of the wedding banquet of Pirithous, son of Ixion, king of the Lapiths, to which centaurs, their neighbors, had been invited and then attempted to abduct the bride. It is not difficult to see how such a story could have become descriptive over time for any events or celebrations that degenerated into drunkenness and debauchery.[32] For Hutten, the relevant experience is the peasant celebration:

> Als in Teütsch land vnder den vollen bauren offt geschicht, daz sye ire Kyrb zů einer Centhaurischen würtschafft machen. (Mettke, 155)

The inclusion of the Leontines into this complex of wine-drinking, unruly, excessively amorous types seems relevant up to a point. Despite numerous references to them in Thucydides, nowhere is there mention of behavior that might have led to them being viewed proverbially as being addicted to drink:[33]

> Leontini seind ein volck in Sicilien [...] daz man ein sprichwort von jn gemacht: Allweg stecketen Leontini hinder den fleschen. (Mettke, 155)

Having stressed the effects of alcohol on the mentality of a person, or, by extension of a people, Hutten then offered a folk solution, a purgative made from 'nyeszwurtz' – *hellebore*[34] – , which had the common attribute of being able to sharpen senses dulled by alcohol abuse.

---

31 The progenitor of the centaurs, Ixion, lusting after Hera, is deceived by Zeus into making love to a cloud from which is borne the race of centaurs.

32 See Pirithous, *Oxford Classical Dictionary*, 835.

33 See Rex Warner, Trans., *Thucydides. The Peloponnesian War*, New York: Penguin, 1954, 245–246; 349–350; 410–412, and others; however, none offer characterizations of the Leontini.

34 *Hellebore* is an herb considered by the ancients to have both poisonous and medicinal qualities, usually related to treatment of mental disease.

> Ein purgatz von nyeszwurtz [...] pflegen etwan zu nemen die sich vnuer-
> nünfftig oder vnsinnig zů werden besorgten, dann die artzney scherpfft die sinn
> des menschen. (Mettke, 156)

Hutten's narrative connection of these elements with the original references to Sol and the role of the Sun in the affairs of humans is consistent with mythological sources:

> [...] von der sonnen kompt gůter vnnd bößer lufft.Darumb tichten die poeten,
> wann pestilentz regiert, so schyessz der Sonnen gott Apollo, mit pfylen herab
> zů vns, als ertzürnet über das menschlich geschlecht. Darauff würt gezogen,
> was hyerinn von der pestilentz geredt. (Mettke, 156)

The speakers in the dialogue, *Die Anschauenden*, are limited to three: Sol, the Sun; Phaeton, his son; and Cajetan, the papal legate.[35] The mythological context is superficial at this point when Sol, who had not had any contact with his son until the fateful borrowing of the sun chariot, to pass the time while resting his horses engaged his son in conversation. Hutten's narrative puts Phaeton in the role of constant companion to his father on the circuit through the heavens and suggests that it had been their custom to observe human behavior along the way. However, for some reason, combined with a gathering of clouds obscuring the view, Sol had been neglecting the affairs of humans:

> Etzliche schiffend, ein teil sich auch mit kryegen vermischen, vnd offt umb eins
> nichtigen dings willen, als do einer dem anderen einen vnnützen titel fürwitz-
> igklich entzogen, bald grosse hör außfůren, vnnd sich also vnder einander
> ertödten. (Mettke, 156)

The general impression is that human activities were for the most part irresponsible, and that might account for Sol's loss of interest in the affairs of men on earth.

The proverb-based characterizations of the introductory material set the tone for critical assessments of ethnic groups that underlay

---

35 Tommaso de vio Cajetanus (Gaetan), (1468/69–1534) papal legate who was responsible for the examination of Martin Luther and author of the document *Exsurge Domine* condemning Luther.

some of the domestic and international conflicts of this early six-teenth-century period. The Italians, for example, are considered un-trained and inexperienced in military matters. It is not unreasonable to suppose that Hutten was drawing on personal observations for such opinions, especially given the attention to details that go beyond a general assessment.

> [...] also das man kaum einen oder zwen [Italiener findet, die] die harnesch recht fůren, die spieß reüterisch schwingen, ordenung wissen, sich vnder dem fänlin halten, oder zů etzwas das die kryegs ordenung innheldt, vnsträfflich geschickt sein. (Mettke, 157)

Perhaps the sharpest critique of Italians, coming from Sol, was the assertion that one saw in them nothing of their Roman ancestors, with the possible exception of the Venetians, among whom were some very skilled individuals. The military personality identified as such was Marcantonio I Colonna, whose skills allegedly were learned from the Germans.[36] But what Hutten gave the Germans with one hand, he took away with the other:

> [...] sye [die Teütschen] künnen nichtes dann wenn sye trincken vnd voll seint, außrichten. (Mettke, 157)

Phaeton suggested further, that the Germans had a certain impetuosity which could serve them well, but as soon as the heat of the moment had worn off, they were useless. His evidence for this fault was the success of the Venetian military leader Bartolomeus d'Alviano in taking back lands that had already been won by German forces, but these forces through drunkenness and lethargy were unable to defend themselves.[37] Assuming that the recounted incident is historically

---

36   Marcantonio I Colonna, (1478–1522), lord of Frascati, one of a number of condottiere, or mercenary military leaders, employed by the City-States. Hutten's reference to Colonna's contact with Germans cannot be verified, but for additional general information, see also: Michael Mallett, *Mercenaries and their Masters:Warfare in Renaissance Italy*. Rowman and Littlefield. 1974.

37   Bartolomeo d'Alviano (1455–1515), Venetian general and captain, in 1508 defeated the imperial Army of Maximilian I, Holy Roman Emperor in Cadore, at Mauria and Pontebba, conquering Gorizia and Trieste. In 1509,

verifiable, the question posed by Phaeton has validity: why would someone involved in a serious matter in enemy territory allow oneself to become incapacitated by excessive drinking? The implication of a lack of seriousness was viewed as a cultural flaw from which courageous impetuosity could lead to negative or no accomplishments. The flaw was most evident in the gap between the military ability of Germans to conquer and their political inability to rule!

> [Sie sind] mit woffen vnüberwindtlich. Wiewol sye zů regieren vngeschickt. Dann sye genůget doran, wann sye andere überfallen, jagen, verwüsten, vmbstossen, berauben, vnd außbrennen. Darnoch habent sye ein frölichen můt, dencken nit weyter, stätt vnd flecken die sye also gewinnnen, zůbehalten. (Mettke, 158)

The emphasis on short-term thinking, especially in a political sense, was more than a casual criticism but rather one that went to the heart of the ideological shortcomings Hutten saw in his fellow Germans. Implicit in the criticisms was the imperial neglect of cities such as Padua, Vicenza, and Treviso, which though under the control of imperial forces were subsequently, with little effort, recaptured by the Venetians.[38] Hutten's comments about the Spaniards, added here almost as an afterthought, saw them primarily as diligent thieves but militarily, i.e., in the field, honest and reliable, experienced, courageous and defiant.

The interwoven threads of mythological and historical material continued as Hutten's Sol turned his attention to Germany, especially the Rhine, taking responsibility for thwarting the various attempts to erect wooden bridges across the mighty river. By doing so, he also reminds Phaeton of the nearly catastrophic results of his effort to drive his father's sun chariot. The center of Sol's attention , however, was

however, he was defeated at the Battle of Agnadello. For additional general information, see Claudio Rendina, *I capitani di ventura*, Rome: Newton Compton, 1994.

38   This may be a reference to the Battle of Valle di Cadore, mentioned earlier, when Bartolomeo d'Alviano defeated the forces of Maximilian I.

the Augsburg Reichstag of 1518.[39] Despite the gravity of the issues before the delegates, Sol and Phaeton are still concerned about the interaction, or lack of interaction between sober Germans and drunken ones. The suggestion was that the sober Germans might drive out the drunken ones, first, on moral grounds, secondly, on the grounds that they were obstructing the progress of those who wanted to accomplish something, and thirdly, on the basis of the harm that excessive drinking did to their bodies. The link between unhealthy over-indulgence and an inability to think rationally seemed not to be something the drunken Germans would have understood. As Sol expressed it, these people find it easier to understand physical matters but have difficulty with matters of mind, or attitude. Among the sober Germans there are those, small in stature and lean of physique, who are deemed to be weak of body but strong of mind. Their rational abilities are endorsed by the preference for water over wine or beer, and they are esteemed by the princes, and others, for their scholar-liness. In some instances, even though the princes themselves may have no evidence of the intellectual abilities of the men in question, they are nevertheless esteemed because others have deemed them to be worthy of the honor.

Behind the elaborate processions and festivities of the Reichstag assembly, the image of Cajetan, the Papal legate, is harshly drawn, and he is clearly identified as the embodiment of exploitation and oppression. Within the conventional context of Christ, the shepherd, tending and caring for his sheep, Hutten inserts the insulting depiction of Germans as sheep who are being sheared and skinned by a less benevolent shepherd, Cajetan. The hypocrisy of Cajetan's public image and posture is as effectively deceptive as the naiveté of the Germans who have succumbed to it.

> [...] der betriger, verwandlet sich wie ein goŭckler, mit etzlichen ver-
> blendungen, also, das wer jn sicht, nit dencken möcht er böß wär, dann er all
> seine geberden, der fromkeit zŭ verglichen weyssz, seine stirn, augen, schül-
> dteren, red, ganck, vnd alles. (Mettke, 162)

39 This Reichstag had three important topics: Imperial succession, funding for the war against the Turks, and the examination of Martin Luther by the Papal Legate, Cajetan.

The thing that might save the Germans, Hutten suggested, was the fact that they have been deceived previously by so many others that they will be able to see through Cajetan and resist his advances. But Cajetan is a worthy adversary; having recognized the resistance to his advances, he cunningly has begun to seek other ways to accomplish his mission. His task was to follow the financial resources, awaken the sleeping Germans, kindle the dying flames of superstition, do anything to create the conditions needed for success. The earlier motif of the son of earth who was unable to recognize his own parents found a new reference here in the person of Cajetan: 'Ich glaub das dißer kaum seinen eygen vatter kenne.' The vocabulary used to describe Cajetan is calculated to convey a demonic, if not satanic image: *bößewicht, list, trug, betrug, boßheit, glessnerye*, all words that imply intentional subversion of the weak-minded away from rational behavior towards acts that are inherently evil but also profitable for the deceiver. The demonization of the enemy is an important element of satirical propaganda, and it served Hutten's purposes well to draw the contrasts between Germans and Romans, i.e., Italians as starkly as possible.

In a cultural reversal, Hutten uses the term 'barbarian' to illustrate how times have changed. The historical reality in which non-Roman germanic tribes were conventionally described as barbarians, and here used to encompass the Germans, French, and any others who are not Roman-Italian, now is converted into Roman 'barbarians' as contrasted with the more civilized Germans.

> Wil man aber gůte sitten, vnd achtung freündtlicher beywonung, auch fleyß der Tugent, beständigkeit der gemůt vnd redlichkeit ansehen [...] dargegen die Römer mit der allerausserlichsten barbarey verstallt. (Mettke, 164)

What constitutes barbarism? In Hutten's view, a people who have been ruined by weakness, 'weychmůtigkeit,' an effeminate lifestyle, 'weybischem leben,' inconsistency, 'wankelmůtigkeit,' feminine fickleness, 'weybische vnbeständigkeit,' little faith, i.e. beliefs, 'glauben,' deception and evil, 'betrug vnd boßheit.'

The discussion of cultural virtues and behavioral flaws, whether German or Roman, is marked for the Germans by a recurrent motif:

151

drunkenness. In an interesting application of the concept of 'noblesse oblige', the curse of drunkenness among Germans is the fault of the princes, those whose bad example has unfortunately become the norm.

> Wär diße vngebärd nit in dem Fürstlichen standt, die gantze geselschafft der trunckenen wer lang zergangen. (Mettke, 165)

But the best representatives of this German societal disease were the Saxons:

> [Sol] Dann allein die Sachszen, auß allen Teütschen, haben noch von irer alten weiß nichts abgelassen [...] Setzent sich wider alle vermanung [...] [Phaeton] O himel vnd erden, welh ein geselschafft syhe ich da, welhe trünck, welhe grollen, welh spewen. Da frisszt vnd saufft man vnzüchtigklich, uber-haufft die gericht, tregt auff das brot mit grossen körben, den tranck in lüst, schweren fläschen, schreyet, růfft, singt, vnd heület. (Mettke, 165)

Hutten followed the lead of Lucilius, the Roman satirist, by viewing people, in this case, the Saxons, as no more than walking bellies, gorged with wine.[40] He also linked his current criticisms with the earlier references to the baudy, drunken, lecherous behavior of the centaurs at the wedding ceremony of a Lapith bride and groom and the notorious Leontines, of whom the Greeks said, as Hutten now says of the Saxons in Latin, they always have a bottle in the hand. Phaeton's assumption that the Saxons, like the Leontines, were wine-guzzlers, was immediately corrected by Sol:

> Sonder kochen sye etzliche kreüter, vnd frucht, vnd von dem selbigen tranck – Byer – werden sye voll. (Mettke, 166)

At this point Hutten abandoned his classical references, his mythological contexts, and resorted to a theme he had in common with Conrad Celtis: the superiority of the germanic past. On one level one may infer an influence of Tacitus, but such a context is not necessary to understand Hutten's view of his contemporaries and their debt to the past. The Saxons, despite their guzzling and vomiting, are still

---

40   Gaius Lucilius (180 B.C.–103 B.C.), Roman poet, original contributor to estab-
      lishment of satire as a genre.

the model Germans, for no other people are capable of governing, ensuring that the people live in safety and security from outside attacks, and maintaining themselves as excellent warriors. If they were able to hold to these standards and somehow become soberer at the same time, no people could surpass them.

> Wo sye [die anderen gůten weiß] behalten möchten, vnd darbey nüchter leben, wüßzte ich kein nation für sye zů setzen. (Mettke, 166)

Hutten went beyond the Tacitean glorification of Germanic primitiveness into the realm of fantasy and stereotypes. The Saxons are healthy, strong, talented, and do not make use of physicians because they are so seldom sick. In addition, they drive away the judges because they are scornful of that type of judgment. In their view, the only reliable form of law is that based on custom and wisdom. No written law can measure up to the standards of tradition and custom. How is it possible, Phaeton asked, that such people despite their drunkenness have become better than others? The fact is, according to Sol, that they perhaps have not become better people but rather that they are better at performing drunk than others are when sober. Despite the setting, the 1518 Augsburg Reichstag, Hutten interrupted the critique to insert material promulgated by Tacitus as regards the natural monogamous relations of the ancient Germans and their respectful, protective, seemingly asexual relations with their women.

Hutten's ethnic criticisms are confusing to the extent that he makes very little distinction between the general grouping, Italians, and the more specific grievances against those who are obviously representatives of the Roman Catholic Church. The rather detailed descriptive diatribe against 'die Italiener' dealt with inner disposition as well as physical appearance.

> Dann die Italiener sycht man zů allen zeiten hässig, karg vnd geytzig sein, vil begeren, nach gewinn stellen, betryegen, glauben brechen, vnd hinterlist üben, sich in hassz vnd misszgunst vntereinander selbs verdecken, heymlich mörden, gifft geben, allweg nach betrug dencken, vnd mit vntrew vmbgehen, irer keiner den anderen glauben, nichts öffentlich oder auffrichtlichen thůn, vnd glaub daz sye darumb bleych von farben seint. (Mettke, 168)

The racial descriptor at the end is followed up by a comment from Sol suggesting that perhaps the air was responsible for the skin color 'Vieleycht thủt es auch der lufft'! Equally improbably, the reddish tint of German skin was attributed to their implicit joyfulness, their trust in the good, and their resistance to things that inflame the passions, sadden the heart, and deplete the blood. It is not clear which Germans Hutten had in mind when he suggested that they did not have the custom of maintaining a common treasury but rather, much like the Lacedaemonians (Spartans),[41] resorted to levying taxes from all groups to support the financial demands of a war. Given the fact that Sparta had been described in terms often derived from mythical sources, having little if anything to do with the historical people, Hutten may be using it here similarly as the model for an idealized group of which his Germany was a derivative example. The idea, for example, that pre-war counsels were unknown to the Germans, relying rather on decisions made during the heat of battle suggests that the wisdom of doing the right thing emerged from the courage and initiative engendered by dangerous situations.

Although Hutten's Sol had earlier criticized the Germans for being able to subjugate peoples but unable to maintain government over them, his description of the governing structure reflected the contemporary conditions of which Hutten was at times very critical. The Germans, in his view, are inherently opposed to being subject to another people. Nevertheless, among themselves they had no problem being obedient to a prince, or to various princes as the regional partitions dictated, or to a supreme prince, or emperor. But while they honor and obey the emperor, they do not fear him, so long as he performs in the interest of their welfare.

41 Aside from the strong military reputation of the Spartans, the source of Hutten's comment about their revenue-raising customs in time of war cannot be verified. Many of the most significant myths about Sparta seem to have been fabricated. Sparta, came to be known as a pure community free from internal dissension and fighting with equality of land ownership and other utopian features that never existed in the historical Sparta. See G. E. M. de Ste. Croix, *The Origins of the PeloponnesianWar* (1972); P. A. Brunt, "Spartan Policy and Strategy in the Archidamian War," Phoenix, 19 (4), 1965, 255–280.

> Vnd seind jm der halben nit vast gehorsam. Darumb sich auch offt auffrûr
> vnd zerteylung vnter jnn erheben. Vnd ist daz die vrsach das sye sich nit
> vastvmb den gemeynen butz bekümern. (Mettke, 169)

But they are not always obedient to him. Consequently, often up-
risings and dissension occurs among them, and that is why they do not
always seem to care about the common welfare. Such differences of
opinion and the need to resolve issues of disagreement have led to
meetings that can last for months, such as the Reichstag assemblies,
and end without agreement. The problem, as Sol pointed out, is that
during these assemblies serious matters are put aside in favor of banquets, celebrations, and rowdy behavior, none of which is conducive
to good goverment. Additionally, the very governance structure has its
problems, since not all princes are the same.

> Vnder den fürsten aber seind etzliche von geburt edel, etzliche durch durch
> die wal auffgeworffen, als seind die bischöff, vnd geystlichen [...] seind die
> selbigen am gewältigsten [...] Dann sye in der zal übertreffen, auch mit reych-
> tumb vnd macht obligen [...] mer dann halb Teütschland von pfaffen besessen
> würt. (Mettke, 170)

Hutten's criticism was directed at the German landowners, who, out
of concern for their souls, turned over significant portions of their
possessions to the Church, while at the same time impoverishing their
descendants. The resulting situation led to greater esteem for the
clerics within the society, because of their wealth and political power,
and disgruntled noble subjects who owed their subservient status to
the generous Church bequests of their fathers and earlier ancestors.
Much of the dissension and internal conflicts among the princes was
attributable to this situation, in Hutten's view. It was to the advantage
of the emperor to allow discontent among the princes to continue
while using their allegiance to him in ways that suited his political
interests. At the next level of nobility, the counts, allegiances tended
to be directed upwards towards the princes from whom the greatest
advantages could be expected. But the base of this structure, the
common nobility, was the large order of imperial knights, in Hutten's
view the strength of the nation:

> Dann jr seind vil vnd geübt in kriegen, vber das, sicht man noch bey jnn einen
> scheyn alter tugent, gůte gewonheit, vnd den Teütschen angeborne redlichkeit.
> Dißen gefelt noch die alte Teütsch weyß, vnnd hassen alle frembde sitten, wo
> die bey jn eynbrechen. (Mettke, 171)

Within German society the knights have the greatest animosity towards merchants, and would drive them out were it not for the support theser merchants have from the princes, some of whom would be happy to be rid of them. Unfortunately, Hutten suggested, the princes need the merchants to protect their power and status. The social manifestation of this dependency is widespread robbery on the highways, unrest and lack of security for the common people, and hatred for merchants and the independent cities where they reside. Hutten's explanation of the animosity towards merchants is at the same time a comment on the prosperity of German society.

> [...] Vmb das sye außlendische war zů jnn bringen, als spetzerey, seyden,
> purpur, vnd andere, die zů nichtes, dann einen vnnutzen pracht vnd überfluß
> gebrauchlich, verkeren die besten vnd manlichen sitten irer nation, mit einbringung
> außlendischer gewohneit, vnd eines weychen lebens, dem die Teüt-
> sche art von natur wider, vnd nit vnbillich, gehassz ist. (Mettke, 172)

The fact that the merchants were seen as sources of corruption and perversion of the traditional German lifestyle, might have been compounded, as Phaeton supposed, by the animosity engendered by the changes which drove nobles from the cities as merchants became the more prosperous city-dwellers. But Sol quickly refuted this assumption by pointing out that the nobles had always lived in the countryside, not in the cities. Hutten's view of German society at this point recedes into the early Germanic past, a time when housing settlements were more detached and independent:

> Anfänglich seind keyne stätt gar im Teütschen land gewesen, alle bew von
> ein ander abgesündert, vnd hat ein yder seine wonung für sich vnd allein
> gehapt. (Mettke, 173)

The lifestyle of the early Germans, as Hutten describes it, was truly primitive in the sense that it was based on the land and the resources that the land could provide. There were no merchants bringing in foreign goods from distant lands; people only desired the things that they could produce themselves through their own efforts. Clothing made from the skins of wild animals, food grown from the soil of their own settlements, freedom from the deceptive practices of traders and merchants, ignorance of a money economy based on gold and silver, this was the true German lifestyle. As Phaeton said, 'Daz ist die beste zeyt der teütschen gewest.' Hutten's perception of the negative influence of commerce amidst the development of settlements, from villages to cities, is cynical in a certain sense but also illustrative of a process that may have had more truth than he realized. The influx or foreigners and their new wares had an appeal that drew the useless and lazy into the new circles of commerce where superfluity had become a way of life. Hutten does not explain how this phenomenon happened or why the appeal was to such people. Nor does he address with any specificity the link between expanding commerce, a more prosperous lifestyle, and the move towards isolation and seclusion in the construction of dwellings.

> Das hatt jnn anreytzung erstlich dörfer, darnoch auch stätt zů bauwen gegeben, die sye nachuolgens mit muren, polwercken, türnen vnd gräben beuestiget, vnd sich also darein verschlossen. In welche versamlung alle trägen, faulen, vnd vnstreitbaren verwilliget. (Mettke, 173)

Hutten did suggest, however, that the aversion of nobles for the urban lifestyle was not just a distaste for the luxury and frivolousness of the activities and the people who supported them but rather a deeper, innate connection to values inherent in the Germanic past. The love of war, a scornful attitude towards money, the love of hunting, and an aversion to the enjoyment of peace and quiet, all served to widen the gap between the nobles and the common people. Following the logic of the argument, the robbery of merchants and others on the open road almost seems like the natural expression of the recognition of the differences between them and the effort to reconcile them. In fact, in a curious example of twisted logic, Phaeton suggested that the fear and insecurity of the city-dwellers may be a good thing, lest their protected way of life within the city walls serve to make them even more objectionable. The localized argument soon gives way to the conclusion

157

that the perverted ways of some are detrimental to the well-being of all; the dissolute lifestyle of the merchants and city-dwellers was merely a reflection of the demise of the country as a whole.

The net effect, as Hutten saw it, was to have opposing forces committed to the elimination of the enemy for the sake of the country. Whether it be nobles driving merchants and foreigners out or merchants and city-dwellers forcefully curtailing the activities of the nobles, the welfare of the country was at stake. The middle ground in this potential confrontation was held by the emperor and his allies, supported by the wealth of the Fuggers. Under normal circumstances, Phaeton suggested, the side wielding the power of wealth would prevail; why not in this instance? The Germans had the advantage of an inborn inclination to honesty and integrity, which made it possible for them to hold virtue in higher esteem than money.

> Sye [die Teütschen] haben auch – wie dann billich – alle reichen in einem Verdacht, vnd werffen jnn das Sprichwort für, das die reychen selten redlich sein.[42] (Mettke, 175)

Given the dichotomies of German nobles versus German merchants and honest nobles versus the dishonest wealthy, it follows that to avoid a general indictment of all Germans, a distinction had to be made between real Germans and non-Germans.

> Nim war, ich sehe auch etzliche, wider landßgewonheit vntrew vnd trugenhafftig, die vast geschickt seint, andere zů betriegen, vnd vervntrewen; die achte ich, wo sye jre sitten nit anderen, vnwirdig daz sye teütschen genennet werden. Dann sye bringen den löblichen namen in ein böß geschrey, vnd verfinsteren die klarheit teütsches gerůches. (Mettke, 176)

Despite the shortcomings of nobles and merchants, the harshest criticism has been reserved for priests. Priests are useless beings and in no way serve the common good. They are idle and gluttonous, they like to sleep and lack chastity, they love entertainment and banquets,

---

42   Cf. the German proverb which says 'Reich sein und gerecht, reimt sich wie krumm und schlecht' (Karl Simrock, *Deutsche Sprichwörter*, 8347) or Horace, Epistle 1, 1, 54 *O cives, cives, quaerenda pecunia primum est / virtus post nummos.*

they love the boisterous, lecherous life, and encourage flatterers. They eat and drink well and to excess, having given themselves over to pleasure, and under the influence of the luxurious lifestyle have become effeminate, ruined by a lack of chastity. They live more like irrational animals than humans. They have an affinity for superfluous things, enjoy a soft life of, gentle tranquility, and they seek pleasure by nature. They also seek security, especially in the things that please them and provide pleasure. They cannot endure the harsher aspects of life, they abhor work, and avoid difficulties. They have no patience for the hard, rough, gruesome elements in life, they hate the sober, honorable life, avoid unrest, and are by nature so tender that they cannot endure even the slightest level of concern. Their favorite activities are going to the baths, lying on their backs, and surrounding themselves with pleasant aromas. Hutten's cryptic reference to a proverb, 'Bischöffliche pancket,' suggested that no celebratory banquet could equal in lavishness and excess one given by a bishop. The life of intemperance, the lack of moderation, and the coarse, animal-like behavior had the effect of making priests impotent in matters of reason, stupid, and dominated by their appetites. The culmination of this list of non-German characteristics was the affirmation of the foreignness of priests and others who enjoyed a similar lifestyle. Once again relying on proverbial wisdom, Hutten summed up with 'Ländlich, sittlich, oder: Die sitten arten sich nach dem land.' (Mettke, 178) Thus, the habits and customs of the priests being incompatible with ancient German values meant that they were in essence non-Germans, even though they may have been born in Germany.

Hutten's comments about monks are rarely mentioned when he is being identified as a strong supporter and, in some cases, a precursor of Martin Luther. In this dialogue, after the harsh, extensive depiction of priests as lazy, lecherous, gluttonous parasites in German society, it seems almost overkill to launch another extended attack against the monks. The justification seemed to be the impression that there were more monks in Germany than anywhere else:

[...] der seint mer in Teütsch land dann anderswo. Sych wie lauffen sye hin vnd wider als ob sye vil zů schaffen hetten, vnd machen sich an allen örteren zůthätig. [Sol] Das seind auch volle fleschen, vnnütz, träg, kläffer, lugenträger, vnd loß fischer. (Mettke, 178)

The descriptive language used to characterize the monks and their activities among the common people is contextually homogeneous: 'misszglauben,' or false beliefs, 'bezauberung,' enchantment, 'betören' (to make foolish), 'verleyten,'and 'verfûren,' to lead astray, or mislead. In a similar vein, the act of confession, mumbling into the ear of a monk or priest, is characterized as an irrational act because it depends on faith in the the trustworthiness of ones confessor.

> [Phaeton: [Was heisst das] in die oren murmelen? [Sol] Das heissen sye beychten. Dann es würt für ein geystlich vnd gotts förchtig ding angesehen, das ein yeder was er gesündet hab, dißen zů erkennen gebe, vnnd nit allein was er mit der thatt begangen sonder auch was jm in gedencken gewest. Vnd also mûssz yederman, diße aller seinen heymlicheiten mitwissend haben. (Mettke, 178)

The reliability of the confessor is a dangerous risk, Hutten suggested via Phaeton, not so much because of malicious or vindictive inclinations but rather because of the consumption of so much wine. An equal distrust might accompany the follow-up to confession, the granting of absolution, releasing penitents from the prison of sin. The conclusion that the discussion of priests, monks, and Catholicism leads to was the timely observation that change was necessary:

> [Phaeton] Ich lobe es nit. Darumb würt disem land einer Reformation, vnd besserung gemeyner sitten von nöten sein.(Mettke, 179)

Interestingly, the suggestion that the Germans should drive out the gluttonous, over-indulging priests and monks in order to bring about the needed reforms was countered by the reminder that excessive eating and drinking was a part of the German makeup:

> Dißer gebrechen ist jnn angeborn, als den Italianer betrug, Hispaniern dieberey, Franzosen stoltz vnd übermut, anderen andere mängel. (Mettke, 180)

After a considerable time away from the Augsburg Reichstag, during which Hutten's mythological observers Sol and Phaeton have dis-

160

cussed in some detail various aspects of German culture, personality, and behavior, Hutten turns once again to the central event and its principal figure, the Papal legate Cajetan. The structure of the dialogue up to this point has been marked by the distance between the observers and the subjects, and it has relied primarily on beliefs and attitudes as opposed to real actions in contemporary time. At this point, however, there is at least visual contact between the observers and the subject, Cajetan, who appeared to be upset at the intrusion of supernatural figures into his realm of activity. The remarkable aspect of Cajetan's discontent is weather-related. Twice he mentioned the failure of the sun to respond to a wave of his, Cajetan's, hand and to shine brighter, though he emphasized that this should not be interpreted as a command. Ten days of cloudy weather in Augsburg seemed to Cajetan to be unfair treatment of a Papal legate and to place a damper on the important activities of the Reichstag. Amusingly, Hutten, as a writer of at least one Prognostication himself,[43] has Sol explain his hiding behind the clouds as obedience to the astrologers and prognosticators, who predicted cloudiness for this period of the calendar. Cajetan's reasoning underlines the arrogance of which he had been earlier accused:

> Du soltest aber mer gedocht haben, was eins Bapstes Legat wölle, dann Was den sternguckern gefalle. Weystu nit do ich aus Italien zohe, was ich dir trawet, wo du nit mit grosser hitz Teütsch land, das zů vnzeyten kaltt ist, erwörmest, vnd mir das gantz summerisch mächtest? Vff daz ich nit wider in Italien begeren dörfft. (Mettke, 181)

The arrogance, however, is not so much a personal trait as it is an extension of the office of Papal legate, serving one who had been given the divine power to bind and loose on earth as it was in Heaven.

> [...] einen Römischen Bischoff – der dann yetzo alle seine macht in mich seinen Legaten, gegossen hat – in himelen vnd vff erden, was er wöll binden vnd lößen Mögen? (Mettke, 181)

Sol's assertion that such power had never been given to a mortal to control the motions of the heavenly bodies was met with the charge of

---

43   *Prognosticon Leonem X*, (1516).

heresy and the suggestion that the sun should be consigned to Hell and the Devil. The solution, such as it is, was for the sun to confess his sins to a valid confessor, or rather to one of Cajetan's subordinates, though the absolution would come from Cajetan himself. This parody of a ritualistic structure, which Hutten had already ridiculed, straddled a line between travesty and blasphemy. From the perspective of a believing Catholic, Hutten's description was blasphemous and a harsh exaggeration of a structure which was integral to the Catholic faith. On the other hand, this type of satirical, parodistic treatment of religious beliefs and rituals, Catholic or Protestant, had become part of the literary treatments of the controversies motivating the Reformation debates. The extent of the parody is best illustrated by Cajetan's response concerning the consequences of Sol's potential confession:

> [...] Dann wil ich dir ein bůssz auff setzen, daz du ettwo mit vasten erhungerest, oder yerget ein schwäre arbeit thůest, oder dich mit walfart besůchung ermühest, oder aber almůß gebest, oder etzwas zů dem Türckischen kryeg jnlegest, oder gelt gebest in den Ablaß, daruon man sanct Peters münster, das zů Rom verfallen, widerumb bawen wil, oder wiltu das gelt sparen, das du dich für deine sund lassest mit růten schlagen. (Mettke, 181–182)

Granting absolution to the sun, in a sense purifying it of its sins, was tantamount to the proverbial 'giving light to the sun,' – der Sunnen liecht geben, (or carrying coals to Newcastle)[44] – , as Sol pointed out, and was such a challenge to reason that he recommended a *hellebore* potion to restore Cajetan's sanity.[45] The ridiculousness of this exchange and the subsequent suggestion that Cajetan might have used his power, derived from the Pope, to warm up and brighten the gloomy, chilly July days leads to a more serious, politically sensitive side of the Sol–Cajetan discussion.

Sol accused Cajetan of having a secret agenda, the success of which depended on keeping the German people in the dark. The central issue was the effort of the Papacy, spearheaded by Cajetan, to prevent the election of Charles V as German king, in keeping with the

---

44   An exact duplicate is found in the Swedish proverb '*Bära ljus till solen,*' i.e., carry light to the sun.

45   See note 33 this section.

wishes of his ancestor, Emperor Maximilian I. Cajetan's response to the suggestion that informed Germans would resent his interference was characteristic: *oderint dum metuant*, i.e., let them hate so long as they fear (attributed to Caligula). The combination of the mythological and the contemporary political underlines again the confusion of persona between Sol, the Sun God Apollo, and Sol, the anthropomorphic sinner who would be subject to Cajetan's threats of excommunication. Sol, as Apollo, could serve Cajetan's purposes by shooting his arrows into Germany, creating plague and destruction that would eliminate the holders and benefactors of ecclesiastical estates. The resources freed up by this action would not only serve the Church but Cajetan as well.

Auch gebiete ich dir, das du pfeil zů richtest, vnnd den Teütschen pestilentz vnnd gehen tott zů schiessest. Vff das vil pfründen vnd geystlicher lehen ledig werden, damit sich pension begeben, gelt geyn Rom gefalle, so vnnd auch mir alhie etzwas werde. Dann es seindt yetzo lange zeyt her nit genůg pfaffen im Teütschen land gestorben [...] Aber erstlich scheüussz zů denn Bischöffen, das die Pallia gekaufft werden. Vnd triff die pröbst vnnd reichen prelaten, vff das die newen Creaturen des Bapstes zů lehen haben. Dann man můossz die ye jrem stand nach bedencken, daz sye nichtes mangelen. (Mettke, 184)

The practicality of Cajetan's approach was designed to highlight the callousness of his feelings towards his fellow prelates. Having been informed that to create a pestilence of the scope he desired would require a considerable cloud cover and pollution of the air, his response was that the pestilence had the highest priority, and that the clouds and pollution accompanying it, if unavoidable, should be kept as limited as possible. Such an insensitive attitude on Cajetan's part led Phaeton to the proverbial assessment:

Yetzo erst hör ich wo jn der schůch truckt, was jm wol, vnd was jm übel thůt, was jn traurig, vnnd was jm frölich macht. (Mettke, 184)

This proverb in its German version is a self-indictment: 'Es weiß niemand besser, wo der Schuh drückt, als der ihn trägt.' In other words, Cajetan has made it clear where his priorities lay, and they are primarily self-serving. The indictment was made even more explicit: 'Ein hirt sol seine schoff weyden, nit ermorden.' (Mettke, 184) The

163

distinction which Cajetan seemed unable to appreciate was that between shearing, collecting the external resource that sheep provided, (wool), and flaying or even murdering the sheep out of an excessive greed and an insensitivity to the value of the resource provided. No sophisticated analysis was required to move across the metaphorical spectrum that not only characterized Cajetan's relationship to the German people but also characterized the Germans themselves. The ultimate indictment, however, went beyond Cajetan to his mentor and instigator, Pope Leo X. The adjectives directed at Cajetan applied as well to Pope Leo: unjust, evil, blood-thirsty. Phaeton's final words to Cajetan were defiantly defensive of the German resentment of the treatment from Rome, but they were perhaps not as revolutionary as Hutten might have wished them to be.

> So schencke ich dich den Teütschen, die du beraubest, zů einer spötterey, das sye dich mit verspottung, gespey, vnd verlachung von jnn jagen, vielleycht auch übel tractiren. Vnd dich dermassen halten, das alle nachkommen, eyn beyspil von dir nemen. Bissz verspottet. Also wil ich dich so gestrafft haben. (Mettke , 185)

Curiously, the condemnation spoken by Phaeton was only a verbal expression of contempt for Cajetan and all that he stood for, but the final words of Sol leave Cajetan to his own devices:

> Es ist zeyt, das wir den wagen abwertz byegen, vnd dem abent sternen statt geben. Lassz jn liegen, triegen, stelen, rauben vnnd plönderen, vff sein abentewer. (Mettke, 185)

It is significant that the dialogue ends as night approaches, as Sol and Phaeton move the Sun Chariot into the transitional phase where darkness prevails and obscures the ominous activities that the observers have highlighted. Hutten's final slogan, 'Ich habs gewagt', usually cited as a German translation of the Latin 'Jacta est alea', might also be heard as a call to arms, but the response was to be carried out by others.

Chapter Six
Conclusion

Ulrich von Hutten's creative impulses were drawn primarily from the past, even though he may have been writing about contemporary events. His frames of reference owed much to his educational background and his familiarity with Latin and Greek literary traditions. The curiosity of the two works given extended analyses here, the *Arminius* dialogue and the dialogue *Inspicientes*, to which Hutten gave the German title *Die Anschauenden,* is that both have mythological contexts: *Arminius*, the timelessness of the Elysian Fields, and *Die Anschauenden*, with its dual perspective, being set during a hiatus in the timeless circuit of Apollo, the sun god. Nevertheless, Apollo and his son, Phaeton, are observing a specific event in Hutten's contentious contemporary sixteenth century. By contrast, the uses to which these works have been put by Hutten's followers, even down to the present day, have had more to do with the future, only marginally with the present, and only idealistically and ideologically with the past. The reverence Hutten and others of his contemporaries had for the ancient Germanic past and the continuity of values they believed to see between that time and their own has no place in the mindset of those who today see Hutten, past and present, as an icon of German patriotism. Hutten may have been in a number of respects ahead of his time but he was also a child of his time in much the same way that Martin Luther was. For example, one looks in vain in Hutten's dialogues for a more than casual awareness of people outside his own social and intellectual class. Aside from generalizations about freedom and independence of thought, Hutten was not a champion of the underdog, even when he was himself an object of scorn and derision. The strongest impression one gets after a reading of *Arminius* or *Die Anschauenden* is that of one man's bitterness and disappointment. Despite the victorious judgment awarded Arminius by Minos in the dialogue, Arminius's story of his trials, tribulations, and ultimate successes is not a happy one, nor one likely to endear a reader to the hero. Similarly, despite the harsh criticisms of sixteenth-century Catholicism and the exploitative, manipulative actions of its representatives, as described in *Die Anschauenden*, the end of the dialogue is not at all optimistic, nor is the characterization of the Germans a very positive one. The exception to both of these representations in the respective dialogues is the extent to which Hutten drew upon the idealized characterizations of early Germanic ancestors, which in each case portrays them as being culturally and morally exemplary. Those who have chosen to use Hutten's writings for ideological reasons must therefore ignore the contemporary realities of which he wrote and concentrate on the glories of an idealized ancient past. Such an approach has for the most part always been indicative of ethnically prideful, patriotic points of view. Whether it is the tribe, the state, the nation, or the Fatherland, the cultural and political realities seem always at some point to give way to ideological fantasies.

Norman Davies, in his history of Europe, in a section sub-titled *Renaissances and Reformations, 1450–1670,* addressed an issue relevant to Ulrich von Hutten's cultural and political role as seen both by his sixteenth century contemporaries and by his supportive successors down to the present day. The issue is reflected in Hutten's identification by Hajo Holborn, for example, as the prototypical patriotic nationalist.[1]

> The 'nation-state' and 'nationalism' are terms which are frequently applied, or misapplied, to the sixteenth century. They are more appropriate to the nineteenth, when they were invented by historians looking for the origins of the nation-states of their own day. They should certainly not be used to convey premature preoccupations with ethnic identity. What they can properly convey, however, is the strong sense of sovereignty which both monarchs and subjects assumed, as the unity of the Middle Ages disintegrated.[2]

---

1   Holborn, 1. 'Humanism, nationalism, and Protestantism [...] constitute the theme of this book and no life is better able to exemplify their interrelations than that of [...] Ulrich von Hutten, who first attempted to bring them into a living synthesis.'

2   Norman Davies, *Europe: A History*, Oxford: Oxford University Press, 1996, 520.

However agreeable one may find Davies's cautions to be, the fact remains that in Germany the idea of an ethnic exclusivity that led subsequently to nationalistic concerns and a patriotic agenda, realistic or not, are to be found in basic forms in the sixteenth century, and not just in the writings of Ulrich von Hutten. The essence of the ethnic pride motivating the respect for Hutten and his works was also evident in an earlier work by Conrad Celtis, the *Germania generalis* (1502).[3] The following text illustrates the mythic-mythological context in which the early Germans were viewed as an aboriginal people, culturally independent, self-sufficient, and bearing traits that were duplicated with minor variations in ethnically chauvinistic texts for centuries afterwards.

Über die Lage Deutschlands und seine Lebensart
Ein unbesiegtes Volk, wohlbekannt in der ganzen Welt, lebt von jeher dort, wo sich die Erde, in ihrer Kugelgestalt gekrummt, herabneigt zum Nordpol. Geduldig erträgt es Sonnenhitze, Kälte mit harter Arbeit; Müßiggang eines trägen Lebens zu erdulden leidet es nicht. Es ist ein Volk von Ureinwohnern, das seinen Ursprung nicht von einem anderen Geschlecht herleitet, sondern unter seinem eigenen Himmel erzeugt wurde, als Demogorgons Leib alles Erschaffene hervorgebracht hatte unter die weiten Lüfte. Germanen pflegen sie die Italiener zu nennen, die Griechen aber 'Adelphoi,' weil sie gewohnt sind, wie Brüder mit einander zu leben: diesen Namen halten unsere Edlen bis heute in Ehren.[4]

This was a group of people, patient, hard-working, intolerant of idleness and laziness, who, as Celtis saw them, became the original inhabitants of a world unto themselves, self-originating and independent. But the harmony of which Celtis spoke was certainly not evident in Hutten's world nor in that of his mythical social critics, Sol and Phaeton. In defense of Celtis, and on a certain level Hutten, the point must be made that in the *Germania generalis* as in *Die*

3   Hans Rupprich, Hrsg., Conrad Celtis *Germania generalis*, In: *Humanismus und Renaissance*, Band 2, *Deutsche Literatur in Entwicklungsreihen*, Stuttgart, 1935.
4   This excerpt is a translation of Celtis's Latin original. For the full text, see Gernot Michael Muller. *Die Germania generalis des Conrad Celtis*, Studien mit Edition, Übersetzung und Kommentar. Tübingen: Niemeyer, 2001 (=Frühe Neuzeit, Bd. 67).

Anschauenden we are in the midst of fictional worlds with all the contours and motifs of myth. To seek a concrete bridge, that is to say historically verifiable links of cultural continuity between these fictional worlds and the real worlds of those who looked to these worlds for models of thought and behavior, would be futile. For the latter have substituted for the mythologically-inspired fictions of the fifteenth and sixteenth centuries equally fanciful notions of historical antecedents for the ideas and attitudes of the nineteenth, twentieth, and twenty-first centuries. This process has been used as a justification for the supposed links between pre-nationalistic and nationalistic attitudes in Germany while at the same time deemphasizing the important role of fabricated structures in their support. To suggest a de-emphasis, however, is not to say that the myth of Aryan superiority has not been used at various times and in various ways by various groups with their own agendas. But in every instance, the myth has been recognizably an ideologically-based fabrication that has served only to deceive and to subvert the truth. Arminius, however, was a real person, not a figment of Hutten's imagination, such as, in another context, Parzival or Siegfried might be viewed. Arminius had personal and political motivations for his actions, we assume, motivations that had real political and cultural ramifications. Hutten's awareness of the realities of Arminius's story allowed him creatively to convert those realities into his own personal and political agenda. However, he was not permitted to interpose his sixteenth century reality into the fictional realm of the dialogue. The dialogue form, so well-suited for such a conversion, was equally restrictive as regards the scope of the narrative. Its thematic and structural characteristics precluded supplying extensive factual details to support Arminius's claims.

Celtis's idealized image of ancient Germans, written when Hutten was fourteen and most probably familiar to him as his study of humanist writers progressed, can be seen as a cultural bridge between the glorification of ancient Germans derived from Tacitus and others[5] and Hutten's development of his own sense of German

5   There is a considerable body of literature concerning the influence of Tacitus's image of Germans and subsequent German cultural and political history. Christopher B. Krebs, *Negotiatio Germaniae*: Tacitus' Germania und Enea Silvio

cultural continuity.[6] He and Celtis had roles as synthesizers and popularizers of views that would influence perceptions of Germans and German history in more important ways than has been generally acknowledged. It is difficult, for example, to gloss over the implicit praise of Hutten in Hajo Holborn's summary:

> *For all time to come*, (emphasis added) however, Hutten made a contribution by evolving the conception of a German national history segregated from the universal stream and the constituent conception of a distinct German character, and by popularizing these ideas among his contemporaries with all the drive of his extraordinary energy and through the medium of a newly forged and emotionally expressive language. His complaints over the deficiency of early German historical literature indicate the source of his conception. We find that Conrad Celt [sic] was disturbed in the same way and in Vienna Hutten would come to know intimately the historical work of his humanist circle.[7]

This complex of images, coupled with a sensitivity to the controversies of his own time and a number of personal disappointments, may provide a sense of the intellectual and emotional background against which Hutten came to be seen as someone whose reality succumbed to the perceptions about him. Unfortunately, relying as we must on the texts alone does not tell us enough about his motivations or about the man. Just as it must remain unknown why Hutten did not publish the *Arminius* dialogue during his lifetime, it must also be a matter of speculation as regards the lack of a more concrete program of action in response to the grievances outlined in the dialogue *Die Anschauenden*. While he called for change, a reformation, the literary

---

Piccolomini, Giannantonio Campano, Conrad Celtis und Heinrich Bebel. *Hypomnemata* 158. Göttingen: Vandenhoeck & Ruprecht, 2005. See also: L. Canfora, *La Germania di Tacito da Engels al nazismo*, Naples, 1979; A. A. Lund, *Germanenideologie im Nationalsozialismus*. Zur Rezeption der 'Germania' des Tacitus im Dritten Reich, Heidelberg 1995; H. W. Benario, 'Tacitus's Germania and Modern Germany', Institute of Classical Studies (ICS) 15 (1990), 163–175; see also Mertens cited earlier.

6   Hutten may also have been familiar with Celtis's edition of Tacitus's *Germania* published in 1500.
7   Holborn, 43.

mandate is a weak one and the line of action Hutten pursued, the alliance with Franz von Sickingen, failed.

The most perplexing aspect of Hutten's role as a cultural icon in Germany has been the appropriation of his name by groups whose motivations are clear even though their knowledge and understanding of Hutten may be questionable. From the alleged interest in historical truth of the *Gesellschaft für Freie Publizistik,* awarders of the Hutten Medaille, to the acknowledged support of neo-Fascism, anti-Semitic views, and opposition to immigration and multiculturalism of the *Freundeskreis Ulrich von Hutten* e.V., the range of mentalities flourishing under the umbrella of Hutten supporters is depressingly broad and active.

Ulrich von Hutten's life was chaotic, uncomfortable, plagued by personal and familial problems that complicated his relationships with those who ought to have been his closest supporters. His personality and his strong sense of a mission also made it difficult for those who understood him intellectually, even though they may not have agreed with him. More importantly, Hutten's literary reputation, which even among his contemporaries was not a subject of disagreement, succumbed early on to the prevalence of those who chose to concentrate more on limited aspects of his message than on the stylistic manner of his writing, the validity of his arguments, or the broader humanistic scope of his convictions. One example of the flexibility of Hutten's persona as reflected in his thought can be seen in his epigram contributions to the *Coryciana* collection of humanist poems, written probably in 1516 but not published until 1524, a year after Hutten's death. As Ijsewin has pointed out, despite Hutten's public animosity towards the activities of the Catholic Church, his participation in the publication of the *Coryciana* poems, that is to say, his agreement, we must assume, to have his poems included in the original collection, provides another perspective on his literary persona.

Der Beitrag Huttens ist besonders erwähnenswert, da er im schroffen Gegensatz steht zu seinen sonstigen in Rom und Italien entstandenen Schöpfungen. In manchen Epigrammen hatte er ja Papst Julius II., die Simonie und die Käuf lichkeit der römischen Kurie scharf angegriffen; in den *Coryciana* jedoch akzeptierte er uneingeschränkt das gesellschaftliche Leben der römischen Prälaten und Humanisten, sogar bis hin zur Heiligenverehrung.[8]

Though this literary effort speaks well of Hutten's ability to adapt to a cosmopolitan environment and to the acceptance of his literary talents outside Germany – though apparently his texts were altered in some ways by the *Coryciana* editors in 1524 – one might also suppose that this is evidence of Hutten's literary persona operating on a different level from the realistic, harshly critical assessments of his political radicalism.

Hutten was a tragic figure but he was not a hero in the conventional sense, i.e., having performed feats of courage or having nobility of purpose. At the same time, he must be given some sympathy and understanding for the years of physical suffering he endured and the selflessness of his efforts to explain syphilis to his contemporaries. Nevertheless, to understand how he became for some the image of patriotic fervor and national feeling requires that one turn away from his personal life, from his personal reactions to greed, extravagant living, injustices, and the self-serving manipulations of authority figures, to see instead how he became in essence a figment of the imaginations of others. While it may be questionable that the reform ideas of Martin Luther '[fanden] weite Verbreitung beim einfachen Volk, das sich in nationaler Einigkeit gegen das römische Papsttum wandte,' (Glaser, 20) a more valid assertion can be made that Hutten's ideas about Germans and Germany, though received by a more limited audience, struck a deeper chord. Many had no difficulty seeing Luther as a heroic figure, but to see Hutten as such required enhancements of persona and personality that no longer needed factual verification. Hutten's Germany was limited by class, in some respects by gender, and by nationality, or ethnic origin. Foreignness for him was essentially defined by the extravagant goods being imported into Germany, the Turkish threat which repeatedly led to increased financial burdens on Germans, and the Roman Church hierarchy which by nationality, behavior, and attitudes towards Germany were in every respect non-German. For Hutten supporters – from the nineteenth to the twenty-

8   Glaser, 288.

171

first centuries – foreignness was a matter of birth and culture, as illustrated in our own time by their opposition to immigration and multi-culturalism. Underlying such views is the fear of cultural adulteration, which was not an idea alien to Hutten but not one that characterized his patriotic view either.

In the strictest sense, German nationalism must be seen to have its beginning in the nineteenth century; as for German ethnic identity, or later, national feeling, one could stretch the point to include Walther von der Vogelweide's paean to German women, 'tiutsche frauen,'[9] but certainly to include the essence of Celtis's *Germania generalis* or Hutten's dialogues and epigrams. They are not 'national' in the modern sense but rather expressions of ethnic pride and a sense of place that bear within them the seeds of ethnic arrogance and cultural exclusivity. One of the ways to combat such cultural exclusivity would be to give greater consideration to the works of writers such as Celtis, Hutten, and others writing in Latin, some of whom have yet to be indentified more fully, other than the fact that they were German, and to move towards a closer understanding of the effect of language on ethnic identity and, by extension, the role of language in determining who we are. Just as these questions were relevant to Hutten and his time as regards the select group who felt more comfortable communicating in Latin without, however, sacrificing their identities as Germans, so today is the issue of German-ness one that is clouded by the external trappings of dress, ritual, and language. The resolution of these issues, then as now, may result in a concept of belonging that goes beyond cultural, geographical matters to get at the heart of what it means to be a part of humanity, wherever one may live, whatever language one may speak.

9   Lied 120, 'Ir sult sprechen willekomen,' Walther von der Vogelweide, *Sprüche-Lieder-DerLeich,* Urtext/ Prosaübertragung. Hrsg., Übers., Paul Stapf., Berlin /Darmstadt: Der Tempel-Verlag, [1955] 1963, 290–293.

Appendix I
In Hutteni Arminium Eobanus Hessus

Tot sua stat populis gestarum gloria rerum salva, suum tot adhuc
secula nomen habent; Audet adhuc veteres reminisci Roma triumphos,
et mortis quadam vivere pate suæ; Quæ nequit ipsa suas ostendere
Troia ruinas, Mœonio clarum carmine nomen habet; Invida non totas
merserunt funera Thebas, vivit adhuc Spartæ non moriturus honor;
Nondum Palladiæ prorsus cecidistis Athenæ, quicquid et eximiæ
Græcia laudis habet; Integra floret adhuc Pellææ gloria gentis,
Persarum nomen fama superstes habet; Innumeræ gentes aliæ sua
nomina servant, quasque supervacuum, quasque referre mora est: Una
suæ merito fraudata est laudis honore semper, et incelebris Teutonis
ora fuit. Cur ita? quæ nobis res hunc invidit honorem? Fida alibi, cur
hic fama maligna fuit? An quia non rebus clari, non Marte potentes?
An quia nos victos saepe fuisse pudet? Non ita: nam rebus nec clarior
ulla per orbem Gens fuit, aut ullo tempore victa minus. Cur igitur?
quia non rebus, sed nomina rebus quæ facerent, scriptis nos caruisse
liquet; Præcipue cum floreret Germanica virtus, et nondum hic nostras
luxus haberet opes: Tunc memoranda aliis nostri gessere parentes;
Tunc rerum virtus unica caussa fuit: Tunc quia scriptorum nos defe-
cere labores, gloria Lethæas nostra subivit aquas: Nondum tota tamen,
quoniam, licet invida, nostrum non potuit totum fama tacere decus:
Et sparsim Romana suis ea littera rebus inseruit, quae nunc pauca, sed
apta vides. Atque ea si quaeras, quae sint et qualia debes Hutteni
patriae vindicis esse memor: Is quaesita suis patriae monumenta
libellis edidit et lucem iussit habere novam; Nam quia sparsa aliis
incognita quæque latebant, qui legeret rarus quique teneret erat: Ille
suas patriae laudes atque eruta passim nomina digna legi fecit ubique
legi: E quibus unus hic est, quem condidit ipse, libellus, sed non
auspiciis edidit ipse suis: Namque immatura præreptus morte reliquit
hunc quoque ceu partem funeris esse sui: In quo si qua leges non
qualia forte requiras, parte bona veniam quo mereatur habet: Condidit

Huttenus, non edidit; ergo futurum, quod fuerat melius coniice quicquid erat. Hunc tibi Mauritius gentili Huttenus honori fidus ab aeternis noctibus adseruit: Hic ferus Arminius, patriis qui victor in armis afflixit vires, Martia Roma, tuas: Qui nisi adhuc iuvenis periisset fraude suorum, Tu dominus Tyberis, Rhene, futurus eras: Hunc quod habes patriae, lector studiose, libellum, Hutteno debes munera prima tuo, altera Mauritio, Ioachimo tertia, nobis quarta, aliquis nobis si locus esse potest.

Nurenbergæ Anno MDXXVIII. Mense Augusto

Böcking *Opera*, II, 439–40.

Appendix II
Arminius Dialogus

Interlocutores: Arminius, Minos, Mercurius, Alexander, Scipio, Annibal, Cornelius Tacitus

Arminius.
Hoc tandem iniquum est, o Minos, judicium, si fuit ullum unquam tuum.
Minos.
Bona verba quaeso, Armini: nam quae hoc nova est calumnia quicquam iustissimum iniuste Minoem statuisse? quod illud vero est iudicium? dic agedum.
Arminius.
Dabis hanc mihi veniam primum, si te offendit dicendi libertas mea. Germanis est peculiare hoc minus blande loqui, cum loquuntur libere et serio: queri me vero decet, quod, cum honorem habes, et veluti præmia statuis Imperatoribus qui ubique fuerunt optimis, ipsum me quasi qui non vixerim, sic præteris; iampridem enim sententiam ferente te Imperatorum primus toto Elysio campo et beatorum hac regione pronunciatus est Alexander Macedo, ab eoque secundus honore Romanus Scipio, et tertius Carthaginensis Hannibal; solus in nullo ego habitus sum numero, qui tamen si certandum mihi cum illis unquam putavissem, equidem in nullo posuerim dubio quin te iudice principem locum obitnuissem.
Minos.
Caussam profecto habes, Germane; sed cum hoc illi certamen apud me inirent, quid non admonebas me ipse quoque?
Arminius.
Quia neque putavi quicquam licere ulli hic ambire, neque unquam dubitavi, quod in vita bene aut male quis meruerit, summa in omnes æquitate abs te distribui.

Minos.

Neque non fit hoc sedulo: sed iudicamus secundum confessa plerumque hic, fitque copia dicendi quod in rem suam quilibet arbitratur; cætera facile transimus occupati, præsertim ad ambitionem quæ sunt nisi postulati, negligentes: vides enim negotiorum quae sit moles, quod iudiciorum onus, quam varium et multiplex, deinde otii quam arcta sint tempora. quanquam si recordatus fuissem quod nunc redigis in memoriam mihi, vocassem ultro et cum aliis audivissem.

Arminius.

Et non audies nunc, revocatis huc de quibus nuper iudicasti?

Minos.

Quid ni audiam? Accerse huc ad nos Imperatores, Mercuri, qui de præstantia in re militari et bellica contenderunt paucos ante dies.

M*ercurius.*

Treis illos? Memini; en adsunt.

Minos.

Hic ille est, optimi, vetus Germanorum dux Arminius, qui pro libertate cum Romanis certavit olim et vicit, cumque vos audiat de Imperatoris præstantia contendisse, ac sententiam ea super re tulisse me, indigne asserit se præteritum ibi: habet enim quæ cum afferet, ostensurum se putat neminem rectius hanc ad palmam pervenire.

Alexander.

Igitur dicat.

Scipio.

Valde.

Annibal.

Haud moror.

Minos.

Dic, Armini.

Arminius.

Prius sisti velim huc Tacitum ex Italia quendam, ut is dicat quid mihi tribuerit in historia.

Minos.

Etiam ipsum voca, Mercuri.

Mercurius.

Huc te, Tacite, huc te, huc ad me, ut loquaris tandem! Eccum hominem.

176

Arminius.
Operæ pretium est, o Itale, elogium illud meum, quod in historiis tuis est, recitare hic te.
Tacitus.
Eo loco, ubi de interitu quoque tuo commemoratum a me est?
Arminius
Eo ipso.
Tacitus.
'Cæterum Arminius, abscedentibus Romanis, et pulso Maroboduo regnum affectans libertatem popularium adversam habuit, petitusque armis, cum varia fortuna certaret, dolo propinquorum cecidit, liberator haud dubie Germaniae, et qui non primordia populi Romani, sicut alii reges ducesque, sed florentissimum imperium lacessierit, præliis ambiguus, bello non victus. Septem et triginta annos vitae, duodecim potentiæ explevit, caniturque adhuc barbaras apud gentes, Graecorum annalibus ignotus, qui sua tantum mirantur, Romanis haud perinde celebris, dum vetera extollimus, recentium incuriosi.'
Arminius.
Fuit alicuius iste in vita fidei, Minos, et vir bonus fuit?
Minos.
Profecto fuit; sed tu melius nosti, Mercuri, qualiter vixerit, coluit te enim peculiariter.
Mercurius.
Sancte vero: Nam candidus inprimis fuit, et quo nemo syncerius scripserit historiam, minusque affectibus tribuerit. etiam autem Germaniam viderat, et gentis ejus mores descripsit, ac rerum ibi gestarum fuit perquam studiosus.
Arminius.
Igitur talis iste cum fuerit, et rerum mearum haud ignarus, sic de me scriptum reliquerit, ut taceam deinceps ego, dubitari non potest quin maximi esse momenti iure debeat, hoc ab hoste perhibitum mihi testimonium. Principio 'liberatorem Germaniae' vocat, quod est aliquid credo eripuisse vi ac armis provinciam Romanis ut tunc fuerunt, et iisdem invitis summoque contra nisu conantibus vindicasse in libertatem quos servire illi decreverant. Deinde, quod recte maximi fit, illud me 'imperium' non cum adolesceret tum et incrementum acciperet, 'sicut alii reges ducesque', Pyrrhus, autumo, Antiochus, et iste

177

Hannibal, sed cum consistebat iam et maxime florebat, non bellum inferens sustenuisse, verum ultro lacessendo armis impetiisse, unumque ex omnibus invicte bellum contra Romanos transegisse dicit. quare etiam dignissimum arbitratur quem Graecorum pariter et Latinorum annales celebrent. Quodsi omnium consensu nulla fuit unquam maior quam Romanorum potestas, nullum amplius a condito ævo imperium, et hos ego vici cum in flore essent ac vigerent plurimum, rectissime summum Imperatorem, et in re bellica omnibus præstantem me iudicandum arbitror, infinitam potentiam, maximas vires, summum Imperium qui bello superaverim: etsi minus nihil velim quam alienam defraudare gloriam aut rerum ab istis gestarum famam premere. nam æquissimo semper animo feram, quantus quisque est, tantum haberi ab omnibus, de meque cum dicam, sine invidia dicam: fuit hoc semper studium mihi propter se virtutem colere; de gloria curavi haud multum, quippe satis esse conscientiam facti existimavi; neque nunc iam ea est arrogantia ut præ me alios duces contemnam, nec illud quidem mihi sumo ut esse nullum me superiorem contendere velim: potius si quis est, æquum censeo ut ipsius quoque habeatur hic ratio: sed dignus venia sum si eorum qui de hac laude certaverunt adhuc, ex conscientia negavero ulli a me concedi oportere. idque haud temere sentire me ostendam, si audient isti, ut audituros pollicentur, bona arbitror ratione.

Minos.

Audient, pro ipsis spondeo.

Arminius.

Primum igitur quia plurimum ferunt in hoc ponere te Hannibal, quod a parvis initiis ad amplissima incrementa progressus sis, docebo, si haec gloria sit, quanto debeatur mihi rectius, quam aut tibi, aut ulli: nam eorum qui res praeclaras gesserunt, nemo maioribus difficultatibus enisus aut gravioribus circa impedimentis eluctatus est. cui potentia quidem esse quæ potuit rebus sic perditis et deploratis? authoritas vero ut esset, ipsa non sinebat aetas: quare solus non fuit Alexander qui immatura aetate gerendis rebus accesserit; etiam ego enim quartum et vigesimum haud dum egressus annum, cum multa prius miles fecissem strenue, dux esse incepi exercitus quem nondum habebam, qui nondum coierat, quemque conscribi celerrime cum oporteret, an existere posset a tanta dispersione dubium quoque fuit; nam pecunia haud vereor ne quis suspicetur valuisse me, quæ tum Germanis nulla erat: itaque in summa rerum atque hominum inopia, misera egestate, desertus ab omnibus, impeditus undique, tamen ad recuperandam libertatem viam mihi communivi, citraque omnem extra opem, omne adiumentum et auxilium, hoc solo præditus et suffultus animo a meipso rerum initia petivi, et bellum extreme periculosum, non antea cœptum, prosequutus sum, sed ab omnibus desperatum et a cogitationibus quoque hominum iam pridem relegatum provocavi, me dignum arbitrans, nihil fortunæ intentum destinatam mihi sortem alacriter movere potius quam expectare sollicite. Nam quemadmodum audivistis, ultro bellum intuli et denunciavi, obstante etiamnum domestica Segestis et Iguiomeri perfidia ac fratre Flavio magna apud hostes vi adversante, cum milite omnis disciplinæ ignaro nec ullius in re militari scientiæ, armorum vero habitu pene inutili et apparatu belli adeo non suppetente ut ne ferri quidem ad telorum fabricam satis esset. at haec omnia animi et consilio et alacritate correxi et sarcivi. Cumque esset permagnus mei contemptus, in hostium eum calamitatem verti ac tanta celeritate irrui, ut prius pugnam conseruerim quam bello ausurum me homines crediderint, ante cædem fecerim quam conflati exercitus fides fuerit; nec levibus vero momentis tantæ molis initia auspicatus sum: tres primo statim impetu legiones, et in iis Martiam, cum auxiliis omnibus fortissimum exercitum et quo non alius disciplina magis ac rei militaris experientia vique et virtute Romanos inter milites tunc valebat, ipsumque simul ducem et legatos ad internicionem usque occidi et delevi. Quo tempore in unius mea persona, patriæ incolumitas constitit: ut dicere non debeat Scipio, tam consternatam se rem Romanam tamque accisam restaurasse quam ego penitus proculcatam et discerptam brevi Germaniam restitui. Quanquam rei ipsius magnitudinem, non est quod verbis ego assequi studeam, ipsi cottidie hic veteres Romani loquuntur hoc, quantæ eis calamitati fuerim tunc, quam misere potentissimam civitatem, imperium florentissimum confuderim, et quod non alius magis illos rerum dominos gentemque togatam metu et trepidatione consternaverit. Certe enim quod tu non effecisti, Hannibal, ad urbis usque portas obequitans, ego in ultima constitutus Germania, tanto intervallo, tot mediis fluminibus ac paludibus, tot interpositis montibus ac locis nullo dum itinere hominum exploratis aut cognitis, ipsis etiam dirimentibus montium altissimis

Alpibus, eo desperationis adegi civitatem Romanam, ut ille Augustus Imperator, quem solum alioqui perpetuo felicem vocant homines, et quo nemo potentior, quod omnes sciunt, imperio illi præfuit, ita obstinate primum mori decreverit, ne videret puto, quod mihi in mentem nunquam venerat, Romam capi a me, ut caput foribus illisisse eum memoriae proditum sit, tandem excubias tota urbe, in portis stationes, extra præsidia disposuerit, rectoribus provinciarum imperium prorogaverit, Iovi optimo maximo, si in meliorem statum vertisset rempublicam, magnos ludos voverit; breviter, ita de rerum summa consultaverit ac in suprema necessitate fieri solet, neque alio tempore sollicitius cautum illud Romæ sit, ne quid detrimenti respublica caperet, pavor ubique confusissimus hominum mentes perculerit: fuit enim gravissima haec Romanis clades, pene exitiabilis etiam. Et hoc cœptum atque perfectum a me est conciso atque pervulso penitusque deposito Germaniæ statu, illius vero reipublicæ florentissimis rebus, fortuna secundissima, maximis incrementis, cum neque ut Alexander a patre regnum, neque ut isti a senatu exercitum cum imperio accepissem. Deinde alios atque alios continue domi motus compressi; omneis undique defectionis authores postulavi, et nonnullos quidem assensu popularium punivi, aliis vero veniam petentibus dedi; qui transfugerant, reprehendi, qui in deditionem erant, recepi; omnia flagitiis perpurgavi; neque pro Germanis habui, qui tributa exteris penderent, aut aliis conditionibus obnoxios teneri se paterentur; summumque nefas proclamavi quod inter Albim et Rhenum virgæ et secures ac Romana illa toga conspecta semel essent. Ibi tum excitatis iterum ad capessendam libertatem popularium animis promisi fore paulo post ne ullae in Germania Romanorum saltem reliquiæ superessent, pene memoria aboleretur: nec id mullto post præstiti, quamvis haud segnius omnia contra hostes conarentur: nam ut maxime strenuus quisque, et primæ in iuventute spei Romæ fuit, ita Germanicum illi bellum, ulciscendi Varianam cladem studio demandatum est; missi haud contemnendus bello vir Tiberius Nero et in paucis connumerandus illius frater, egregie cordatus homo Drusus, atque alii sic mecum certaverunt, ut Romam reversi ipsi quidem triumpharint, ego vero gliscente indies libertate immunem et sui iuris Germaniam obtinuerim. Tunc et vigentem animi alacritate imperatorem Germanicum et longo militiæ usu pollentem illius legatum Cæcinnam, cum mille etiam naves, tanquam ad expugnandam Troiam, adversus me agerentur, magnis ac miseris cum populi Romani cladibus sustinui ac repressi, et Cariovaldum, Batavorum ducem, inter auxilia Romana multis cum nobilibus cecidi; Cattos ac Phrysios a diversa et ipsos parte vindice bello contudi. Interea machinante illinc fratre Flavio, Iguiomero domi connivente, flagitiosa facta a Segeste transitio est, qua nefarius proditor ne filiæ quidem suæ, uxori meæ et eidem gravidæ pepercit, sed et hanc et alias quasdam nobiles fœminas in pudendam secum captivitatem et ad triumphum Romam abduxit. Item Segimerus cum filio perfugit ad hostes; multi domesticorum pecunia corrupti insidias vitæ meæ construxerunt; popularium non nulli hostilia omnia machinati sunt, Adgandestrio Catto imprimis adeo nihil non pertentante ut, inauditum illa tempestate Germaniæ scelus, venenum a Romanis quo me conficeret petierit. Ipse nihil motus vero constantissime cœptis institi, neque aliquid prius habui quam fas patriæ et avitum Germaniæ decus; cumque esset efficacissima tunc permovendi Germanorum animas caussa, si cuius uxor apud hostes teneretur, neque alio magis nomine captivitatem timerent homines, meamque ego amarem ardentissime et ab ipsa præstanti invicem fide redamarer, quodque omnium dolentissime afficiebat, gravidam amisissem, tamen vel sic immotum me præstiti, neque passus sum privatum dolorem patriæ in me caritatem minuere: quin vero in iram versus dolor, alacrius omnia conari impulit quam conatus ante essem: ubi et mihi testes esse oportet inferos, quantam quotidie Romanorum multitudinem huc demiserim, vehementi ac varia in patriæ proditores cæde pergrassatus funestumque et atrox per adversarios bellum circumferens: plane ostendi Romanis ibi magno iniecto pudore non proditione me neque adversus fœminas gravidas rem gerere, sed palam armatos deposcere mihi in quos dignæ ultionis aculeos defigerem. qua re factum brevi est, ut Romanos Germania penitus eiecerim. a quo deinde tempore usque in hunc puto diem nullum fuit illorum ibi imperium. Restabat Maraboduus Suevus, qui cum mihi ex fœdere quod cum Romanis ipsi fuit adversaretur, tota a me belli mole petitus est: gravissimum id difficillimumque certamen fuit cum rege potentissimo, ac bellicæ omnis rei scientissimo, bellicosos Suevorum populos, ingentem sociorum vim, immensa auxilia post se trahente, cum interim a Romanis iuvaretur pecunia et Iguiomeri perfugio magnam mihi manum abrupisset: tamen vel sic varie, ultro citroque tentata Fortuna tandem inclinante ad æquioris caussæ partes, deorum voluntate victum atroci proelio in ultimos Hercyniæ secessus propuli; unde paulo post de ulteriori cavens periculo in Italiam confugit, ibique pulchre fallentibus Romanis qui liberaliter omnia promiserant, et spe frustratus sua inglorius consenuit. ego Germaniam intra se coniunctam reddidi et unanimem, ac olim iam optato libertatis bono tandemque adsecuto frui cœpi. His oportet ampliora gesserit qui me sibi secundum esse velit aut quo præ ad primam ego palmam venire non debeam. Sed quia de rei militaris peritia et imperandi scientia ac ducendi exercitus industria certamen est, præferat aliquis ibi se mihi ac neget affuisse hæc illi, qui tantas in huiuscemodi difficultatibus talem contra hostem res gesserit, easque ad finem usque vitæ bello invictus continuaverit. Nihil alienam æmulor gloriam; sed isti, absit dicto invidia, mediocrem quisque potentiam et dispertitas ut plurimum vires aggressi sunt: ego terrarum orbis imperium idque, ut dictum est, valentissimum tunc, tot in unum coactas nationum vires, ac renascens ab omni clade bellum, et diutissime nulla intermissione succedentes sibi vices ultro audensque in me concitavi et ad ultimum, quod ne hostes quidem negant, vici ac profligavi, patriam externo decusso iugo, ex omnium prope mundi gentium in communem servitutem consensu immunem et libertatis memorem retinui. neque ulla hoc siverit ratio, iudex, ut persuadeat Alexander tibi tam facile debellaturum se fuisse, vel ut illa fuerunt tempestate Romanos, quam aut molles Asiæ populos, quibus de postea ex Romanis quidam nullo negotio ab se devictis memorabile hoc triumpho suo prætulit, 'Veni,vidi,vici,' aut inermes Indiæ nationes, quas bellorum insolentes commessabundus iste ebriolorum et bacchantium circa se militum exercitu, quatenus adire potuit, in fugam et deditionem coegit: nam quos magnifacit Scythas, vidit tantum. certe ipsius avunculus, clarus Epirotarum rex, negat, qui non cum Romanis quidem sed in Italia tamen bellum gerens, dicere solitus est se in viros, nepotem suum in fœminas incidisse. Præterea summum fuit semper virtutis studium mihi, nulla gloriæ sitis aut avaritiæ: neque enim ita erexi trophæa mihi, ut Romanis deieci, aut pro opibus vel imperio decertavi, sed fuit mihi scopus, ad quem direxi omnia, reddere vi ademptam patriæ libertatem; egique totam in summus virtutibus ætatem, donec premente domestica invidia et propinquorum dolo facinus patrante liberum et omnium victorem huc animum ex conscientia optimorum in patriam meritorum, ac vitæ per omnia bene actæ transmisi. Iam tuum, Minos, est consyderare quem mihi præferre velis, qui vel ex graviori angustia ad tantam sua virtute amplitudinem emerserit, vel maiora bella gesserit, vel scientius rem militarem tractaverit, vel æquabilius imperium administraverit, vel meliore pro caussa arma sumpserit, vel maiores vires contriverit, vel minus in vita cupiditatibus dederit, vel constantius in bono perstiterit: in summa, quis sit omnium qui his laudibus excelluerunt, ad quem tu primas optimo jure referas.

Minos.

Generosam profecto et non summo tantum imperatore, verum bono etiam viro dignam habuit orationem iste: atque ita esse ut narravit, omnia, neque aliquid affinxisse eum scio; equidem memini admiratum me tunc, istiusmodi ferre industriam barbaricum. quam ob rem, cum et optimam iste conatus sui causam habuerit, et tantum animo ac virtute militarique scientia valuerit, neque aliter quam ad patriæ commodum periclitatus sit, minimumque vitiis concesserit, non video, per Iovem, quis rectius Imperatorum summus haberi debeat; nec dubium est quin, si primo statim vobiscum, o Alexander, contendisset hic, palmam ei ultro addixissem; nunc iam, quia quod iudicatum semel hic est rescindere illud fas prohibet, neque constitutum ante ordinem movere licet, satis habere decet te, Armini, hoc in animi sententia esse mihi, quod verbis quoque pronunciassem, si cum istis ambitiosus tu esse voluisses; quia vero fuisti liberator Germaniæ, et bello pro libertate suscepto invictum omnes confitentur, neque ibi vel periculi plus exhausit quisquam vel commodi in publicum assecutus est, placet cum Brutis ponere te, et inter patriæ libertatis vindices primo loco; Mercurio autem huic negotium do, ut in foro, plateis, circo, triviis, et ubiubi hominum ac deorum frequentia est, pronunciet Arminium Cheruscum liberrimum, invictissimum et Germanissimum, sicque iubeat passim ab omnibus acclamari tibi: Id quod decretum et constitutum esto, neque ulli posthac refragari liceat.

Alexander.

At servivit aliquando hic; ego semper rex, semper fui liber.

Arminius.

Ego minime vero mente obnoxius ulli unquam fui; semper enim libertatis memor, cum aliud nihil agitarem animo nisi quomodo possem oblata occasione iuvare patriam, in illa popularium servitutis patientia, donec facta præstare non potui, consilium quoque dissimulavi, et clausam intra me libertatis curam tenui.

Alexander.

Hoc est, quod ferunt illi, non licuisse tibi desciscere ab iis quorum semel iugum accepisses.

Arminius.

Atque hoc est, quod ego contra respondeo, neque accepisse iugum me, vel animo in servitutem consisse, neque si eo necessitatis iniquo aliquo tempore coactus me impedivissem, non licuisse per occasionem, quandocunque ea se dedisset, inde rursus expediri: nam quod jus habere potest qui naturæ beneficium alteri eripit? vel quæ iniuria est suum sibi violenter detractum pari violentia recuperare?

Alexander.

At fidem dederas.

Arminius.

Ut indigne aliquid paterer., non dederam: potui tamen honeste et liberaliter parere, si modeste illi et civiliter imperare voluissent; sed ut dedissem extortam vi et iniuria, communis hoc vita sancivit, fidem non esse quam raptores exigunt ab eis qui necessitate coacti ea concedunt facile, quibus nec ipsi carere debent nec uti, qui rapiunt. Porro, qui alteri iugum iniecit, nonne eatenus sibi obnoxium habet, quatenus vi tenere potest? aut non licet armis per iniuriam adempta armis per occasionem repetere? neque puto, contra naturam cum sit ex libero servum fieri, contra leges esse debere ad naturæ donum respicere: ea demum fides est, qua damus quod debemus. Age autem, quis tam iniuriae patiens esse debet, ut ea ferat quæ in Germania faciebant Romani tunc, quæque Varus, homo omnium puto quos terra protulit avarissimus et iniquissimus? qui cum Syriam ante spoliando circumrasisset, Germanos ex toto consumere peculando instituerat; ibique ea fuit superbia et animi impotentia, ut mente conciperet bestias esse Germanos et ratione carentia bruta, non homines, neque ullam tantam esse indignitatem, quam aversari nos deceret aut contra quam resistere. itaque nihil amentiæ suæ temperavit, omne flagitium et omne ausus est scelus. Quapropter ego illud cum conscivi facinus, non erga legitimos dominos fidem fefelli, sed contra iniquissimos tyrannos ius patriæ, et commune fas obtinui.

Minos.

Ingenue caussam tutatus est, et sic ego existimo neminem ita alteri pace obstrictum esse, ut talibus percitus caussis mutandæ jus non habeat.

Scipio.

Et tamen perfidiam obiiciunt huic nostri, ac nimis crudeliter videtur Varianam exercuisse victoriam.

Arminius.

Eadem, Scipio, ratione perfidi fuerint tyrannicidæ ubique omnes et patriæ libertatis adsertores; vestri præsertim, qui Tarquinios eiecerunt, et Cæsarem interfecerunt, ac summam ob id laudem sempiternam inter vos gloriam consecuti sunt. denique eorum est perfidia, qui ad fortunæ motus spectant, et mutabilem ad hos fidem circumferunt: me caussæ æquitas contra adversos quoque casus niti perpulit. Dicat iste vero Minos, talem tamque importunam Quintilii atrocitatem, an non licuerit mihi, cum occasionem dii tribuissent, alia invicem atrocitate punire.

Minos.

Censeo, licuit.

Annibal.

Ecce autem qui iactas nihil tam necessarium tibi visum, quin patriæ studium pervicerit, tamen regnum affectasse diceris, et qui alienum gloriaris amolitum te iugum a popularibus, tuum iisdem intentasti, quod nefas in meum animum nunquam cecidit, ut vel huius ergo præponi ipse tibi debeam.

Arminius.

Minime tu quidem hanc ob causam, siquando apud se esse volet hic Minos: nam regnum capessendi nunquam mihi cupido incessit; sed fuit inimicorum ea invidia quæ suspicionem hanc hominibus iniecit. Omnes autem intelligimus sic humanitus comparatum esse, ut quorum plurimæ sunt virtutes, eorum par contra sit invidia: nam soli invidiam non sentiunt quorum in conspicuo virtus non est; eos maxime illa petit quos altissime erexit haec. Necesse est autem multum in commune possit cui rerum summa procuranda est: quam facile pessum rediisset publica libertas, si ad uniuscuiusque pravam de me opinionem vires quibus tuenda ea fuit dimisissem: in hoc propositum cum potentiam retinerem gratumque id bonis facerem, in affectatæ tyrannidis calumniam apud malos incidi. Quodsi regnum occupassem etiam, cui id magis conveniebat quam ei qui ab externa servitute redemerat quos sub patrium regnum collecturus erat? mihi nondum parem retulisset gratiam patria, si pro restituta sibi libertate seque ab interitu prope vindicata regnum ultro detulisset; at vero languescente post temporis intervalla accepti beneficii memoria, passa est impeti calumnia primum, deinde opprimi scelere. Quod nec primo mihi, nec ultimo reor contigit. tuis enim bene meritis grati fuerunt Carthaginenses? aut non fuit, quæ te premeret, imo quæ oppressit tandem, inimicorum domi insectatio?

Annibal.

Fateor, fuit.

Arminius.

Nam Scipioni, credo, vicem reddidit patria, in qua ab se amplissime décorata post tot edita præclara facinora, ne mori quidem permissus est. certe Alexandro domestica invidia mortem concinnavit.

Minos.

Etiam hoc expedivit. ita enim est: nemo clarus unquam fuit, cui non aliquando fraudi sua esset virtus. Necesse est vero hunc qui norunt Arminium, præclaram ob indolem valde ament. proinde auctum honore decet esse te, Germane, neque nos tuarum virtutum fas est unquam fieri immemores. Sed iam ipsum iube sequi te, Mercuri, ac facesse actutum iussa. vos ad vestra hinc redite!

Mercurius.

Sequere.

Böcking *Opera* IV, 407–418

Bibliography

Balke, Gustav, Hrsg., *Thomas Murner. Die Deutschen Dichtungen des Ulrich von Hutten*, In: *Deutsche Nationalliteratur*, Bd.17/2. Darmstadt: Wissenschaftliche Buchgesellschaft, 1967.

Becker, Reinhard Paul. *A War of Fools.The Letters of Obscure Men. A Study of the Satire and the Satirized*. Bern, Frankfurt am Main, Las Vegas: Peter Lang, 1981.

Benzing, Josef. *Ulrich von Hutten und seine Drucker*. Wiesbaden: Otto Harrassowitz. 1956. In: Carl Wehmer, Hrsg. *Beiträge zum Buch- und Bibliothekswesen*. Bd. 6.

Bernstein, Eckhard, *Ulrich von Hutten mit Selbstzeugnissen und Bilddokumenten*. Reinbek bei Hamburg: Rowohlt Taschenbuch Verlag, 1988.

——. 'Creating Humanist Myths: Two Poems by Ulrich von Hutten.' In: *Acta Conventus Neo-Latini Totontonensis. Proceedings of the Seventh International Congress of Neo-Latin Studies*. Binghamton: Medieval & Renaissance Texts & Studies, 1991.

Best, Thomas W. *The humanist Ulrich von Hutten; a reappraisal of his humor*. Chapel Hill: University of North Carolina Press, 1969.

Böcking, Edward. *Opera Ulrichi Hutteni equiti Germani*. Five volumes. Leipzig: F.A. Brockhaus. 1859–62. Two supplementary volumes. Leipzig, 1864.

——. *Index bibliographicvs Hvttenianus*, Verzeichniss der Schriften Ulrichs von Hutten. Leipzig: B. G. Teubner. 1858.

——. *Ulrichi Hutteni equitis germani opera quae reperiri potuerunt omnia*. Aalen: Zeller. 1963.

Bömer, Aloys, Hrsg. *Epistolae obscurorum virorum*. Heidelberg: Weissbach Verlag. 1924.

Brady, Thomas, Heiko Obermann, James Tracy, Eds. *Handbook of European History. 1400–1600*. Volume I: Structures and Assertions. Grand Rapids, MI: Erdmanns Press. 1996.

Burckhard, Jacob, *De Ulrici de Hutten fatis ac meritis commentarius,* 3 Bde. Wolfenbüttel, 1717–1723.

Clemen, Otto, Hrsg. *David Friedrich Strauss. Ulrich von Hutten.* Leipzig: Insel Verlag. 1914.

——. 'Ulrich v. Hutten: Ein Bücherdieb?' *Archiv für Reformationsgeschichte.* No. 89/90. XXIII. Jahrg. 150–155.

Davies, Norman. *A History of Europe.* Oxford: Oxford University Press. 1996.

DeBoor, Helmut and Richard Newald. *Geschichte der Deutschen Literatur.* Vol. 4/1. Hans Rupprich, Hrsg. München: C. H. Beck-Verlag. 1970.

Fuller, J. F. C. *Decisive Battles of the Western World and their influence upon history.* 3 Vols. London: Cassell & Co. 2001.

Füssel, Stephan. *Akten des Internationalen Ulrich von Hutten Symposions,* 15.–17. Juli 1988. München: Wilhelm Fink Verlag. 1989.

Gardels, Nathan. 'Two Concepts of Nationalism: An Interview with Isaiah Berlin.' *New York Review of Books.* Vol. 38. No. 19. 1991.

Garland, Henry and Mary, Eds., *The Oxford Companion to German Literature,* 3rd ed. by Mary Garland, Oxford: Oxford University Press, 1997

Gewerstock, Olga. *Lucian und Hutten: Zur Geschichte des Dialogs im 16. Jahrhundert.* [Berlin: E. Ebering. 1924] Nendeln / Liechtenstein: Kraus Reprint. 1967.

Glaser, Horst Albert. Hrsg. *Deutsche Literatur: Eine Sozialgeschichte.* Bd. 2. Hrsg. Ingrid Bennewitz and Ulrich Müller. 1320–1572. Reinbek bei Hamburg: Rowohlt Taschenbuch Verlag. 1991.

Goethe, Johann Wolfgang von, *Götz von Berlichingen.* DTV Gesamt-ausgabe, Bd. 8. Hrsg. Peter Boerner. Nördlingen: Deutscher Taschenbuch Verlag. 1962.

Grimm, Günter E. *Johann Gottfried Herder. Werke in zehn Bänden.* Schriften zur Aesthetik und Literatur. 1767–1781. Frankfurt am Main. 1993.

Grimm, Heinrich. *Ulrich von Hutten; Wille und Schicksal.* Göttingen: Musterschmidt. 1971.

Hahn, Reinhard: 'Huttens Anteil an den *Epistolae obscurorum virorum.*' In: Füssel, Stephan. *Ulrich von Hutten 1488–1988.* 79–111.

Hahn, Rahel L. *Witnessing disease: Autopathographies of AIDS and Syphilis in 16th and 20th Century Germany.* Ann Arbor, MI: UMI. 1998.

Hohoff, Curt, *Kleist.* Rowohlt Monographien. Hamburg: Rowohlt Taschenbuchverlag. 1958.

Holborn, Hajo. *Ulrich von Hutten and the German Reformation,* [German, 1929]. English trans. Roland H. Bainton (1937). New Haven: Yale University Press. Harper Torchbook. New York: Harper & Row, 1966

Jensen, Minna Skafte. *16th century nationalism: the case of Erasmus Lætus.* In: Eckhard Keßler & Heinrich C. Kuhn, Eds, Conference Proceedings. *Germania latina-Latinitas teutonica*: Humanistische Bibliothek. Reihe I (Abhandlungen). Vol. 54. München: Wilhelm Fink Verlag. 2002.

Jillings, Lewis. 'The Aggression of the Cured Syphilitic: Ulrich von Hutten's Projection of his Disease as Metaphor,' *The German Quarterly,* Vol. 68, No. 1. (Winter, 1995).

Johnson, Paul. *The Renaissance. A Short History.* New York: The Modern Library. 2002.

Jordan, David Starr. *Ulrich von Hutten. A knight of the order of poets.* Boston,: The Beacon Press. 1910.

Kalkoff, Paul. *Ulrich von Hutten und die Reformation:*Eine kritische Geschichte seiner wichtigsten Lebenszeit und der Entscheidungsjahre der Reformation (1517–1523). Leipzig: Verein für Reformationsgeschichte. R. Haupt Kommissionsverlag. 1920.

——. *Huttens Vagantenzeit und Untergang:* Der geschichtliche Ulrich von Hutten und seine Umwelt. Weimar: H. Böhlaus Nachf. 1925.

Kampe, Jürgen. *Problem 'Reformationsdialog.'* Untersuchungen zu einer Gattung im reformatorischen Medienwettstreit. *Beiträge zur Dialogforschung.* Bd. 14. Tübingen: Max Niemeyer Verlag. 1997.

Keller, Hans Gustav. *Hutten und Zwingli.* Aarau: H. R. Sauerländer. 1952.

Killy, Walther, Hrsg. *Die Deutsche Literatur. Texte und Zeugnisse.* Hedwig Heger, Hrsg. 2. Teilband. München: C. H. Beck'sche Verlagsbuchhandlung. 1978.

Kivistö, Sari. *Creating anti-eloquence.* 'Epistolae obscurorum Virorum' and the humanist polemics on style. Helsinki. *Commentationes Humanarum Litterarum,* Vol. 118. Helsinki: *Societas Scientiarum Fennica.* Diss.2002.

——. 'On the Concept of Obscurity in the Humanist Polemics of the Early Sixteenth Century.' In: Rhoda Schnur et alia. Eds. *Conventus Neo-Latini Bonnensis. Proceedings of the Twelfth International Congress of Neo-Latin Studies (Bonn 2003).* Tempe: Arizona Center for Medieval and Renaissance Studies. 2006.

Klawiter, Randolph J. *The Polemics of Erasmus of Rotterdam and Ulrich von Hutten.* Notre Dame, Ind.: University of Notre Dame Press. N.d.

Kleinschmidt, Karl. *Ulrich von Hutten, Ritter, Humanist und Patriot.* Berlin: Kongress-Verlag. 1955.

Kloft, Hans. 'Die *Germania* des Tacitus und das Problem eines deutschen Nationalbewußtseins.' In: *Archiv für Kulturgeschichte* 71 (1990).

——. 'Die Idee einer deutschen Nation zu Beginn der frühen Neuzeit. Überlegungen zur *Germania* des Tacitus und zum *Arminius* Ulrichs von Hütten.' In: Rainer Wiegels, & Winfried Woesler. Hrsg. *Arminius und die Varusschlacht: Geschichte – Mythos – Literatur.* Paderborn, München, Wien, Zürich: Ferdinand Schöningh. 2003.

Krebs, Christopher B. *Negotiatio Germaniae: Tacitus' Germania und Enea Silvio Piccolomini, Giannantonio Campano, Conrad Celtis und Heirich Bebel.* Hypomnemata 158. Göttingen: Vandenhoeck & Ruprecht. 2005.

Kreutz, Wilhelm. *Die Deutschen und Ulrich von Hutten.* Rezeption von Autor und Werk seit dem 16. Jhdt. München: Wilhelm Fink Verlag. 1984

Krueger, Karl Eberhard. *The Image of Hutten in German Fictional Literature.* Ann Arbor, MI: Dissertation Abstracts. 1980.

Kuhlmann, Petra. *Untersuchungen zum Verhältnis von Latein und Deutsch in den Schriften Ulrichs von Hutten.* Frankfurt am Main: P. Kulhmann. 1986.

Lohenstein, Danial Casper von. *Grossmüthiger Feldherr Arminius.* Reprint of the Leipzig 1689 Edition. Intro. Elida Maria Szarota. Hildesheim, New York: Georg Olms Verlag. 1973.

Lucian. *Mortuorum dialogi.* (*Totengespräche*). Translated from the Greek by Christoph Martin Wieland. 6 Bde, 1788–1789. via http://gutenberg. spiegel.de /lukian/totengsp/totengsp.htm.

Madej, W. Victor. *German Army Order of Battle.* 2 Vols., Allentown, PA: Game Marketing Company. 1981.

Martini, Fritz, Hrsg. *Christoph Martin Wieland. Werke*, Bd.3. München: Carl Hanser Verlag. 1967.

———. *Deutsche Literaturgeschichte.* Von den Anfängen bis zur Gegenwart. 15. Aufl. Stuttgart: Alferd Kröner Verlag. 1968.

Mehl, James. 'Language, Class, and Mimic Satire in the Characterization of Correspondents in the *Epistolae obscurorum virorum.* 'Sixteenth Century Journal*, Vol. 25, No. 2 (Summer, 1994), 289–305.

Mettke, Heinz, Hrsg. Ulrich von Hutten. *Deutsche Schriften.* Leipzig: Bibliographisches Institut. 1972.

Meyer, Conrad Ferdinand. *Sämtliche Werke in vier Bänden.* Intro. Robert Faesi. Berlin: Th. Knaur Verlag. 1920.

———. *Huttens letzte Tage.* Leipzig: H. Haessel, 1921.

Moore, Merrill, Harry C Solomon. *Contributors to the history of syphilis of the nervous system:* Ulrich von Hutten (1488–1523) Chicago, IL: American Medical Association. 1935.

Mosse, George L. *The Crisis of German Ideology.* Intellectual Origins of the Third Reich. New York: Grosset & Dunlap. 1964.

Münch, Ernst Joseph Herman. *Des teutschen Ritters Ulrich von Hutten sämmtliche Werke.* Berlin: G. Reimer Verlag. 1825.

Nauert, Charles, 'The Clash of Humanists and Scholastics: An Approach to Pre-Reformation Controversies.' *The Sixteenth Century Journal* 4 (1973).

Overfield, James H. *Humanism and Scholasticism in Late Medieval Germany.* Princeton: Princeton University Press, 1984.

Pagan, Victoria E. 'Beyond Teutoburg: Transgression and Transformation in Tacitus Annales 1.61–62.' *Classical Philology*, Vol. 94, No. 3 (Jul., 1999). 302–320

Potton, François Ferdinand Ariste. *Livre du chevalier allemand Ulric de Hutten sur la maladie française et sur les propriétés du bois de gayac: orné d'un portrait de l'auteur, précédé d'une notice historique sur sa vie et ses ouvrages.* Lyon: L. Perrin. 1865.

Rehfisch, Hans J., ed., *In Tyrannos, Four Centuries of Struggle against Tyranny in Germany.* A Symposium.[The Club 1943]. London: Lindsay Drummond, 1944.

Röhr, Helmut. *Ulrich von Hutten und das Werden des Deutschen Nationalbewusstseins.* Hamburg: Evert. 1936.

Roloff, Hans-Gert. 'Der *Arminius* des Ulrich von Hütten.' In: Rainer Wiegels and Winfried Woesler. Eds. *Arminius und die Varusschlacht.* Paderborn, München, Wien, Zürich: Ferdinand Schöningh. 2003.

Roulston, Robert Bruce. *Huttens letzte Tage.* Baltimore: Johns Hopkins University Press. 1933.

Rueb, Franz. Ulrich von Hutten: ein radikaler Intellektueller im 16. Jahrhundert. Berlin: Wagenbach. 1981.

Rummel, Erika. *The Humanist - Scholastic Debate in the Renaissance and the Reformation.* Cambridge, MA: Harvard University Press, 1995.

Schama, Simon. *Landscape and Memory.* New York: Alfred A. Knopf. 1995. Vintage Canada. 1996

Scherer, Wilhelm. *Geschichte der Deutschen Literatur.* [Berlin, 1883] Complete Text-Edition, Hrsg. Heinz Amelung. Berlin: Th. Knaur, 1929.

Schilling, Johannes. *Ulrich von Hutten in seiner Zeit* : Schlüchterner Vorträge zu seinem 500. Geburtstag. Kassel: Verlag Evangelischer Presseverband. 1988.

Scholz, Günter, Sabine Ferlein. *Ulrich von Hutten, 1488-1523: glanzvoller Humanist, gescheiterter Reichsreformer.* Ausstellung. Bauernkriegsmuseum. Böblingen: Stadtarchiv und Museen. 1989.

Scribner, Robert, Ed. *Germany: A New Social and Economic History.* Vol. I. 1450–1630. London: Arnold. 1996.

Shipley, Frederick W. Trans. *Velleius Paterculus* and *Res Gestae Divi Augusti. Loeb Classical Library.* London: William Heinemann. 1924.

Stammler, Wolfgang. *Von der Mystik zum Barock.* 1400–1600. *Epochen der deutschen Literatur.* Bd. II. Teil 1. Stuttgart: J. B. Metzler'sche Verlagsbuchhandlung. 1927.

Stockley, V. *German Literature as Known in England 1750–1830.* Port Washington, NY / London: Kennikat Press.[1929] 1969.

Strauss, David Friedrich. *Ulrich von Hutten.* Leipzig: F.A. Brockhaus, 1857/58, rev. ed. Otto Clemen. Leipzig: Insel Verlag, 1914.

Strauss, Gerald. *Manifestations of Discontent in Germany on the Eve of the Reformation.* Bloomington: Indiana University Press, 1971.

Suphan, Bernhard, Hrsg. *Johann Gottfried Herder, Sämtliche Werke.* Vol. XVI. Hildesheim: Georg Olms Verlagsbuchhandlung. 1967.

Szamatólski, Siegfried. Ulrichs von Hutten deutsche Schriften. Untersuchungen nebst einer Nachlese. Strassburg: K. J. Trübner, 1891.

Tacitus, Gaius Cornelius. *Historiae.* Ed. K. Wellesley. Stuttgart, 1989.

———. *Tacitus in Five Volumes.* Vol. IV: The Annals. Books IV-VI, XI-XII. English Translation by John Jackson. (*The Loeb Classical Library* 312). Cambridge, Mass. and London. 1970 (first ed. 1937).

———. *Annales.* [*Annalen*]. German translation by August Horneffer. Stuttgart: Alfred Kröner Verlag.

———. *Germania.* Lateinisch/Deutsch. UB Nr. 9391. Hrsg. Manfred Fuhrmann. Stuttgart: Philipp Reclam Jun. 1972.

Thion, Edmond, Trans. *Arminius Dialogue. Ulrich de Hutten.* Latin-French. Paris: C. Motteroz. 1877.

Treu, Martin, Hrsg. *Die Schule des Tyrannen: Ulrich von Hutten. Lateinische Schriften.* [Leipzig: Reclam. 1991] Darmstadt: Wissenschaftliche Buchgesellschaft, 1996.

Trillitzsch, Winfried. Ed. and Trans. *Der Deutsche Renaissance-Humanismus.* Historischer Abriß. Leipzig: Philipp Reclam Jun.Verlag. 1981.

Vitz, Paul C. *Sigmund Freud's Christian Unconscious.* New York, London: The Guilford Press. 1988.

Walser, Fritz. *Die politische Entwicklung Ulrichs von Hutten während der Entscheidungsjahre der Reformation.* München, Berlin: R. Oldenbourg, 1928.

Weiss, James Michael. 'Kennst du das Land wo die Humanisten blühen?' References to Italy in the Biographies of German Humanists. In: Eckhard Keßler & Heinrich C. Kuhn, Eds. Conference Proceedings. *Germania latina-Latinitas teutonica*: Humanistische Bibliothek. Reihe I (Abhandlungen). Vol. 54. München: Wilhelm Fink Verlag. 2002.

Wells, Peter S. *The Battle That Stopped Rome*. New York, London: W. W. Norton. 2003.

Wiegels, Rainer & Winfried Woesler. Eds. *Arminius und die Varusschlacht Geschichte – Mythos – Literatur*. Paderborn, München, Wien, Zürich: Ferdinand Schöningh. 2003.

Wimmer, Andreas. Lecture transcript: 'Voice or Exit: Comparative Perspectives on Ethnic Minorities in 20th Century Europe.' Humboldt University, Berlin, June 14-16, 2001.

Zoozmann, Richard. *Das Gesprächbüchlein Ulrichs von Hutten*. Angermanns Bibliothek für Bibliophilen, Bd. 4. Dresden: Hugo Angermann. 1905.